A Fierce Commitment:

The First Ten Years of Washtenaw Community College

By Cynthia Furlong Reynolds

 Washtenaw Community College

The proceeds from the sale of this book will benefit Washtenaw Community College.

Washtenaw Community College

A Fierce Commitment: The First Ten Years of Washtenaw Community College
by Cynthia Furlong Reynolds
ISBN 0-9627691-4-2

Thank You!

Washtenaw Community College is an extraordinary place, a place built by and for the people of Washtenaw County. Just as the College would not exist without the contributions of dedicated and farsighted people, this book would not have been possible without the help of the people who transformed a good idea into a great educational institution.

This College owes its existence to the generosity and farsightedness of more people than history remembers: people who worked on the Ann Arbor Chamber of Commerce Education Committee in the early 1960s; people who worked diligently and unselfishly to persuade voters to approve a revolutionary new educational institution in 1965; and people who contributed their time, talents, and money to the College throughout its decades. Our admiration and heartfelt thanks go out to all those people, particularly to the early members of the Board of Trustees; to WCC's first President, David Ponitz; and to the first and highly versatile administrator, David Pollock. Their dedication to the youth and the dispossessed of Washtenaw County will always be gratefully appreciated and remembered.

Thanks are due to the early faculty, administrators, and staff members who pioneered teaching methods, administrative structures, and operations for this new breed of college. They reached out with care and concern to the new College's students. They worked far, far beyond job descriptions and union-mandated hours. They created a College out of a derelict and abandoned elementary school, and later out of an apple orchard. They listened, advised, swept, painted, typed, delivered, mowed, dusted, shined, polished, arranged, rearranged, organized, reorganized, lifted, loaded, made mistakes, learned, and loved. Some of them taught "out of the trunks of their cars," as Psychology Instructor Bill Moy remembers. Many of those people also dedicated their time and recollections so that the history of the College would become the story of a community triumph.

Thanks are due to the current students who designed this book and to the early students who endured muddy parking lots and a scarcity of books, facilities, plans, classrooms, and tools in the pursuit of learning. They created a newspaper, student government, sports teams, bands, orchestras, clubs, precedents, excitement, challenges, and a reason for being. This College, after all, exists solely because of, and for, them.

Thanks are also due to the present Board of Trustees and administrators, particularly President Larry Whitworth, who had the desire and drive to tell this story and preserve the memories before it was too late.

I am very grateful for the oral histories History Instructor Flavia Reps collected in the 1980s. In addition, more than fifty past and present instructors, Trustees, counselors, staff members, and administrators sat down with me and shared their memories and photographs. Each person I interviewed deserves his or her own book—the contributions were monumental and memorable to the creation of the College. Their stories of WCC's early years gave flesh and blood to this book.

With Sincere Admiration and Appreciation,

Cynthia Furlong Reynolds

Acknowledgments

Production of this book would not have happened without the assistance of the following individuals:

Editorial Review
Dr. Richard W. Bailey, Board of Trustees
Lucinda Bingham, Copy Editor
Edith Croake, English Instructor
David Pollock ,Vice President Emeritus
Mehran Thomson, Dean Emeritus
Tom Zimmerman, English Instructor

Proofreaders
Linda Conroy
Mary Faulkner
Jean Nelson
John Phibbs
Deborah Shillington
Valerie Wenger

Washtenaw Community College Instructors and Classes
Lind Babcock, Graphic Design Instructor
GDT 220 Publication Design Class
Kristine Willimann, Graphic Design Instructor
GDT 239 Imaging & Illustration Class
Susan Westhoff, Student, Layout Designer
Melissa Wylie, Contributing Cover Designer
Lin Zhang Jones, Student, Scanner

Currier Service
Michael Quail, Math Instructor
Jill Beauchamp, Culinary Arts Instructor

Production Services
Judith Corkran Hommel, Production Coordinator
Nicholas G. Maher, Production Artist
Mary Hashman, Proofreader
William Upton, President of Malloy
Patrice Smith, Malloy Sales Representative
Lynn Rohkohl, Malloy Customer Service Representative

Our heartfelt thanks goes out to all these people!

Cynthia Furlong Reynolds

This book is dedicated to the people of Washtenaw County, who created a community college with the desire to serve the needs of all county residents, to the people of Washtenaw Community College, who dedicated their time, support, memories, and efforts to this history, and to the special people in my family, who gave me great encouragement and support throughout this project: my husband, Mark, sons Chip and Ben, and daughter Elizabeth.

Cynthia Furlong Reynolds

Table of Contents

- Lyndon Baines Johnson is inaugurated as 36th U.S. president.

- Malcolm X, Black Muslim leader, is assassinated in Harlem.

- Violence breaks out in Selma, Alabama. Martin Luther King heads procession of 4,000 civil rights demonstrators in "Freedom March" from Selma to Montgomery. Ku Klux Klan shootings in Selma.

- Students demonstrate in Washington, D.C., against U.S. bombing of North Vietnam. They chant, "Hey, Hey, L.B.J., how many kids did you kill today?"

- Severe race riots in Watts, Los Angeles result in 35 dead, 4,000 arrested, $40 million property damage.

- U.S. astronaut Edward White walks from Gemini 4 for 21 minutes.

- Congress passes a bill making it an offense to mutilate or destroy a draft card.

- The average union hourly wage scale in the U.S. has doubled for workers in the building trades since 1949, more than doubled in the trucking and transit industries, and increased by 75 percent for those in printing trades.

- Vietnam: U.S. troop strength: 190,000; U.S. dead: 1,350; wounded: 5,300; enemy dead: 34,585.

History & Politics

- America is reading *A Thousand Days* (Arthur Schlesinger Jr.'s Pulitzer Prize winner); *Thunderball* and *the Man with the Golden Gun* (Ian Fleming); *Unsafe at Any Speed* (Ralph Nader); *The Green Berets* (Robin Moore); *Manchild in the Promised Land* (Claude Brown); *The Autobiography of Malcolm X; The Kandy-Kolored, Tangerine-flake Streamline Baby* (Tom Wolfe); *The Psychedelic Reader* (Timothy Leary); *The Americans: The National Experience* (Daniel Boorstin).

Books

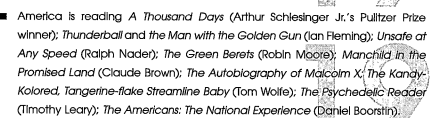

Music

- Radio stations are playing *King of the Road, It Was a Very Good Year, Downtown, A Hard Day's Night.*

New Words

- Kook, camp, computerize, degradable, discotheque, quark, printout, program, skateboard, crash, dude, do your own thing, groupie, no way, old lady, old man, rap, vibes, straight.

Education

- A $2.2 billion Higher Education Act is passed.
- U.S. spends more than $26.2 billion for public school education, $654 per student.
- Out of 3.52 million seventeen year olds, 2.63 million are expected to graduate from high school.
- American colleges confer 709,332 degrees; 551,040 are bachelors, 140,055 are masters, 18,237 are doctorates.
- Michigan triumphs over Oregon State, 34-7, in the Rose Bowl.
- The first Teach-in is held March 2 at the University of Michigan. Later, 100,000 students on 100 campuses attend the National Teach-in on Vietnam.
- Allen Ginsberg coins the phrase "Flower Power" at a Berkeley antiwar rally.
- Harvard professor Timothy Leary urges "Drop out, turn on, tune in."

Prologue

The Time Was Right for Change

By President Larry Whitworth

The decade from 1965 to 1975 was a time like no other. Those were the years of civil unrest, urban riots, assassinations, civil disobedience, the Civil Rights Movement, the Women's Movement, the Antiwar Movement, the beginning of the drug culture, flower children, the pill that brought about the beginning of the sexual revolution, and the Free Love Movement. Music changed dramatically with the appearance of the Stones, the Doors, Led Zeppelin, Jimi Hendrix, the Grateful Dead, and James Brown. Visual art headed in a new direction with Andy Warhol, pop art, and psychedelic art. Fashion trends were out of control and the fashion police had fallen asleep on the job.

The guideposts that provided direction for collective behavior—these included tradition, common culture, and common civility—were all under attack from the members of the baby boom generation. The generations that preceded the baby boom generation were struck with disbelief as the fundamental foundations that had guided their lives were destroyed by the onslaught of this new generation. These were exciting times, depressing times, a time for great creativity, and a time of great anxiety. It is during this time that the community college and the community college movement were born.

Historians will argue that the community college grew out of the junior college movement. As one who was there at the beginning, I can say with assurance that this is a significant misinterpretation of what was truly happening. Yes, there were several hundred junior colleges throughout the country; these two-year liberal arts colleges served as feeders for four-year colleges and universities. Although these schools were valuable in providing access to a college education for many who would have otherwise been denied, the junior colleges did not share the soul of the community college. Community colleges sprang forth not as an adaptation of the junior college tradition, but rather as a brand-new institution with an egalitarian mission to serve the educational needs of a community in every way possible. The massive growth and expansion of community college enrollments first occurred in the urban areas, beginning in about 1965. Miami, Los Angeles, New York, Cleveland, Pittsburgh, and Chicago each opened their doors within months of each other and each started with enrollments in the thousands. But it wasn't just urban communities that hosted the new breed of educational institution, they could also be found in suburban and rural communities in each and every state. Some community colleges were sponsored by cities, some by counties, some by school districts. Some were created and sponsored as a statewide system. Each had its unique qualities, but they all were similar in purpose. The breakdown of historic traditions allowed for the creation of a new institution and new traditions. Community colleges all across the country simultaneously adopted a five-part mission statement dedicated to the educational needs of their communities. Each institution developed high-quality, low-cost educational programs that would provide access to all adults with its "open door" admission policy. Each school would focus programming on the following five areas:

■ Occupational / Vocational Technical
■ Transfer Preparation
■ Developmental / Remediation
■ Non-credit / Continuing Adult Education
■ Community Service

Occupational / vocational technical educational programs were the cornerstone of every community college. Although the specific programs were different at each community college, the philosophy of preparing people for the workplace near their homes was the driver for the creation of each and every program. Most community colleges developed nursing programs because of expanding needs within the health care system. Similarly, community colleges developed other allied health programs, such as inhalation therapy, radiography, dental assistant, and physical therapy. Schools also developed occupational programs in areas such as business management, accounting, computer technology, and clerical services. At this time, communities were also facing a tremendous shortage of highly skilled industrial workers in areas such as machine tool, robotics, welding, and other areas of mechanics. Each institution, as a result of community assessment, determined which programs would best fit its community's special needs. These were the programs created and these were the programs that drove incredible enrollment growth throughout these first ten years of the life of the community college.

Transfer preparation programs became the second part of the five-part mission. All community colleges continued the tradition established by junior colleges to develop a transfer program. Substantial tension existed between occupational / vocational technical faculty and the general education faculty. The debate raged for nearly ten years concerning the proportion of general education and occupational education that ought to be contained within a specific program. Over time, it became nearly universally accepted that the three degrees offered by the community college—the associate in applied science; the associate in science, and the associate in arts— would each require a general education foundation. The associate in applied science would require a minimum of eighteen credits of general education, the associate in science a minimum of twenty-six credits in general education, and the associate in arts, thirty-six credits in general education. The successful outcome of this struggle between the occupational and the transfer faculty has in fact insured the long-term health and viability of the community college. Today, although 65 percent of our students indicate that they are attending in order to pursue an occupational program, nearly 70 percent of students indicate an interest in transferring and continuing their education. No longer are the occupational programs referred to as "the terminal track program." Instead, students from nearly every program—particularly nursing, welding, robotics, and graphic arts— transfer to four-year institutions to pursue the bachelor's degree and beyond. Lifelong learning has become a reality, not just a slogan.

Developmental / remediation education was also an important mission priority at every community college. Research has demonstrated on many occasions that students out of school for five years or longer would probably need at least one area of remediation in either mathematics, English composition, or reading comprehension. It was evident from the very beginning that the community colleges would be enrolling a non-traditional population, where more than half of their students would have been out of school for substantially more than five years. Additionally, a large portion of the traditional-age students starting at a community college had not pursued a college preparatory track in high school and also required remediation in at least one of the fundamental academic skills areas. Remediation was the key to keeping the open door open and providing access to literally millions of people. Without this fundamental opportunity to develop academic skills in preparation for college-level work, these people would have been denied access. It was our commitment to remediation that prevented the "open door" from becoming the "revolving door."

Non-credit / continuing adult education was another important cornerstone of the community college mission. In order to attend to the educational needs of a community, community colleges took very seriously their commitment to provide a wide variety of curricula. Many courses had traditionally been considered outside the realm of responsibility for a college or university. By offering non-credit courses, community colleges helped to bring people together to pursue common intellectual, social, and recreational experiences. Community colleges also offered—and continue to offer—a wide variety of non-credit courses designed to respond to the business and economic climate of a particular community. Continuing education experiences for nurses, accountants, lawyers, and real estate agents are just a few of the vast array of instructional components offered by community colleges. In many respects, the continuing education program was the community college's most responsive division in filling a community's specific needs. In other words, continuing education really put "community" into the community college.

Community service has always been an important part of the underlying egalitarian mission of the community college. Community colleges operate on the generosity of public funds. After all, they were created to attend to the educational needs of their community. But, somewhere in that initial breath of life, community colleges took on a social mission. No matter which community college you visit from border to border or coast to coast, you will find a deep commitment to serving the needs of the less fortunate: those who are economically disadvantaged, those who are handicapped, and those who are socially disenfranchised. In order to serve these particular needs, community colleges learned to leverage their time, talent, and resources by working with local agencies in order to help attend to the needs of the most needy.

This five-part mission is nearly universal for all community colleges, and it remains essentially intact from 1965 through today. It is this five-part mission that differentiates community colleges from junior colleges and universities. As you read *A Fierce Commitment: The First Ten Years of Washtenaw Community College* remember that during this dynamic and dramatic ten-year period, the country moved from a few hundred small two-year liberal arts (junior) colleges to more than a thousand community colleges. Some of these community colleges developed from two-year junior colleges, but on balance the vast majority were a part of this great expansion of wholly new institutions created by local needs. And, although each was unique, each was based on the same fundamental principles. This book is not merely the story of one community college. It is, in fact, the story of nearly a thousand community colleges, all of them created in the churning social and cultural cauldron that existed from the mid-sixties to the mid-seventies.

■ International Days of Protest are held, objecting to U.S. policy in Vietnam.

■ "Black Power" is introduced into the civil rights movement, defining the rift between the pacifist followers of Martin Luther King Jr. and the militants following Stokeley Carmichael and Floyd McKissick.

■ U.S. population totals 195,827,000.

■ U.C.L.A. defeats Michigan State 14-12 in Rose Bowl.

■ Blanket student deferments are abolished and draft calls reach 50,000 a month.

■ *Time* magazine's "Man of the Year" is actually a group: the "Twenty-five and Under Generation."

■ Russia makes first soft moon landing.

■ L.B.J. asks Congress for $4 billion more for defense, $3 billion for Great Society.

■ Roman Catholic bishops rule that U.S. Catholics no longer must abstain from eating meat on Fridays, except during Lent.

■ Vietnam: U.S. troop strength: 400,000; U.S. dead: 6,458; enemy dead: 77,115.

History & Politics

■ Best-selling books include Truman Capote's *In Cold Blood*, Jacqueline Susann's *Valley of the Dolls*, *Quotations of Mao Tse-tung*, *Human Sexual Response* by William Howard Masters and Virginia E. Johnson, *Everything but Money* by Sam Levenson, and Phyllis Diller's *Housekeeping Hints*.

Books

■ British model Twiggy takes American fashion by storm. Women are wearing hip-hugging mini-skirts, T-shirt dresses with chin-high necklines, turtlenecks, headbands, scarves, tent dresses, and military-style coats with epaulettes and brass buttons.

■ Hair is long and straight and parted in the middle, although Mia Farrow sets a style with hair cut close to the scalp. Op art glasses are seen everywhere.

■ Men and women wear low-slung bell bottoms with wide belts. Women appear in daytime pantsuits and elaborate jumpsuits.

Fashion

Movies

- Americans flock to theaters to see *Torn Curtain, The Bible, Alfie, Masculin-Feminin, A Man for All Seasons* (Academy Award winner), and *Who's Afraid of Virginia Woolf?*
- Walt Disney dies.

Music

- Hit songs: *Born Free, Eleanor Rigby, Strangers in the Night, Ballad of the Green Berets, Winchester Cathedral, Georgy Girl, The Sound of Silence, The Impossible Dream, Good Vibrations.*

Television

- Americans are watching *The Newlywed Game, Mission: Impossible, Batman, The Monkees, That Girl, The Smothers Brothers Comedy Hour.*

New Words

- Abort, big-bang theory, bowser bag, cable TV, glitch, commune, flower children, psychedelic, acid rock, mind-blowing, zap, go-go, hawk, hippy, LSD, miniskirt, mod, pop, Third World.

Quotes

- "Their symbol is the black panther, a bold, beautiful animal, representing the strength and dignity of black demands today."—Stokeley Carmichael, describing a new party in Lowndes County, Alabama.
- "We have stopped losing the war."—General William Westmoreland.
- "The time has come to confront with concrete action the conditions which now prevent women from enjoying equality of opportunity and freedom of choice which is their right as individual Americans and as human beings."—NOW manifesto

Chapter 1:

Setting The Stage

The golden era of community colleges took place in the 1960s. Post-World War II baby boomers began jamming the nation's high schools and pounding on the doors of unprepared colleges and universities, which began struggling with enrollment and expansion pressures. An entirely new breed of higher education suddenly appeared all over the country: the community college, which found a place in education somewhere between high schools and colleges, trade schools, junior colleges, and universities. Throughout the 1960s, on average, one community college opened somewhere in the United States every week.

Community colleges were neither junior colleges nor trade schools, but something else. Each community college lived up to its name: the school and its programs were tailored to its community. However, some fared better than others in those heady, hurried, up-and-coming days. Success or failure depended on the amount of community support, the vision of the community leaders, how astute early administrators proved to be, the commitment of faculty and staff, and the types and variety of programs offered.

In Michigan, the community college movement has been traced back to 1914, when Grand Rapids Junior College opened its doors to 49 students and 6 instructors. By 1965, Grand Rapids had grown to 3,500 students and 108 faculty members. Schoolcraft Community College opened its doors in Livonia in September 1964, with 1,860 students and 47 faculty members. By the mid-1960s, all of Michigan's community colleges were providing three programs: liberal arts for college transfer candidates, one- and two-year terminal technical vocational programs, and two years of general education "for those not interested in or qualified for four-year college work."

By January 1, 1965, five hundred public two-year colleges were teaching and training students in the United States. The previous fall, twenty-five percent of all American students entering college matriculated at community colleges. In fact, the trend was so strong that *The Saturday Review* estimated that within five years, eighty percent of all students entering college would start at the community college level. The *Review's* statistics were overstated, but the strength of the trend was not.

In 1965, the *Ypsilanti Press* asked rhetorically, "What accounts for the rise of the community college concept?" and then answered its own question: "The modern community college is a product of American educational philosophy and economic necessity." The *Review* also noted that the goal of higher education has been expanded to include training adults of all ages for hundreds of professional and semi-professional occupations.

As Director of the Ann Arbor Chamber of Commerce, Bill Bott worked closely with the Chamber's Education Committee, which fathered Washtenaw Community College.

ESTABLISHING A NEED

"There is something extraordinary about Washtenaw Community College. It was actually and entirely the direct result of a citizens' movement," observed Dave Pollock, one of the earliest WCC administrators. "In the early 1960s, the Michigan State Legislature authorized the establishment of community colleges either by school districts or on a county basis. The Ann Arbor Chamber of Commerce took the ball and ran with it after the Ann Arbor School Board discussed it, decided they weren't interested in taking it on as a project, but said that they saw great value in the idea."

In the 1950s and 1960s, a healthy economy, booming population, Cold War, and emerging new technologies and industries began to change the course of Washtenaw County's business world. Industry began spilling over into its borders from Wayne County, and Ann Arbor began to vie with other cities for high-tech companies. Shortly after Bill Bott arrived in Ann Arbor in 1957, as Director of the Chamber of Commerce, he started hearing rumblings about the need for a new and different educational institution. "I was present when Washtenaw Community College became more than just a twinkle in someone's eye," he said.

"In the 1950s, Ann Arbor was going through big changes," Bott pointed out. "Manufacturing jobs weren't available. The industrial base hadn't changed one bit. But our population was increasing and the future looked as though it would be tied to research. We were competing with areas like Chapel Hill for research companies, but we

Anthony Procassini was a member the Ann Arbor Chamber of Commerce Education Committee, which spearheaded the creation of Washtenaw Community College. Narrowly defeated in the first election for the College's Board of Trustees, he ran again in 1966, with a catchy slogan created by his children: "Don't be a meanie—Vote for Procassini!" Procassini served as Board Chair from 1973 until 1981.

needed a place to put the companies and people to work for them. We needed kids with specialized training to fill those jobs—and Washtenaw kids had no way of getting that kind of training here. Suddenly, the Chamber of Commerce had a thrust."

Forty years later, Tony Procassini clearly remembered how his interest in a community college developed. As human resources director for Bendix, he knew the company was looking for people who could be electronics technicians. "These people needed more than a high school education, but didn't necessarily need the four-year baccalaureate," he said. "We needed people who were knowledgeable in the practical aspects of electronics; our engineers would worry about the theoretical aspects. Also, at this time, computers were in their infancy and we needed trained technicians in that field." Procassini discussed his corporate needs with Bill Bott and Bott asked him to serve on the Chamber's Education Committee, which Procassini eventually chaired.

As David Ponitz explained many years later, "In the 1960s, Americans were just starting to begin to realize that not everyone needs to be educated the same way; we were beginning to understand that a formula existed. These are the facts that we were working with: In 1950, the percentage of our population requiring four years of post-high school education ranged between twenty and twenty-two percent. Sixty-five percent of Americans in the work force were semi-skilled workers; fifteen percent required technical training. But we knew those numbers were about to change, that increasingly more people would need technical training."

"We were moving into a new age, where workers required technical skills beyond the high schools in order to get jobs," Tony Procassini added.

In the late 1950s, Washtenaw voters rejected a proposal for a technical high school. Shortly afterwards, the Ann Arbor Board of Education approached the Chamber of Commerce Education Committee, chaired by Jim McDonald, to say that the members felt that Ann Arbor had a strong and growing need for a community college that would provide vocational training. The school board asked the Chamber to look into the feasibility of a local community college.

"In those days, few of us were familiar with the concept of a community college. We didn't know what they were talking about," Bill Bott recalled. "Jim McDonald was skeptical, but he called the Education Committee together and decided to find out what a community college was and whether we needed one." On that committee was Tony Procassini.

The Education Committee members logged countless hours in Lansing doing their homework with state education officials and visiting with the president of Lansing Community College ("a very sharp man who was very helpful," Bott recalled). Committee members also visited the Dearborn Community College campus. "As we looked into the community college concept, we became increasingly more convinced that it might work for us," Bott said. "We became very enthused about the idea of what a community college could offer Washtenaw youngsters."

After six months of study, the Education Committee decided to get the community involved in the discussions. "After all, no one else knew what a community college was either," Bott pointed out.

The Education Committee formed a citizens' steering committee headed by Ann Arbor High School Principal Nicholas Schreiber, which quickly decided to survey the local business community. "We put together a team that wouldn't quit," Bott said with admiration.

The committee needed ten thousand dollars for the survey and members were having difficulty raising the funds—until they turned to Chelsea Milling Company President Howard Holmes, Ralph Wenrich recalled many years later. "Within twenty-four hours, Howard told us he had the funds. He never received the kind of recognition he deserved for his crucial role in this process. Without his help, I'm not sure the project would have proceeded."

University of Michigan Professor Raymond Young was asked to conduct the survey, starting June 30, 1962. Before the results were tabulated and released, on September 18, 1962, *The Ann Arbor News* printed an article with the headline "School Drop-Out Problem Will Get Worse Here, Committee Says." The article pointed out:

> Ann Arbor is faced with the serious problem of unemployed school drop-outs. The problem is not nearly as acute here as in major metropolitan cities, but it is nonetheless crucial and will become more so. This was the sobering theme of the annual report of the Youth Commission established in 1961 by the City Council.

Chamber and committee members were amazed at the high percentage of people who responded to their survey saying they were interested in the idea of starting—and attending—a community college. "That encouraged us to keep going," Bott said.

In September 1963, the commission announced the results and recommendations from the Citizens' Survey of Washtenaw County

Community College Possibilities (July, 1963; 195 pp). The survey reported a "demonstrated demand by county youth and employers for a post-high school program offering technical and semi-professional occupational training." High school juniors and seniors had indicated that "a financial barrier appears to be denying a significant proportion of youth an opportunity for additional education." Fifteen percent of the seniors said they were not planning on college, but indicated that their plans would change if more money for educational purposes were available. Another eighteen percent of the high school seniors said they would have continued their education if finances were not a problem.

Some professionals believed that the number of county teenagers able to go on to higher education was even lower. "Only 10 percent—at best—of the students I have talked to over the years have a chance at further education," suggested Willow Run High School teacher Mildred K. Bjornstad in 1965. "The community college would give these students that chance."

At the top of the list of commission recommendations was the establishment of a local community college. The commission identified three different populations that would benefit from a community college: First, people right out of high school who lacked skills or the financial wherewithal to go to college. Second, adults who needed to sharpen their skills or learn new skills because the job place had changed. Third, the "late bloomers" who hadn't lived up to their potential academically, either in high school or college, and needed a second chance.

The next step the committee took was to meet with leaders in the business community, including the hospitals. These meetings helped identify supporters and pinpoint the professional areas that were suffering from a lack of training programs: nursing, business education, electrical and electronics technology, laboratory technology, drafting and design, mechanical technology, and computer graphics. The business leaders also suggested that the proposed educational institution should offer additional preprofessional and liberal arts education, as well as vocational training.

"For that reason, I pushed, and other people pushed, to make sure that we would have a community college with its own identity," Tony Procassini said. "We strongly believed that the community college should not be a part of another educational system."

"I told the business people that a community college would want operational dollars and scholarships," Bill Bott said. " 'They're going to want money,' I warned them. 'That's fine,' they told us. 'Let's stop fussing and get the job done.'"

At that point, the Education Committee and citizens' steering committee decided to reach out throughout Washtenaw County to spread the word. Members talked to the School Officers' Association and the president said they'd take the proposal to the school districts. Interest began growing in outlying regions. Committee members spent hours with Bill Bott, listing the county's movers and shakers, then identifying institutions and businesses that could be effective and affected. Each committee member was assigned a cluster of businesses and individuals and each man and woman began making phone calls and public appearances.

"This was truly a grass-roots movement," Procassini said.

With a smile and a handshake, Trustee Anthony Procassini (left) confers on Ralph Wenrich the Board's appreciation for his six years on the Board of Trustees.

Wyeth Allen, a civic leader and University of Michigan professor emeritus of industrial engineering, was named director of the community college implementation committee, which included County Treasurer Sylvester Leonard. With Robert Harrington coordinating the information drive, newspapers were flooded with information, editorials, reports, and advertisements urging voters to support the referendum to establish a community college.

Meanwhile, committee members were making presentations throughout the county to school boards, PTAs, civic organizations—

"and anyone else we could think of," Bott said. "Early on, John McKevitt had told me, 'You and I know this is a tough town. Everybody goes his own way. Ann Arbor has a show-me attitude. Let's show them this is what they need!' "

When the time seemed right, in January 1965, the committee decided to put the proposal to establish a Washtenaw County Community College up for a county-wide vote. A slate of nominees for the College's first Board of Trustees would also be proposed, to save time and money. Mrs. Florence Mayer of Chelsea, one of the committee members, was the first to file for election to the Community College Board of Trustees.

"The year 1965 is crucial for Michigan higher education," Stuart Gross wrote in the *Manchester Enterprise:*

> The crest of the World War II baby crop graduates from high school next June...Colleges recognize their selectivity now is high, and don't want to get more selective. They point out there are so many students who qualify for admission that the time is approaching when the postmark on a letter will determine final placement.

Writing again a week later in the *Enterprise,* Gross warned, "Enrollment pressures on Michigan's 10 four-year state colleges and universities reach a climax this school year."

Prospects for endorsement of the referendum looked strong, but committee members were taking no chances. They continued to talk to community organizations, write letters, speak to reporters, and make phone calls to voters. Parents of high school students and educators quickly jumped on the bandwagon—for good reason. "For the first time every high school student will be able to look forward to going to college if he wants to...Up until now, this county has offered advanced schooling only to the select and the few," observed Marion Carr, assistant English professor at Eastern Michigan University, when she announced that she, too, would run for the new Board of Trustees.

The dissenting voices came from people who asked one question: Why did Washtenaw County need another college when it already had the University of Michigan, Eastern Michigan University, and Cleary College?

"We had a tremendous challenge in fitting a new concept of education into a community full of educational institutions," Dave Ponitz recalled nearly forty years later. "We had to carve our own niche. That was a tall order."

Proponents of the community college listed five important primary functions for Washtenaw Community College that were not being addressed by the other local institutions of higher education:

■ Occupational education. The community college would not duplicate the efforts of Eastern Michigan University, Cleary College, or the University of Michigan, proponents promised.

■ General studies classes open to everyone, regardless of past academic experience.

■ A transfer program where students in good academic standing would be welcomed by Eastern or Michigan, with all relevant community college credits accepted.

■ Trade-related instruction, which included classroom work, apprenticeship programs, and industrial contacts.

■ A wide array of continuing education programs open to all community members at a reasonable price. (In 1965, few continuing education programs existed within the K-12 school districts.)

Community college proponents promised that the new institution would not duplicate or interfere with any existing continuing education program. "Over and over again as we made our presentation, we'd explain that this new college would be entirely different. This institution would focus on training and educating a different population, with different needs, requiring different skills," Bott said. "And," he added, "we'd tell them that it's not just for youngsters. It's for adults, too."

Early on, it became apparent that the community college idea could go nowhere without support from the University of Michigan. Dave Pollock, who was then the university's public relations director, as well as a member of the Ann Arbor Chamber of Commerce, went to work. "Several of us in the university administration felt that the university should demonstrate its support in some way, so we held a lunch at the Michigan Union for three hundred people representing local industries and banks," Pollock said. University of Michigan President Harlan Hatcher made a speech strongly in favor of the community college proposal, emphasizing the importance of the kind of education a community college would offer. For the first time, the university president publicly stated that the new community college would complement—not detract from—the university's activities. He also promised that the university would allow community college graduates in good academic standing to transfer to the university. All appropriate community college credits would be accepted.

David Pollock was the College's first administrator hired after President David Ponitz was appointed.

17 Of 38 Trustee Candidates Connected With Education

*Newspapers through-
out the county reported
on the progress of the
grass–roots community
college movement.*

"That was exactly what we needed," Bill Bott said. "We were on our way."

From that point on, there was no strong opposition, "except from individuals worried about their taxes," Pollock said.

By January, thirty-eight business leaders, professional educators, and community volunteers had put their names on the ballot for the Board of Trustees.

On January 19, 1965, *The Ann Arbor News* reported,

> Choosing six candidates for the posts of trustees of the proposed Washtenaw Community College is going to be difficult for county voters Friday because of the generally high caliber of the candidates and the large number on the ballot.

The newspaper printed its "preferred list" and the reasons for its selections:

Edward Adams Jr., "who has many years of experience in education, is highly regarded by county school superintendents, and is on the Board of Cleary College."

Richard C. Creal, "active in education and studies of youth problems and young enough to identify with the age group most concerned with the proposed college."

Anthony J. Procassini, "who has had considerable experience in personnel work and job training with industry."

Ralph C. Wenrich, "a consultant to community colleges and with thirty-three years' experience in vocational-technical education."

Samuel T. Harmon, "head of a research company and with a strong interest in the college as a source of technically trained students."

Kenneth L. Yourd, "attorney with considerable education-associated administrative experience."

Elvira Vogel, "The only Manchester candidate, Mrs. Vogel is active in school and church work in that village and is a member of the Washtenaw Area Intermediate School District Board and past president of the Western Washtenaw Area Parent-Teacher Association Council and Pleasant Lake PTA."

> *The Ann Arbor News* went on to note...one of the most
> heartening things about the candidates' meetings last week was
> the enthusiasm of all the group and their often expressed willing-
> ness to serve the proposed college in some capacity, regardless of
> their own fortunes as candidates for trustees. The wealth of can-
> didates...not only attests to the enthusiasm with which the col-
> lege project is meeting, but to the civic interest of many
> Washtenaw County residents.

The vote for trustees will mean nothing, however, if county residents do not approve the two propositions on the ballot, the
newspaper reminded readers.

ELECTION DAY

A county-wide election was held on a snowy January day in 1965.
Voters were asked to approve the referendum to establish a community college and to agree to a one and one-quarter-per-mil levy. Then
they were asked to select six people for the Washtenaw Community
College Board of Trustees. That night, despite forbidding weather and
a lower than expected voter turnout, Washtenaw Community College
became a reality.

Banner headlines in the *Ypsilanti Press* were the first to announce
"New County College Approved by 2 to 1."

Almost one-fourth of the 72,000 registered voters in Washtenaw
County cast their ballots in the special election. The vote was 11,109
in favor of creating a community college, with 5,085 opposed.

"Interestingly, the strength of the vote came from Ann Arbor—the
ballot option didn't pass anyplace else," Dave Pollock recalled.
"Despite the fact that the millage vote was raised every three years,
it was endorsed every time but one. Yet many years passed before the
vote reached a 50:50 margin in Ypsilanti. Although Ypsilanti sent
many, many students to the community college and the people recognized the College's value to the community, its voters didn't want to
pay the taxes to support it."

ELECTED BY THE PEOPLE

After the votes had been counted on election night, officials
announced that Samuel Harmon, Evart Ardis, Ralph Wenrich,
Edward Adams Jr., Richard Creal, and Elvira Vogel had been selected for the Washtenaw Community College Board of Trustees. *The
Michigan Daily* noted that Samuel Harmon was the top vote-getter,
with 5,798 votes. Dick Creal received 4,802 votes; Evart Ardis, 4,649;
Ed Adams, 4,178; and Ralph Wenrich, 4,131.

Two days later, errors were found in the vote tabulation. Elvira Vogel dropped to seventh place, edged out of a seat on the Board by Kenneth Yourd. Vogel's vote was 4,028 instead of 4,088; Yourd's was 4,109. Tony Procassini received 4,104 votes. One year later, he was elected to the Board.

Ralph Wenrich was on a trip to South America at the time of the election. When he received word of his win, he went to the U.S. Embassy to be sworn into his new position.

"The first Board consisted of very diverse personalities and strengths, but they worked very effectively together for the good of the College," Dave Pollock observed many years later.

"The Board had a lot of different points of view and that fact became evident as we grappled with all the crucial decisions that had to be made immediately," Evart Ardis said in an interview with WCC history instructor Flavia Reps in 1982. "The Board was committed to a lot of openness. They felt that it would give the institution credibility if the people felt it was truly their College. We listened very carefully to the citizens and we tried to reflect the majority opinions as nearly as we could."

A member of the first Board of Trustees, Ralph Wenrich was Chair of the Department of Vocational Education and Practical Arts at the University of Michigan.

PRESENTING:
THE WCC BOARD OF TRUSTEES

In local newspapers throughout the county, the thirty-eight candidates for Board of Trustees had been given the opportunity to explain their qualifications for the job and their platforms. These were the winners and close runners-up, along with their statements for *The Ann Arbor News* taken directly from the newspaper.

Ralph Wenrich

Chairman of the Department of Vocational Education and Practical Arts at the University of Michigan. He was formerly Associate State Superintendent of Public Instruction and State Director of Vocational Education.

"I definitely think the community college should give major emphasis to vocational-technical programs and occupational guidance. It should also provide general and pre-professional programs for those who plan to transfer to four-year colleges. Programs in the business field should supplement, rather than compete with, those now offered at Cleary College...I favor locating the community college where it would be accessible to the greatest number of persons to be served. More information is needed to determine the exact location."

Kenneth L. Yourd

Assistant Dean to the University of Michigan Medical School. He was formerly senior attorney for the Columbia Broadcasting System and director of its business affairs. He was later vice president and treasurer of the National Educational Television and Radio Center in Ann Arbor.

"There is a three-part need which the county community college should satisfy: vocational-technical programs to prepare young people for useful employment; training programs for mature adults which will sharpen old skills or retrain for new skills; and a two-year liberal arts course of study. No one program should be emphasized to the detriment of the others. All should be done well....

"I see no need to duplicate courses of instruction where Cleary College is already satisfying the need. There are many other areas where instruction and training are needed and in which the community college should start as soon as is feasible.

"This will be a community college serving the whole county. For this reason I do not feel that it should be physically located in the City of Ann Arbor or the City of Ypsilanti. On the other hand the college should not be too far from the population and geographic centers of the county and must have adequate water and sewer facilities plus roads."

Edward Adams Jr.

Rutgers University graduate, "nationally known and respected for his valuable contributions to banking and finance." President of the National Bank & Trust Company of Ann Arbor and a director and trustee of several state and local institutions. In his thirty years of service, Mr. Adams has shown a unique capability for coping with all facets of economic development.

"One does not have to look far to realize the dilemma we face in education in Washtenaw. The high school population has outrun growth of higher educational facilities, while student cost of higher education has gone up faster than family disposable income. The result is that many young people are denied equal educational opportunity.

"A community college is the most convenient, pliable, and economical means of filling the void between secondary and higher education. In addition, a community college is essential for meeting the demands of modern day business for better trained technicians. We must not only provide new trained individuals; we must also provide means of upgrading those now employed."

Richard Creal

A life-long resident of Ann Arbor, Richard Creal graduated from the University of Michigan in 1952, obtained an M.A. degree in school administration and supervision in 1956. For the past twelve years, he has participated in virtually all phases of local public school education.

"My primary concern is that the curriculum include a strong basic vocational training program for all interested youth backed up by a solid counseling service. It is of prime importance that the viewpoint of youth, especially those most in need of vocational training, be represented on the Board...I hope to represent the needs of this segment of our population in the determination of the training programs.

"The Community College will...help to upgrade the programs of the employment-bound students."

Evart Ardis

Director of the University of Michigan Bureau of Appointments and Occupational Education. He served for many years as superintendent of schools in Ypsilanti.

"I believe the Washtenaw Community College should offer terminal courses in the vocational-technical fields, and also a rich two-year liberal arts curriculum for those who will not be able to enter a four-year college due to finances or overcrowding. It should fill all the needs not now being met by existing institutions in Washtenaw County.

"My 25 years as a superintendent of schools, including seven at Ypsilanti, combined with my five years as Director of Placement at the University of Michigan, should enable me to help the trustees make sound, sensible decisions relative to the sites, construction, curriculum development, counseling and placement of terminal graduates."

Samuel T. Harmon

Owner of Sensor Dynamics, he was formerly with Bendix Systems Division. He holds a master's degree in electrical engineering from the University of Michigan.

"I believe the community college should be a multipurpose institution with an open door admissions policy offering post-high school education to anyone who can profit from it. The curriculum in my opinion should emphasize technical-vocational occupational education in fields where the community offers present and future employment opportunities. In addition, the college should offer to a lesser degree a liberal arts transfer curriculum and an adult education expansion program."

■■■

Nearly forty years after running for election to the first Board of Trustees, Harmon reflected on his attitudes about education in the mid-1960s.

"I am an African-American man with a strong concern for the underdog in society," he said. A native of Detroit, he attended Cass Technical High School, but quit when he was fifteen. After eight years in the Navy, he entered the University of Michigan's engineering program at a time when, he remembered, the University had thirty African-American students.

After earning his master's degree and settling into his career, he decided to put his efforts toward "working for community betterment." He joined the Democratic Party, the Ann Arbor Chamber of Commerce, the

Originally published Jan. 14, 1965 (© 2004, The Ann Arbor News. All rights reserved. Reprinted with permission.)

United Way, and the local chapter of the National Association for the Advancement of Colored People. Between 1958 and 1963, he was a board member of the of seventeen community organizations, but in 1963, when he began hearing discussions about establishing a community college, he decided to focus his attention on helping to establish a college that would offer technical training. Along with Tony Procassini, he was a member of the Chamber of Commerce Education Committee.

This advertisement ran in local newspapers preceding the county referendum on a new community college.

"In the early 1960s, *Fortune* magazine ran an article showing the trends taking place with black versus white families. It showed that the percentage of African-American families in the middle and upper ranks of our society had been declining. I also noted that local employment of African-American men and white children of farmers was lagging behind the national growth. To me, that meant that we had a strong need for technical training," he explained.

Harmon was the only African-American running for election in 1965.

Elvira Vogel

A housewife, formerly employed in personnel work. A member of the County Board of Education for the past five years.

"To meet the specific needs in our county, I believe primary emphasis should be for a technical-vocational and semi-professional program.

Originally published Dec. 17, 1964 (© 2004, The Ann Arbor News. All rights reserved. Reprinted with permission.)

An active community member, Elvira Vogel never served on the College Board of Trustees, but remained a staunch College supporter.

An accredited liberal arts course should be offered for those interested in general education and for those who will be transferring to a four-year program. A good guidance, counseling, and placement program is fundamental.

"A general admissions policy for any high school graduate over 21 who is interested should be accepted....

"I am genuinely interested in people and in the educational opportunities offered to them so that they might help themselves."

■ ■ ■

In a 1982 interview for history instructor Flavia Reps' oral history project focusing on the early years of the College, Elvira Vogel remembered, "I was really sold on the fact of the great need for such a College...Out county, Manchester and the western end of the county, offered more resistance than any other area."

She told the interviewer, "I felt so deeply bothered (by the opposition to the idea of a community college) that I did consent to be one of the persons to run for the initial board. I remember that there were only two or three women and we were a very diverse group. One of the men...said he looked at the group of thirty-eight candidates and said the only thing we really have in common is our temperature!"

Despite her election loss, Vogel remained active in helping establish the new Community College and served on the committee that selected Gunder Myran as second President of the College.

"Elvira Vogel is a fine example of someone who doesn't need an elected office to make a difference in a place," observed the current Assistant to the Board of Trustees Mary Faulkner. "She worked very hard to make the new College meet community needs."

Anthony J. Procassini

Director of Human Resources for the Bendix Corporation. He was chairman of the Education Committee that spearheaded the efforts on behalf of the community college.

"My experience in industrial management and manpower retraining should provide the board with a required understanding of both the individual and industrial needs of the community.

"As chairman of the City Council's Economic Development and Manpower Commission, I am aware of the complex problems confronting some individuals within our community to cope with the increasing demands stimulated by an expanding technology. This, combined with my understanding of the needs of the business and industrial communities gained from 18 years' experience, should permit me to anticipate the needs of our community and to recommend and implement programs designed to best satisfy these ever-changing demands."

■ ■ ■

The father of ten children, Tony Procassini was enthusiastically endorsed by his family, whose election motto was "Don't be a meanie—Vote for Procassini!"

His parents had emigrated to America from Italy and Procassini grew up in New Jersey. He became the first in his family to attend college; he graduated from the University of Michigan with a psychology major in 1947.

As a member of the Ann Arbor Chamber of Commerce Education Committee, Procassini always had a "deep interest in making sure that the educational process worked well for the people of Ann Arbor and Washtenaw County," he said. "Because Washtenaw County had no institution to educate people beyond the high school level unless they attended a four-year college or university, a lot of opportunities were passing our high school graduates by." Along with his committee, Procassini realized that Washtenaw County had an international reputation for its educational programs–"but the community college was the one missing link."

"I can't tell you who first introduced the idea of establishing a community college here—probably several people deserve credit—but I wish I could say I was the one!" he remembered, forty years later with a grin.

"When the idea of a community college was introduced to the voters of Washtenaw County, it was easier for people to understand that we needed technical people and programs than to convince them that we needed another place to teach English. Still, we always stayed true to the idea that we would offer a complete education to anyone who came to our door."

OFF TO WORK

At the first Board of Trustees meeting, Samuel Harmon was elected Chair; Richard Creal, Secretary; and Edward Adams, Treasurer. Kenneth Yourd was asked to begin work on a preliminary statement of purpose and by-laws, while Adams was authorized to negotiate loans of up to one hundred thousand dollars against future tax collections for "interim operating expenses."

*The first Board of
Trustees was a
collection of hard-
working and dedicat-
ed men:
(Top l-r)
Edward Adams,
Evart Ardis,
Richard Creal,
(Bottom l-r)
Samuel Harmon,
Ralph Wenrich,
Kenneth Yourd.*

By March 3, Adams had suggested that the new Community College not wait for a permanent campus and buildings before opening classrooms for the public. He proposed finding a temporary site, explaining, "This would alleviate the current pressure on the board to select a site early."

The Board was in business.

■ ■ ■

Fifty-three years after the 1950 survey of the American workforce and its educational needs, some of the numbers had changed significantly—and the changes validated the work and foresight of community colleges like Washtenaw's. The number of people requiring four years of higher education has remained twenty percent, but the number of semi-skilled workers and the number of technically-trained workers have been transposed. Nowadays, the American workforce requires fifteen percent semi-skilled workers and sixty-five percent technically-trained workers. "This is where community colleges have become the single-most important educational function in any community," former WCC President David Ponitz pointed out. "The sixty-five percent are people who use math and physics and work between the highly educated engineer and the hands-on people. These folks learn differently and they need to be taught differently. That's where community colleges come in."

Sam Harmon remembered the groundbreaking process as being "both exciting and stressful."

"The Board of Trustees faced tremendous challenges," he said. "We had to determine course offerings, outline the needs for staff, select qualified people, and formulate administrative policy. Our basic policy was to make the college hospitable to every student from every part of the county who wanted to go—not just the brightest. We believed that we should focus on what a person was ready to do, rather than on what they had done in the past, that a student just needed to be sincere in order to be welcomed to this institution."

Tony Procassini added, "What we were trying to establish in 1965 was to provide a major opportunity for everybody—whether or not they had money—to get an education. In order to do that, we had to keep tuition low. If we could put education within everyone's financial grasp, we knew a lot more people would take advantage of what the College offered. We bent over backwards to make education easier for everybody. In my opinion, since 1966 here in Washtenaw County, there has been no reason why anyone in the county cannot get a college education

A desolate, deserted Willow Run Village was transformed into a vital, vibrant, and very busy Community College campus in the summer and fall of 1966.

1967

- In Newark, riots end after six days with 26 dead.

- Detroit riots end after eight days with 43 dead.

- More than 70,000 march in Fifth Avenue parade supporting American soldiers.

- Vietnam: U.S. troop strength: 525,000, which exceeds total troop strength in Korea during that war; U.S. dead: 15,997. U.S. total bombing tonnage exceeds that of World War II.

History & Politics

- Americans are watching *Mannix, N.Y.P.D., The Flying Nun, Ironside, The Carol Burnett Show, The Phil Donahue Show, Mission: Impossible, Get Smart, I Spy.*

Television

- On the big screen: *Bonnie and Clyde, The Graduate, Guess Who's Coming to Dinner?, In Cold Blood, Cool Hand Luke, The Dirty Dozen, Barefoot in the Park, Elvira Madigan.*

Movies

- Americans are reading *The Confessions of Nat Turner* (William Styron), *The Chosen* (Chaim Potok), *Christy* (Catherine Marshall), *Rosemary's Baby* (Ira Levin), *The Naked Ape* (Desmond Morris), *Death of a President* (William Manchester), *Better Homes & Gardens Favorite Ways in Chicken.*

Books

- Men wear unrestrained colors, double-breasted plaid jackets, turtlenecks, and boldly striped shirts with spread collars and French cuffs. Fashion model Twiggy arrives in New York wearing short skirts, boots, pin-striped jumpsuits and wildly contrasting colors. The maxi is worn over the mini. Tights replace stockings. Underwear becomes an issue. Bras are burned.

Fashion

- "There (in Haight-Ashbury), in a daily street-fair atmosphere, upwards of 15,000 unbonded girls and boys interact in a tribal love-seeking, free-winging, acid-based society, where if you are a hippie and you have a dime, you can put it in a parking meter and lie down in the street for an hour's sunshine."—Warren Hinckle, *Social History of the Hippies*

Quotes

Quotes

- "'An Investigation into Sex' is now offered at Dartmouth. 'Analogues to the LSD Experience' can now be studied at Penn. 'Guerrilla Warfare' is being examined by DePauw students. Stanford undergraduates are studying 'American Youth in Revolt,' and 'The Origins and Meaning of Black Power' is a course at Brooklyn College. Has higher education finally caught up with the times?"—Ralph Keyes, "The Free Universities"

Education

- Coed dorms open at numerous colleges across the country.
- U.S. college enrollment has almost doubled since 1960.
- In the fall, the WCC student population nearly doubles, from 1,205 to 2,374. The number of students in general studies and occupational studies are equal; nine percent of WCC's students are undecided about their major. The ratio of men to women: 2.4 to 1.

New Words

- Guru, blow your cool, narc, beautiful, head shop, shades, peacenik, boondocks.

WCC in 1967

WCC's student newspaper, *The Voice*, chronicles the rise and fall of concerns and issues on campus:

- In March, nearly one hundred students hear two University of Michigan doctoral candidates argue the issue of Vietnam. *The Voice*, in an unpartisan voice, reports, "Both men...provided entertainment, as well as being educational for students and faculty." Dave Pollock says he is "surprised and pleased" at the size of the turnout for the controversial topic.
- In May, *The Voice* says, "Here's the announcement you've been waiting for: a chance to come to a function and really have a groovy session. The Student Senate is presenting the second big dance of the semester, Psychedelic Weekend."

- During the same month, WCC's first—and last—fraternity obtains a residence at 2312 Packard Road. Zeta Sigma Phi offers each of its 17 members "a place to go when he is troubled, someone he can trust and trust him, people who will cry with him, people who will laugh with him, people who will help him when he needs help." Officers include Mike Purdy, Dan Nissly, Bill Cheatham, Pete Toggerson, and George Schwimmer.

- The Student Senate holds its second election. Bill Bush wins the presidency, with Kathi Nelson as vice president. On the agenda: parking problems and developing school spirit.

- Two basketball players, Tom Baldwin and Gary Owen, launch the Inter-Racial Relations Club to discuss important issues of the day: "civil rights, the Negro revolution, white backlash, and Vietnam." Baldwin tells *The Voice* "the club will provide a place for everyone—white, black and blue—to intelligently discuss the problems of our society. The main objective will be to promote a better understanding of the problems facing Negroes and whites today."

- WCC earns temporary accreditation from the North Central Association.

- Gary Owen, managing editor of *The Voice*, editorializes: *Look around, let's quit pretending. There is as much or more segregation at WCC as there is at any Mississippi university. The whites have the Ski Club, the Negroes the Jestettes. It took a lot of work just to get white girls to go out for the cheerleading squad because some said it was Negro dominated....If both black and white will drop their silly group norms and accept the basic fact of equality, then and only then will WCC be free of this ancient idea of racial prejudice.*

- *The Voice* conducts a survey of narcotics use. A similar Gallup poll estimates 13 percent of U.S. students have used narcotics, but discovers that only 6 percent had tried "grass," while WCC learns that a hefty 41 percent of its students had smoked "grass."

- The Board of Trustees approves the architectural drawings for the Exact Sciences Building on the new campus.

WCC in 1967

Chapter 2:
"The One Hundred Days"

The election had been held, the mission of the new Washtenaw Community College had been endorsed, the money had been allocated, a Board of Trustees had been elected. It was time to find the right person to lead the College from an impressive idea to an impressive institution.

The Board received applications for the president's position from all over the country, narrowed the candidates down to five, and began to get to know David Ponitz, a University of Michigan graduate and Harvard-trained educator.

The son of a former assistant superintendent of public instruction for the state of Michigan, Dave Ponitz earned his bachelor's and master's degrees at the University of Michigan before heading to Harvard for his doctorate. At the time the Community College was up for a vote in Washtenaw County, Ponitz was the superintendent of schools for Freeport, Illinois, as well as president of its small new community college. One day he happened to call Evart "Slim" Ardis in Ann Arbor to ask him for a recommendation for someone to fill a position in his school district. Ardis, the former superintendent of Ypsilanti schools, was at this time the Director of Career Planning and Placement at the University of Michigan and a member of the first WCC Board of Trustees. He told Dave Ponitz that Washtenaw was about to launch a community college in Ann Arbor and suggested that he apply.

"I wasn't sure that made sense," Ponitz recalled many years later. "I worried that some people would want to replicate the University of Michigan's programs, and I felt that any new college would have to be really different in order to meet the needs of people whose needs

The first Washtenaw Community College President, David Ponitz

weren't being met by the University of Michigan or Eastern Michigan University."

Ponitz walked the beach of Wisconsin's Door County for hours and hours one vacation, debating about whether to investigate the Washtenaw job. "It wasn't Ann Arbor that was the drawing card, but the fact that the community college movement could be the wave of the future," he said.

Ralph Wenrich, another WCC Trustee, also worked hard to convince Ponitz to become a candidate for president. Still reluctant, Ponitz arrived in Ann Arbor to talk to the Board. "It was an exciting idea, but daunting," he said. "At that point, the college possessed not a pencil or piece of paper."

Ponitz did decide to apply and was eventually offered the position— but not before Chairman of the Board Sam Harmon became convinced that Dave Ponitz was the right man.

"We had some very, very good candidates for the position of President," Sam Harmon said. "Evart Ardis knew Dave Ponitz well from his days at the University of Michigan, and he encouraged us to look at him closely, but there were many struggles and discussions among board members about who was the best among a group of very good candidates."

Although Dave Ponitz had the right academic background combined with experience as a high school and community college administrator, he was very young—thirty-two, to be exact, Harmon noted. Also, Ponitz came across as fairly conservative in a decidedly unconservative place and time. That was an attraction for some Board members and a point of concern for Sam Harmon. "Some of us wondered if that would go over well in Ann Arbor," he said. "I was the lone holdout for a while. It was clear that he was very, very competitive, but not clear if he would have a passion for the population I was most concerned with."

So, one day Harmon hopped into his car and drove to Illinois to meet with the young educator. "Both of us persuaded each other that we had the same vision of what this college should and could become. I became Dave's greatest supporter, while he became one of my greatest friends," Harmon said. "He was—and is—a damn good man with a social conscience. I suspect he knew where he wanted his career to go, and he was way ahead of the pack."

On August 13, the Board of Trustees announced its selection of David Ponitz as the first president for the new Washtenaw Community College. Ponitz told a reporter for *The Ann Arbor News*, "I am here because this appears to be one of the finest challenges in education."

The Washtenaw Community College Board of Trustees offered Dave Ponitz the opportunity to try things that he wouldn't have been able to try anywhere else in the country at that time, Harmon believed. Dave Ponitz accepted the challenge and the job. Together, the Board, the community, and the President formed a partnership that gave birth to a new community college and allowed it to flourish.

Years later, when Dave Ponitz left WCC, another search committee member, Neal Stabler, wrote him a letter saying that at the time Ponitz was appointed President, Stabler thought the wrong man had been selected, that he didn't think Ponitz was creative enough to create an institution from scratch or in tune with the needs of the broad-based population. Stabler confessed that he had been wrong about that. "I have always appreciated that letter," Ponitz said, nearly three decades after the letter was written.

DIVISION OF RESPONSIBILITIES

"One important point we made early in the process of creating this community college was the distinction between policy and administration," Sam Harmon said. "The Board was the policy maker and the President was the administrator." The selection of administrators, staff, faculty members, office procedures, and day-to-day decisions would belong to the President and his administrators.

With housing difficult to find in Ann Arbor, Dave Ponitz temporarily moved into the YMCA and set up an informal office there. Eventually, the fledgling community college leased offices at 204 Huron Street—appropriately, in the building the Chamber of Commerce had vacated.

The first thing the new President did was to create a long list of the kinds of people the College would need, the positions the College would need to fill, and the time frame. Trustee Ralph Wenrich remembered drawing numerous organizational charts and finally choosing an administrative structure with two academic deans, one for Occupational Education, the other for General Education. All other academicians would report to them. "There was a strong sense of urgency, a great number of jobs to get done. We felt strongly that everyone associated with WCC would have to have a fierce commitment to our mission," Ponitz said. "This was not the place for mediocrity."

On February 1, 1966, when Washtenaw Community College moved a few desks, chairs, and files into the Huron Street office, the College consisted of three people: Dave Ponitz, Dave Pollock, and Lloyd Van Buskirk. Pollock had left a University of Michigan job in public relations to become assistant to the president. Van Buskirk was the business manager.

Within weeks, Lee Luchsinger was hired as Executive Assistant, Norm Olmsted as Dean of General Studies, and Douglas Woolley as Registrar. It would take longer to fill the Dean of Occupational Education position; eventually Paul Hunt was lured from his job in Detroit. Together, those men formed the cornerstone for the new College. Then John Wooden was hired as Division Director of General Studies, Andy Ford was named Director of Technical and Industrial Studies, and Mehran Thomson, Director of Exact Sciences.

"Without exception, every one of those administrators pulled his weight—and then some—but Dave Pollock especially played a very, very key role in putting the first year together," Ponitz said. "People in Washtenaw County had voted for the levy, but there was still a lot of suspicion about what we were going to do. We needed someone who knew the labyrinth of the university system and the community in spades and could maneuver there. Dave did that for us; he had been working at the university for a number of years before coming to WCC. When we had questions, Dave would call someone at U of M and we would get $5,000 worth of advice free of charge."

WHO ARE WE?

"We started at the basic level, asking ourselves if everyone needed a college experience, who the targeted population would be, and whether a community college should be a glorified high school, a college, or something in between," Ponitz recalled.

Although the community college movement was snowballing around the nation and two nearby community colleges could provide some insight, no other institution shared WCC's precise goal and mission; most were more like junior colleges, preparing students for transfer to a four-year college or university after a year or two of academics. WCC's mission was much broader, with a strong emphasis on occupational training. "We knew that our occupational programs had to be strong because they provided the division of labor between WCC and the University of Michigan and Eastern Michigan," Ponitz pointed out.

Ponitz addressing a crowd. "Those early days were heady days," WCC's first President, recalled many years later. "We were always concerned about meeting the needs of our community and our students."

The University of Michigan and its experts in education were invaluable resources. Ponitz also conferred with people across the nation who were heading community colleges or struggling to establish community colleges, sharing wisdom, information, experiences, and viewpoints.

"Those early days were heady days," Ponitz recalled many years later. "We felt like we were inventing the wheel. We were always concerned about meeting the needs of our community and our students, but we were also concerned about growing too fast. With two large universities nearby and one-third of the county population attending college, I spent a lot of time pondering the uniqueness of the WCC campus and curriculum. I also spent a lot of time trying to define how we wanted to be different and how best to become involved in the economic development of our community. Our mission was very broad."

Susan Thomson, wife of Division Director Mehran Thomson, remembered the compelling way Dave Ponitz could present the College's case. "When Tommy told me about his job offer, I was not enthusiastic. As I saw it, junior colleges were second-class entities," she admitted. Then Dave Ponitz had a meeting with the wives of all the directors and teachers, explaining his vision of the school and its mission. In one hour, he convinced her that the community college was an innovative and "most-needed thing," something that hadn't been done before, she said. "I was really turned on to the idea that day—and I've been a strong supporter ever since."

"Dave was a good 'front man,'" Andy Ford said. "He had a gift for presenting the vision of the new College. He had strong connections with Lansing. He could negotiate the political system to our advantage. And he had the ability to hire top-notch people."

"Dr. Ponitz was the right man at the right time," Douglas Woolley observed, as have many others. "He was very energetic and he had a good understanding of the community college philosophy. He was excellent at promoting the college and he did an outstanding job in establishing and running the organization. He was the driving force and spirit behind the College."

Other people quickly caught the spirit. The President worked around the clock seven days a week and so did everyone else who moved into the Huron Street offices. "We made use of every inch of that space, even the stone basement; eventually we had twenty-eight people working there," Ponitz remembered. Thomson distinctly remembered the place as being "a fascinating spot." "We were all jammed into a little office with desks shared by two or three people," he said. "I came in at night to interview people." The purchasing director, Dick Mallory, had so little room to work that he would walk to a nearby park, spread his catalogues, bid proposals, faculty requests, and purchase order forms on picnic benches, and use rocks to prevent the winds from carrying them away while he worked. ("He did a monumental job almost overnight," Dave Pollock recalled.) William Cherniak interviewed Edith Croake for a teaching job in his living room, while one daughter played in a playpen and another modeled her Brownie uniform.

While President Ponitz focused on coordinating the overall direction of the College and its role in the community, many of the nuts-and-bolts decisions were coordinated by Lee Luchsinger, executive assistant to the Board of Trustees. "He came with a strong background in post-secondary schools, and he knew how to put the pieces together," Andy Ford said.

WORKING HAND IN HAND

"Time was too short for petty issues to intrude," Douglas Woolley said. "We all had our jobs and we did them—sometimes inventing them as we went along." The Board of Trustees followed the same approach. "The Board was full of resourceful people committed to identifying and providing whatever the new Community College students would need, whether it was training in specialized fields or academic work that could lead to transfers to four-year institutions," Andy Ford said. "All the Board members worked hard and were willing to take risks if they believed the risks could benefit the students," Ponitz added.

The early Board faced jobs as daunting as the job facing the President. They were grappling with big questions: how the College would find its niche in the community, how fast the College could and should grow, how accommodating to be to students and faculty qualifications, how to establish a permanent campus, and what programs to create—among countless others. Each Board member represented a unique area of expertise and they relied upon each other for their knowledge and wisdom.

Bank president Ed Adams, for instance, concentrated his efforts on financial issues. He traveled to New York City on WCC's behalf and managed to secure a loan for one-half a percent less interest than could be obtained locally. "That represented a major savings to the taxpayer," Ponitz said.

Attorney Ken Yourd "was smooth and helpful in dealing with people," Ponitz said.

Bob Forman, head of the University of Michigan alumni group, was an excellent speaker and writer. He used those skills to introduce the public and industry to the College. Sam Harmon was an inventor and a strong advocate for minority rights and issues. He gave invaluable perspectives on diversity and occupational issues. Evart "Slim" Ardis focused on helping recruit instructors and staff. An administrator in the Ann Arbor Public Schools, Dick Creal concentrated on academic and staffing issues. Ralph Wenrich was the expert on occupational education.

Active community members were also committed to helping the fledgling College. More than once, Dave Ponitz called upon Neal Stabler, particularly when the first levy renewal was endorsed county-wide but failed in Ypsilanti Township by a nine-to-one ratio. "He was a consummate politician in the best sense of the word," Ponitz said. "He suggested the names of four involved citizens who might help us and they worked hard; in the next election, the levy vote was one to one, a significant improvement."

WHEN DO WE START?

The first major decision the administration and Board tackled together made history—and serves as the basis for WCC lore. Most new community colleges were spending between two and four years to organize and build a campus before opening their doors, but WCC decided to ignore that precedent. Board members and President Ponitz agreed that the College should open that fall—which gave them just one hundred days to create a college from thin air.

"The community need was so great," Ponitz explained.

To meet the need and time crunch, President Ponitz created a unique administrative style. In time, faculty and staff members would label the President Ponitz system of management "the undulating cone." Andy Ford explained, "It was a pyramid-style form of management, with the Board and President at the apex. It was undulating because decisions traveled up and down and across. It wasn't a rigid system. We were allowed to do our jobs to the best of our abilities. We all recognized that one does need checks and balances, but there was no micromanaging. The deans and directors were a bunch of 'shoot-from-the-hip' people. We were intellectually and pragmatically movers and doers. We had to be if we were going to get the College up and running in such a short span of time."

The voters had given the new College enough funding for a full year without students, but WCC decided instead to use a substantial amount of that funding to buy equipment to start its occupational programs.

The decision to open immediately meant that temporary campus facilities would have to be found quickly, in an era when real estate was tight and huge vacant spaces were extremely rare. It also meant that the Board and President would be conducting a two-front campaign: discovering and preparing a temporary campus; while scouting for land, and designing and building a permanent campus. And, meanwhile, they had to get an administration in place, hire faculty and staff members, identify their potential students, design a curriculum, decide how to market the new College's existence and programs, create a course list and catalogue, establish a library and other resources, and make countless short- and long-term policy decisions.

All this in one hundred days.

Despite the fierce commitment, the countless hours of overtime, and the sacrifices everyone involved was making, worries lurked constantly in the background: Could everything possibly get done quickly enough? Would anything be forgotten or overlooked? Would a suitable location for a temporary campus be found in time? "While we waited for a decision about a campus, we did as much advance work as possible," Sociology Instructor Don Bylsma said. "We set up courses, wrote book lists, appointed faculty members. It was total chaos—we were always robbing Peter to pay Paul to get the equipment we needed to get started."

"A lot of people said we were nuts," Andy Ford said.

IDENTIFYING LIKELY STUDENTS

"Dave Ponitz was the perfect person to start a new college," recalled former student and former Michigan Speaker of the House Gary Owen. "He was very sensitive to the people who, for whatever reason, were disenfranchised from the system. He and the Board of Trustees

Temporary quarters mushroomed as quickly as the number of students during the early College years, when the campus was located on the Willow Run Village grounds. When the number of students rose to 2,394 during the College's second year, WCC scrambled for additional classrooms and laboratories. When even temporaries failed to accommodate all the students, classes were held at the library, the YMCA, in church basements and even in Ann Arbor's Council Chambers.

believed that it was vitally important that all people everywhere in the county be given an opportunity to get an education. He wanted to prepare students so they could go anywhere they wanted after earning their degree: into industry, good jobs, or a four-year college. His attitude was that WCC would be doing the University of Michigan a favor to send them bright, well-established, competitive students. When he accepted the presidency, he made a commitment to build something important."

Relying on research the Chamber of Commerce had gathered, the Board and President decided on an open-door admissions policy. By the late spring of 1966, Washtenaw Community College announced that it would admit everyone over the age of eighteen who knocked— regardless of whether or not they held a high school diploma and regardless of whether or not they required remedial education to bring them up to college speed. In addition, some teenagers still in high school would be permitted to enroll in classes not offered by their school districts. Initially, the Board declined to admit foreign students, believing that Washtenaw residents were their primary responsibility. A few years later, that decision was reversed. The new Community College would be the place where people who were unable, for whatever reason, to enroll in the local universities or Cleary College would be able to get an education.

As soon as Guy Hower was hired as the first counselor, the College started registering students. "We were throwing together courses as the need arose—even before having faculty members to teach them," he said. "My office at 204 Huron Street consisted of a folding chair and two typing boxes. The desks were on order, but we couldn't wait for them before getting started."

"This College was a godsend for the community—Willow Run in particular and Washtenaw County in general—because it targeted what we call the non-traditional student. It offered those students a tremendous opportunity," said Bill Moy, instructor in behavioral sciences. "Some people just glow when given an unexpected opportunity and that's what we saw happening in those days."

CURRICULUM

Creating the curriculum required countless discussions and endless research, meetings, and decisions. Experts in education at the University of Michigan told WCC's President and Board that they would be wise to start no more than three programs a year, but WCC decided once again to ignore advice and offer as many courses as the College could design. Newly hired faculty members, administrators, and Trustees put their heads together and outlined twenty-seven programs. In September, all but one of them, library science, would have enough students to open. (WCC learned that a huge surplus of librarians existed in Ann Arbor, and few openings were available.)

"The early years of WCC were fantastic, great fun," said Guy Hower. "The atmosphere seemed charged with energy. A bunch of us—the Registrar, myself, and all the division people—would go to Bill Knapp's for lunch once a week, and we'd sit there and discuss, then add new courses. We'd go back to the office and brief President Ponitz and he'd tell us, 'Go for it.' Times are very different nowadays. To add a new course, we have to make proposals, which are referred to the Curriculum Committee, then to the Deans, then the President.

The Registrar's Office was the scene of unending surprises. During the first Registration, supervised by Douglas Woolley, more than 1,200 students enrolled in the brand-new Community College. Administrators had hoped for as many as 700 students. The following year, the number of students matriculating doubled.

The process now takes years. In the old days, the process took no more than a week."

With the leadership of Trustee Ralph Wenrich and members of the Chamber of Commerce's Education Committee, President Ponitz, instructors, and counselors introduced themselves to local industries to identify which programs would best serve the community.

Dave Ponitz had learned a vital lesson about establishing a relationship between industry and a community college while he was in Illinois, and he strove to avoid traditional pitfalls. "I learned that often industry didn't understand our mission; they just wanted to acquire cheap labor," he said. "We wanted to avoid that trap at WCC, to let industry know right away that we were training our students for skilled positions that would warrant excellent pay." At the other end of the spectrum, he also had to pacify people who worried that four-year college and university degrees would be diluted if community college students could transfer their credits to prestigious institutions.

Washtenaw created an advisory committee for every occupational education program. The committee members, who always included one or two students as well as middle- and top-level managers in the related industries, helped select equipment and recruit students; they also offered advice on curriculum matters and spread the word about the new College programs throughout their industry. Later, they became invaluable in helping WCC students land jobs after graduation. "The advisory committees were extremely helpful," Dave Pollock said. Every department and division head would agree.

In the early years, WCC offered academic courses, the Health Sciences Program, the Dental Assistant Program, and classes to become an office administrator, medical secretary, x-ray technician, auto mechanic, auto body repairman, and welder. There were also classes teaching drafting, electronics, mechanical technologies, and accounting. "Because we had such a loose and adaptable structure, we were able to react to events, particularly the unrest of the 1960s and the '70s, quickly, with new classes and even new programs," Hower said. The Black Students and Women's Studies programs are just two examples.

To encourage the sense of shared mission, Dave Ponitz and Lee Luchsinger created a policy called "the mix," where all faculty members—general and occupational—would share office space. "That was a terrific way to promote interaction and communication," Guy Hower said.

Lee Luchsinger wrote and produced the first Washtenaw Community College catalogue, typing it himself on his manual typewriter. The office staff made mimeographed copies and started circulating the catalogue to potential faculty, students, community members, and local businesses.

The staff was just as busy, overworked, and overcommitted. Office assistants created work spaces, started brand new files, and in some cases tracked down their own supplies and furnishings. Library Director Harold Young and his assistant, Judy Hicks, left jobs at the Dearborn campus of the University of Michigan to set up the WCC library even before there was a facility. They were among the people crowded deep in the basement of the Huron Street offices. "We had no books when I was hired," Judy Hicks remembered. "We were in the process of just starting the collection. As new instructors were hired, they supplied us with suggestions of what books their students would need and we scrambled to get what we could. We were a small family, wedged into a crowded space, but I always looked forward to coming to work because everyone liked and cared for everyone else so much."

Many early administrators credit Lee Luchsinger with the smooth running of business affairs. "I can't really say that we had financial concerns in those days," Andy Ford said. The county's financial support and state grants gave the College money in the bank to work with before the doors even opened.

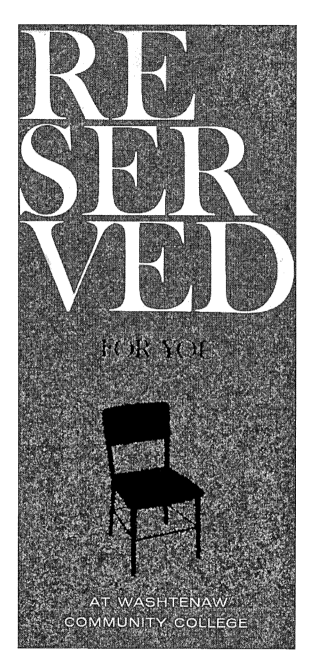

The College's first recruiting brochure.

Administrators weren't given blank checks, but they were given the go-ahead to get the equipment they needed. "We were all reasonable in our requests; we had an unspoken understanding that we had to share from the same pot, and we all wanted to make this new college work," Andy Ford said. "The Board of Trustees was extremely supportive. Most of the members had run on platforms stressing the

A FIERCE COMMITMENT

To Teaching

Positions for teacher-counselors in Communication Arts, Paramedical Technology, Science and Mathematics, Electrical-Electronics, Social Sciences, Automotive Technology, Materials and Processes, and Drafting and Design. College opening September 1966. Responsibilities are one-third time teaching, one-third preparation and self improvement, one-third work with individual students. Salary range $6,500 to $12,500. Excellent collateral benefit program: unlimited sick leave; life, hospitalization, major-medical, and long-term disability insurance; accidental death and travel accident coverage; tax-sheltered annuity program; sabbatical leave policy.

Write for brochure and application:
Dr. David H. Ponitz, President
Washtenaw Community College
204 East Huron Street, Ann Arbor, Michigan 48108

*New York Times
May 15, 1966*

importance of occupational training. They stood behind their campaign pledges."

Dave Pollock and Lee Luchsinger were responsible for publicizing the new College to potential students. They decided to advertise by circulating brochures in supermarket bags, hoping people would bring them home and look at them. The first brochure featured a red and white chair on the cover with the words "Reserved for You." Dave Pollock remembered the lengthy discussion of just what kind of chair should be on that cover. He insisted it be a "modern chair."

FINDING & HIRING THE RIGHT PEOPLE

No model existed to provide a blueprint for creating, designing, then building a community college. Nor was there a blueprint for identifying appropriate faculty and staff members. "Hiring was another immense challenge," Dave Ponitz remembered. "Some people wanted to rely on high school as a model, some wanted to rely on the university as a model, others wanted to create something very different."

Because WCC was located in a community with so many educational institutions, the educational community assumed that the Community College instructors would all hold doctorates. The Board and President took a different stand. "Our priority was to find people who could really connect with our students," Ponitz said. "We developed a hiring profile for our faculty members—which is where the phrase 'A Fierce Commitment' came into play. There was a shortage of teachers in those days, but we still focused on finding the best people, people with real world experience as well as good teaching skills, people who cared about students, and shared our vision."

According to Dave Pollock, the best policy the new President made was to insist that everyone within a program—men and women, African-American and whites—be paid the same salary for the same work. "That was revolutionary in the mid-1960s," Pollock said. Char Hanson, hired to teach Speech, agreed, pointing out, "Not many institutions were similarly enlightened."

"One important thing to understand about WCC was that the school was looking for the best faculty and administrators—and they weren't interested in pulling everyone from either Eastern Michigan University or the University of Michigan," Hanson added. Flavia Reps, for example, learned about WCC

William Pittman, director of Buildings & Grounds, helped with the final decision to move the new College onto the grounds at Willow Run Village. "Bill walked on the roof of the old elementary school to see if it was good and it held him," David Pollock remembered. "That convinced us there was potential."

on the East Coast, when she read a job posting in *The New York Times*. Stuart Susnick drove a taxicab in New York City prior to landing his teaching position. Edith Croake had been teaching in Chicago, David Byrd in Washington, D.C. "Dr. Ponitz did a brilliant job of bringing qualified people from all over the country and then letting them do what they did best," Hanson said.

Dave Ponitz and his staff created the title "teacher-counselor" to describe the faculty's role. The decision was controversial at the time. More than one job applicant with strong academic credentials was incredulous and dismayed to see WCC hire someone with fewer academic qualifications. "But our issue was which candidate would really work well with our students," Ponitz said. He recalled one teacher who wore jeans, faded T-shirts, and sandals to class, to the dismay of some administrators and Board members, who considered this highly unprofessional. Students later told Ponitz this instructor was one of the most effective faculty members, someone they could connect with. "That's the trick: to find the right person to connect," Ponitz told his administrators.

The College's open-door policy meant new and different challenges for incoming faculty members. It also meant that WCC needed to provide remedial as well as vocational and academic opportunities for students. "We had to find faculty willing to take on that challenge," Don Bylsma pointed out.

"We were in a hurry and we did amazingly well in our hiring, considering how needy we were. But there is no question that we made some mistakes," Ponitz said in retrospect. "Sometimes we should have checked more thoroughly on individuals' backgrounds, but that can always be said when someone is in the midst of a massive hiring campaign."

By the time WCC opened its doors in the fall of 1966, the faculty consisted of fifty full-time instructor-counselors recruited from all over the country, with very different backgrounds.

FINDING A TEMPORARY CAMPUS

By May of 1966, the decision was made to open the first classes in the fall—which didn't give WCC much time to pull everything and everybody together. Dave Pollock's first assignment was to find a suitable temporary site for the College.

Everyone helped whenever they could. Assistant to the President David Pollock paints the old cafeteria, supervised by William Pittman.

Pollock checked every lead, but none seemed appropriate. It was Roy Smith, state representative from Ypsilanti, who suggested Willow Run as a possibility. The old Foster School had been built to educate the children of employees working at the bomber plant during World War II, and it stood empty. One Sunday afternoon, Pollock and his wife, Joanne, drove out to Willow Run Village, the housing community built for bomber plant workers at the start of

World War II. Besides the old elementary school, they found a fire station that had been converted into a meat market, a bowling alley, and the old bachelors' quarters for the military, a long, barn-shaped building. "I walked around the school, saw the broken windows and overgrown site, then got into the car and said, 'There is no way this place is appropriate,'" Dave Pollock remembered with a grin, adding, "I would later have to eat those words!"

Douglas Woolley drove out to Willow Run with his wife one night and didn't even bother to get out of the car. "It looked too far gone to be of use," he remembered. Guy Hower's experience was similar. "I can still remember the first time I saw the temporary campus. Willow Run was full of condemned buildings with hundreds of broken windows. We had to break a door down at the bowling alley to get in because the key had been lost."

When the new College President saw the former site of the village that had served workers at the bomber plant during World War II, he was appalled. "My first response was, 'My God! We can do better than this!'" Ponitz said. "However, I had looked around at many unusable places by that time, and we hadn't seen anything else that would work."

The few other options seemed even less appropriate. "I drove everywhere," Pollock recalled. In desperation, he returned to Willow Run. He decided that it offered two things no other site offered: the new Community College could be self-contained there, and the location was adjacent to two low-income neighborhoods that might provide students.

"Bill Pittman (head of Buildings and Grounds), who weighed somewhere around 300 pounds, walked the roof of the old school to see if it was good and it held him," Pollock remembered. "That convinced us there was potential."

The Trustees had hired a planning group to help the College locate grounds for the new campus; Pollock asked the group to look at the site. "The shortcoming of the location was that it wasn't central; it was almost on the Wayne County line," Pollock pointed out. "On the other

A divine setting, St. Alexis Church was the location for the Registrar's Office and faculty quarters for the second wave of new-hires. Andy Ford, the first Director of Technical & Industrial Studies, remembered the days of student revolts, when a bomb was lobbed through the window of St. Alexis.

The first Registrar's Offices were located in Willow Run Village's former meat market. One administrator recalls sitting on a pillowcase full of students' tuition dollars during Registration, then locking the money in the meat freezer until the next day, when the banks were open.

hand, it was in the heart of a depressed community and those kids who had been throwing rocks at the vacant buildings might be the kids who would benefit most from a community college."

With the planners' blessing, WCC invited state officials to inspect the place. They approved the location for one year—which stretched into two, and then three years. "The saving grace turned out to be the fact that the boiler in the school was in good shape and that each classroom had two exits—one off the hallway and one leading outside," Pollock said.

Mehran Thomson thought the old school building was "a gem." "I remember the beauty of the architectural plans," he said. "The blueprints had been drawn by a nationally renowned architect, one of the Saarinens, at a time when the government had put some of the nation's best architects to work on federal projects." Because metal was needed for the war effort, the building was all made of wood. The only drawback was that this meant that each classroom had a wooden post in the middle of the room, Thomson remembered. Art Instructor Fred Horowitz admired the eighteen-inch-tall clerestory windows that ran just below the ceiling of every classroom.

But the school had gone downhill dramatically once the war ended. The tar roof leaked badly. Hundreds of windows were broken. Paint was flaking. As soon as the Trustees gave their approval, Bill Pittman hired a team of "commandos" to paint, fix broken windows, fix plumbing and lighting, pull weeds, mow hayfields, and make necessary repairs. "They worked faster than fast," marveled David Ponitz. "Then we furnished our classrooms with long, new desks and comfortable chairs so the place wouldn't look like a high school."

"I was twenty-eight when I started teaching at WCC, young and foolish enough to think the temporary quarters at Willow Run were wonderful," Roger Bertoia said.

One thing the old school lacked was a science lab, so Thomson furnished the old kindergarten room with science tables and cupboards he discovered at the University of Michigan surplus shop. Plumbers installed plumbing lines and hooked them to the sewer. "It was fun to design and supervise my own lab," he remembered.

Dirt roads meandered onto the site of the temporary College campus. After the old school was transformed into the new College Hall, it housed the majority of General Studies classes and a scattering of Occupational Studies classes.

Administrators' offices were located in the former firehouse-turned-meat market. Faculty and staff members would joke that that was "where you could find the meatheads." "The original organization of the College called for the President to be the outside person, working with organizations within the community, while Lee [Luchsinger] would in essence be the provost, or vice president, supervising every aspect of running the campus," Roger Bertoia said. "Dr. Ponitz was definitely a hands-on administrator, however. His office at Willow Run sat on the spot where the fire trucks used to park. He would point out, 'This is where the fires will still be put out.' When we moved to the new campus, he had another saying: 'Whatever happens at this institution happens across my desk.'"

At first, the only functioning women's bathroom outside of College Hall was in the fire station/meat market, so faculty frequently visited, Edith Croake remembered. Registration, Student Services, and Admissions set up shop in the old St. Alexis Church. The auto repair and body shops found quarters on Carpenter Road in the former Sealtest Dairy distribution plant; they remained there for nearly ten years.

A ten-minute walk from College Hall, the former bowling alley became home to WCC's counseling offices, faculty offices, and the

"This is where you could find the meatheads," faculty members joked about WCC's first administrative building, a former meat market.

When Executive Assistant to the President David Pollock first saw the abandoned elementary school at Willow Run Village, he told his wife, "There is no way this place is appropriate." Weeks later, after searching the county for an appropriate temporary campus, he would have to eat those words. The College launched the 100 Day "Commando Raid" on the abandoned bomber plant village in order to prepare it for the College's first school year.

library. "We had everything we needed and it was actually quite convenient," Judy Hicks said. "We could park right at the door. We had room for study tables. Hal Young was very, very resourceful. We had books coming from everywhere, often given to us gratis when people or other libraries were getting rid of books." Faculty members and administrators could find the secretarial pool in the old bowling alley; department heads would bring their tests to be typed, materials to be mimeographed, and letters to be typed and mailed. Andy Ford's first office was there, and he didn't mind the cramped, open quarters that he shared with Bill Cherniak, Director of the English, Speech, and Language Division. "My office in the Detroit schools had been a converted lavatory wedged between two home economics rooms, you see, so the Willow Run office looked good to me—despite an occasional infestation of mice!"

At first, the five other faculty members sharing space with Edith Croake all shared one phone. The library contained the most modern technology—"a machine that fascinated us all," she remembered. "It was a single Xerox machine. Soon, you had to stand in line to make one copy of an important memo. We had only one mimeograph machine to print materials and tests for classes. The textbooks didn't arrive on time for the first semester, so I typed up, ran off, and handed out dittos to study."

As the numbers of students, staff members, and faculty rose, the College would appropriate several remaining Quonset huts and temporary structures for faculty offices, classrooms, bookstore, and the day care center. In the summer of 1967, six faculty members were

The public response to the College was overwhelming; 1,207 students registered for the fall of 1966.

Friendly toddlers housed in a Quonset hut occasionally visited faculty offices.

asked to move their offices from the bowling alley to a Quonset hut. Gerry Rees, a physics instructor, remembered that on at least one occasion, there was a diaper underneath the water fountain, a product of the adjacent day care center. "It was very unusual in those days for a college to offer childcare," Croake said. One day, a friendly toddler wandered into her office, then accepted her hand. "I enjoyed walking him back to the center."

Years later, Rees reminded Croake how hard it was to hang anything—a chart, for instance—on the curved walls of their Quonset hut. He also reminded her of the thermostat wars. "The hut had only one control," she said. "The physics teachers wanted the building cool enough that their students would stay awake. Shirley Roberts wanted the children's center warm for the children. Each party would change the thermostat when the other wasn't looking. I always brought an extra sweater in case it was a day when the physics teachers won the battle of the thermostat."

Heat was a problem for everyone. "The buildings at Willow Run weren't plush, but everyone knew that they were only temporary and that we could anticipate better quarters in a short while," Lola Jones, a former counselor, said. Jones remembered that the counseling offices were drafty in the winter and hot in the summer. Because the buildings had been abandoned for some years, mice shared space with faculty, staff, and students, and they form part of the College lore. Char Hanson loves to tell the story of her early teaching days in College Hall. "Because I was a speech teacher, I often stood in the

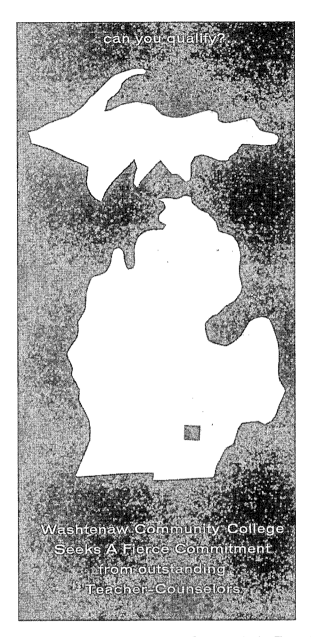

can you qualify?

Washtenaw Community College
Seeks A Fierce Commitment
from outstanding
Teacher-Counselors

Faculty members and administrators hailed from all parts of the state and the country.

back of the classroom so I could hear my students better. One day I saw a mouse running down the wall. A student motioned to me, asking if I wanted him to get the mouse. I vigorously nodded my head, and he caught the mouse and deposited it outside."

Don Bylsma remembered the way the old school suffered during rainstorms. "It leaked like a sieve, so whenever it rained, we ran for buckets and wastebaskets and anything else that could catch the water." Counselors' offices were carved out of the former Foster School's lobby and the clerestory windows just under the ceiling leaked every time it rained. "We'd have to get out twenty or twenty-five wastebaskets to catch the rain-water," Guy Hower said. "No one got upset; we regarded everything as a new adventure. We had great fun."

Before the College arrived, the only occupied building in Willow Run Village was Sunshine Nursing Home, which stood behind the old bowling alley. Judy Hicks fondly remembered an elderly man named Gus greeting everyone as they arrived in the mornings and saying goodbye when they left at night. "He was our mascot."

EARLY SCHOOL DAYS

The brand-new Washtenaw Community College was prepared to launch seventy-two classes by the time Registration Day, September 15, 1966, arrived. "Looking back on that statistic, I'm still impressed," Andy Ford said.

"One of the things that strikes me about the beginning of the school was that it never occurred to us that we couldn't make it work, even though none of us had ever done this before," Edith Croake said. "There was a real sense of urgency, not only about teaching our craft to the best of our abilities, but also contributing to the larger good, to make education a success for people who hadn't had the opportunity to attend college before."

The first year "took off like a dream," according to Char Hanson. "WCC opened to great success. The students who enrolled knew they were being offered something good."

Many faculty members and Trustees credit President Ponitz with carrying the College on his shoulders during the early days. "Dave Ponitz had the height and stature to be a commanding authority figure," said Don Bylsma. "He didn't speak loudly, but he spoke calmly, clearly, and with authority." In the early days of the College, the President knew every faculty, staff member, and student by name— and something about each one's family. People could count on him to be the first person on campus in the morning and the last person to leave at night, to sit down and chat at lunch or break times. He also made rounds to local and civic organizations to present the goals and mission of the new Washtenaw Community College.

Everyone associated with the early days remembers the great sense of excitement, the feeling of working together to build something important, and the feeling of togetherness. "Students, staff, and teachers all felt that we were in this together," said Bill Figg, who enrolled in the automotive program in the fall of 1966 and returned years later as an instructor. "There's a story that the guys in the auto center like to tell about Dave Ponitz. One day he dropped by the auto center, bringing the paychecks to Dan Gray and Bruce Welch, who were sitting around eating lunch with a bunch of students and instructors. Someone casually asked, 'Dave, what the hell do you do here?' He said, 'Well, Dan, I'm the President.' The instructor said in surprise, 'Yeah? No shit!' There was a great sense of camaraderie, of

College Hall on the Willow Run campus was located in the converted and formerly deserted Foster Elementary School, which had been designed by noted architects at the start of World War II for the children of bomber plant workers.

equality. Everyone was working together to help this new College take off."

Some faculty and staff members discovered that they just couldn't maintain the frantic pace over a long period of time. Registrar Douglas Woolley left WCC on August 1, 1968, to become associate registrar at the University of Michigan. Al Klineman took his place, just as he had years before when Woolley left MSU. "The reason I left after two and half years was just that my people were so terribly overworked and we couldn't get additional help," Woolley said. "It was both exciting and frustrating to be on the ground floor. I very much enjoyed the students and I continued to believe in the philosophy and mission of the College very much." In fact, Woolley ran for Trustee in 1970.

"It was tremendously exciting to help create a school from scratch, a terrific, once-in-a-lifetime experience," Roger Bertoia said.

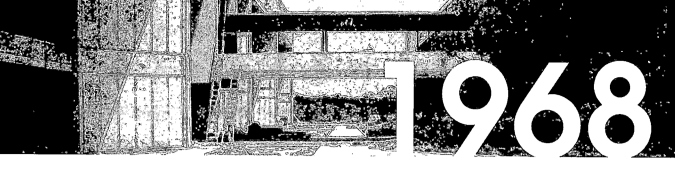

1968

1969 1970 1971 1972 1973

History & Politics

- President Lyndon Johnson announces he will not run for another term in office.

- The Viet Cong begin the Tet Offensive. Saigon is invaded. Hue is recaptured.

- Dr. Martin Luther King Jr., leader of the Civil Rights Movement and winner of the 1964 Nobel Peace Prize, is assassinated in a Memphis hotel. Massive rioting erupts in 125 cities; 46 are killed.

- Senator Robert Kennedy announces his candidacy for the Democratic presidential nomination and, following victory in the California primary in June, is assassinated.

- The 1968 Civil Rights Act passes.

- Yippies lead major riots at the Democratic Convention in Chicago. Hubert Humphrey is selected Democratic candidate.

- Richard Nixon, promising to end the Vietnam War, is elected 37th President of U.S. by the narrowest margin since 1912.

- Vietnam: U.S. troop strength: 540,000; U.S. dead: 30,857; enemy dead: 422,979.

Sports

- Detroit wins the World Series, beating St. Louis 4-3.

- Denny McLain, who shares the Cy Young Award with Bob Gibson, is the first since Dizzy Dean in 1934 to win 30 games.

Theater

- Off-off-Broadway's production of *Hair*, billed as "the first tribal-love-rock musical," hits the stage and revolutionizes theater with its nudity, sexuality, and anti-establishment values.

Movies

- On the big screen: *The Thomas Crown Affair, Star!, Funny Girl, Romeo and Juliet, The Odd Couple, In Cold Blood, The Lion in Winter, 2001: A Space Odyssey.*

Television

- Nielsen's Top Ten shows: *Rowan and Martin's Laugh-In; Gomer Pyle, U.S.M.C.; Bonanza; Mayberry, R.F.D.; Family Affair; Gunsmoke; Julia; The Dean Martin Show; Here's Lucy; The Beverly Hillbillies.*

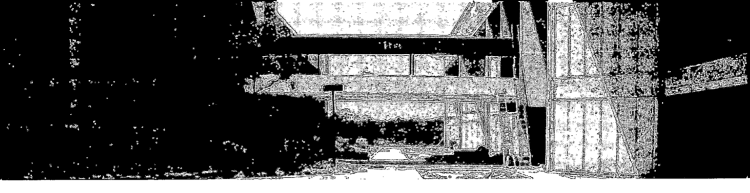

Music

- Hit songs: "Folsom Prison Blues," "Sunshine of Your Love," "The Windmills of Your Mind," "Galveston," "Spinning Wheel," "Lady Madonna," "Do Your Own Thing," "Hey, Jude," "Mrs. Robinson," "Stoned Soul Picnic."

Books

- *Airport* (Alex Hailey), *Myra Breckenridge* (Gore Vidal), *Soul on Ice* (Eldridge Cleaver), *The Electric Kool-Aid Acid Test* (Tom Wolfe), *The Whole Earth Catalogue* (Stewart Brand), *The Weight Watcher's Cook Book.*

Fashion

- Women of all ages wear pants for every occasion, also shirt jackets, long white sweaters, hip-length vests, and multiple chains. Jumpers and sweater-tunics are worn over pants with large belts. Leather dresses, vests, and belted leather skirts are worn with turtlenecks and matching tights. Accessories: novelty rings on all five fingers, long scarves, and safari pouch bags.

- Men choose plaid suits blazing in colors. White blazers trimmed with blue are worn with bright-colored shirts. Ties widen.

Education

- Columbia University is occupied by student rebels.

- Yale admits women.

- Black Studies programs are developed at numerous colleges and universities.

- Black militancy increases on campuses; the president of San Francisco State resigns as black instructors urge black students to bring guns to campus.

- Occupational and graduate school military deferments are cut back.

Quotes

- "We've got some difficult days ahead. But it really doesn't matter with me now. Because I've been to the mountain top. Like anybody, I would like to live a long life, (but) I've seen the Promised Land...Mine eyes have seen the glory of the coming of the Lord."—Martin Luther King Jr., in Memphis, shortly before his assassination.

- "We are at a crisis point in the history of American education and probably in that of the Western world."—Richard Hofstadter, Columbia University professor

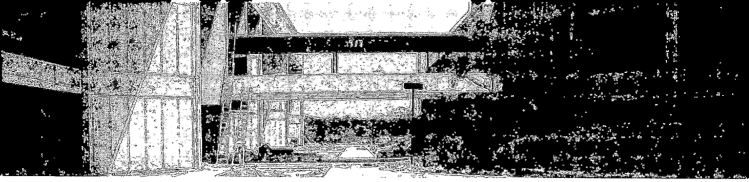

■ "The youth rebellion is a worldwide phenomenon that has not been seen before in history. I do not believe they will calm down and be ad execs at thirty as the Establishment would have us believe."—William Burroughs

■ "No girl child born today should responsibly be brought up to be a housewife. Too much has been made of defining human personality and destiny in terms of sex organs. After all, we share the human brain." —Betty Friedan

The WCC student newspaper, *The Voice*, chronicles the highlights of the year:

■ WCC's secretarial and clerical staff vote to establish a labor bargaining organization.

■ Instructor-counselor Franklin Ferguson offers a new course, "History of the American Negro."

■ WCC Warriors' basketball season ends with a 5-10 record.

■ A center "to help draft victims" opens in Ann Arbor. Half the counselors are ministers and all advise about alternatives to military service, including deferments, non-combatant alternatives, prison, and Canada.

■ Students conduct memorial services commemorating Martin Luther King Jr.'s life and WCC renames the Student Center "Martin Luther King Hall" in Dr. King's memory.

■ Mechanical tech students meet with Dean Paul Hunt to protest the deficiencies in the shop area. The list of concerns: "(1). Upon graduation we want to be competent machine operators. (2). We need tools for the machines we already have and more machines. (3). Most of the students have taken three shop classes and have not learned to operate the basic machine tools." The students propose a remedy: to have the shop open during the summer from 8 a.m. to 10 p.m., at the College's expense, so that all students can obtain adequate training. "We are not threatening the college, we are just concerned about not being able to secure a job after graduation," the proposal reads.

WCC in 1968

- April 22, students urge President Ponitz to appoint a "qualified Negro" to the position of Executive Assistant to the President vacated by Lee Luchsinger. Dr. Ponitz acknowledges "the problem of Negro identification," but notes that WCC is "the most integrated Junior College in Michigan," that 22 percent of the student body and 17 percent of the faculty are blacks.

- On June 8, WCC holds its first commencement; 52 graduate.

- Of the 1,207 WCC students eligible to vote, 309 cast their ballots during the spring, in a mock election; 111 vote for Robert Kennedy, 56 for Senator Eugene McCarthy, and 25 for Governor Nelson Rockefeller.

- College enrollment rises to 3,358 at the third fall registration, with 52 percent of the students registering for the Occupational Studies Program, 35 percent for General Studies, and 13 percent undecided. The College adds 200 new parking spaces, 8 new temporary classrooms at College Hall, 2 temporaries at the Automotive Center on Carpenter Road, and 5 new portables to house the new Bookstore and faculty offices.

- Groundbreaking for the new campus takes place October 17.

- In November, a nursery school opens in Holmes Hall, with services free of charge to student parents.

- The Washtenaw Community College Education Association charges WCC with unfair labor practices because the administration refuses to allow the association to inspect the faculty personnel files in an effort to determine salaries.

Chapter 3:
The Times

Shortly before the College opened in 1966, faculty members received a congratulatory telegram from President Ponitz thanking them for their *fierce commitment* to teaching, but no major social event was planned to launch the College. "We were all moving so fast that summer trying to get ready for the students that we probably didn't have time," English Instructor Edith Croake surmised. "Everyone had a spirit of adventure about the start of this new college in an era when new and exciting things were happening everywhere. On campus, the times were exciting, energizing, hectic, and sometimes even hazardous."

Those adjectives also describe America during the late 1960s. Washtenaw Community College opened in a time of great social turmoil. Students around the world were protesting, picketing, marching, demonstrating, dropping out, sitting-in, and organizing teach-ins to express their views about students' rights, civil rights, women's rights, Earth's rights, and the war in Vietnam.

This was also an era when education was undergoing enormous changes in curriculum, teaching styles, programs, and in the way students and faculty regarded institutions and authority figures. "Dress codes were dropped. Students rioted, marched, and demonstrated—and so did our faculty members," Math Instructor Dennis Bila recalled. "I was opposed to the war and I supported Eugene McCarthy. Most of our faculty members were like me: young and going to school ourselves. The University of Michigan's politics had a strong influence on the people here. Remember, the SDS (Students for a Democratic Society) was founded in Michigan."

Through the late 1960s and early 1970s, pro-civil rights and antiwar riots swept across the nation's campuses and through city

neighborhoods. Police and National Guard troops were sent into the streets of Boston, Cincinnati, and Detroit. Michigan's governor had to call federal troops to Detroit to restore order. Although WCC's campus, with some noteworthy exceptions, remained relatively calm, for years police struggled with student protestors at the nearby University of Michigan and Eastern Michigan University.

"There was a lot of excitement in the air in those days," former WCC student Gary Owen remembered. "People were marching for civil rights. People were marching in protest of the Vietnam War. Women were marching for their rights. The student body at WCC was probably more energized than students in other parts of the state because we had EMU and the university here and they were centers of unrest."

"It wasn't just the students who marched. Faculty marched as well," Bill Moy said. "There was quite a feeling of solidarity on campus." Instructor Stuart Susnick wasn't the only faculty member who

Civil rights, black issues, and racial equality were hot topics on campus during the College's early years. Director of Student Affairs Jim Jones and President David Ponitz met with concerned students repeatedly during these turbulent times.

climbed aboard a bus to participate in a massive antiwar rally in Washington in 1969. "The late 1960s and early 1970s were times of great anxiety, yet no one quite knew what they were anxious about," Susnick said. "There was a sense of normlessness, of a full-blown cultural crisis. I was twenty-three when I came to teach in 1968, a very young man influenced by the war and the turbulence in our social and economic order. I remember hanging out with students and discussing what was happening. Everything seemed up for grabs: the economic structure, social mores, sexual mores, politics. There was a great deal of doubt and uncertainty. When an old order falls away, people can become very anxious. Teaching became hard because to teach well you need faith that what you're teaching has truth and value." He was teaching a government class at the time.

The national unrest resounded on WCC's campus. "We suffered from our share of traumas," President Ponitz said. "Several times during the days of the riots, when Detroit was burning, Dave Pollock and I linked arms with folks from the Willow Run area—black and white—and we stood arm-and-arm all night, afraid that the campus would be torched. Those community leaders told us, 'No one is going to take this college away from us—this is our hope.'"

President Ponitz returned home from a vacation in 1968 to hear that Martin Luther King Jr., had been assassinated. "For the next week, all I did was walk the campus, talking to students and faculty members and community leaders," he said. "Those were hard, tough days." During those days, the President was driving home from a meeting in Detroit one night when he saw a big fire off in the distance. "My God, it's the College!" he said—but learned, to his great relief, that the fire was actually the Ypsilanti dump burning dried Christmas trees. "It was a symptom of the times that my first thought was that the campus had been torched."

At one point, the head of the regional state police came to campus and talked about the ongoing riots at universities. He told the College President that there would be several hundred students demonstrating on the WCC campus the next day and he described how two of them—undercover policemen—would be dressed. "He told us that they would yell, scream, holler, and then march everyone off campus," Ponitz remembered. "He was right."

During the height of the riots, filling stations refused to sell gasoline because gasoline was being used to start fires and police shut down party stores in Washtenaw County because they were afraid drinking would inflame the crowds even more, Registrar Douglas Woolley recalled. Edith Croake remembered watching Detroit burning on national news and learning that curfews had been imposed from Detroit to Ypsilanti. "We had to end some evening classes early and we all worried and wondered if the turmoil would come and affect the College," she said. "I was impressed by how the community members were willing to risk their safety, guarding the new Community College. We all had a sense of urgency, of history in the making—whether for good or bad, we weren't sure." Speech Instructor Char Hanson remembered asking one student agitator why the students were unwilling to take change more slowly. He answered, "First you have to get their attention."

One night someone lobbed a bomb onto the President's desk through the front window of the office building. "I found it Monday morning and it scared the hell out of all of us," Ponitz said. "Dave Pollock called the FBI and the FBI told us the information would be on President Nixon's desk the next morning."

For several years, WCC phones periodically rang with bomb threats. The first time the State Police responded to a bomb threat here, they didn't know any more than WCC officials did about what to do—and not to do. Dave Pollock remembered that several faculty members and administrators volunteered to search the buildings for bombs. "Once we found a black box and lifted it down to see what was inside—about the dumbest thing in the world to do," he said. "That was when we realized we didn't even know what a bomb looked like."

After a while, bomb scares were so frequent that Pollock became convinced that they were phoned in by students who wanted a day off or to miss an exam. "It was my responsibility to determine if we should clear the classrooms. That authority weighed heavily," he said. "What if I assessed the situation incorrectly?"

"Passions about Vietnam and civil rights would ebb and flow on campuses around the country," Dave Ponitz said. "I know of other colleges where students would plan to protest every Thursday—and they would spend an hour beforehand debating about what the issue of the week would be."

Actually, despite a decade of excitement, threats, demonstrations, student demands, and marches, the new College's students were far less politically active than those at the local universities. "Many of our students were older and had families. They were working full time and taking classes, so they didn't have the time or inclination to get involved in political movements," Psychology Instructor Bill Moy said.

"Aside from some issues about race, WCC students weren't in the forefront of the student movements," Trustee Richard W. Bailey said. "Probably because this was a commuter campus, our students weren't the ones leading demonstrations and strikes. In commuter colleges, students have an affiliation to their program and they see the people in their program as their group. They're not sitting around their dorms at night drinking beer and talking about overthrowing the people in charge. They're working towards a personal goal. Those were contentious times, but the most glaring issue facing students was really about Vietnam and whether or not a student would have to go off to fight."

Assisted by the G.I. Bill, many Vietnam veterans started their college studies at WCC after returning to the States. "Many of them arrived with problems," librarian Kathleen Scott said. "My husband, Dennis Burden, was a WCC counselor and a veteran himself. He had been a Navy medic in Korea and he himself was educated because of the G.I. Bill, so he was very committed to having everyone eligible for the G.I. Bill take advantage of it. But there were many emotionally scarred veterans throughout the 1970s, and his counseling job often encompassed much more than preparing them for college life." Burden had a close relationship with the Veterans Administration Hospital and several times had to drive a student there for emergency help.

According to Technical Education Instructor Roger Bertoia, "The biggest concern for most of the faculty at WCC was getting the marching done and the students headed for home before the night students arrived."

BRINGING THE TIMES INTO THE CLASSROOM

One reason for WCC's success in averting major incidents was the fact that from the beginning, the College took a strong stand in favor of affirmative action, Andy Ford said. A significant percentage of staff, administrators, and faculty members were female and minority members. Faculty members willingly discussed race and politics in their classrooms. Students in Edith Croake's composition class read Martin

THE VOICE

Volume 2, Number 11   WASHTENAW COMMUNITY COLLEGE   May 9, 1968

Owen Says: "There Is A Need For A Black Administrator"

The Voice has reported on the state of faculty and administrative issues throughout the College's history.

Luther King Jr.'s, "Letter from the Birmingham Jail," then discussed factors that cause people to change their minds. They also discussed the Freedom Riders (people from the North, many of them college students, who had ridden to the South during the Civil Rights Movement to help with voter registration). Croake, who was in her mid-twenties at the time, mentioned that some of her classmates had been on those buses. A young man her age in the back row of the classroom tipped his chair back and spoke up in his deep southern drawl. "You know, when those Freedom Riders came to Montgomery, they were met with angry, shouting crowds, streams of water from fire hoses, and barking, jumping dogs. I was one of the folks in the crowd holding onto the dogs." Since that day, he added, he had done a lot of thinking and had come to see how wrong that was. "Now I want to do what I can to create a more equal society."

"No one spoke for some time after his remarks," Edith Croake recalled. That student, Gary Owen, later became active in Michigan politics and served as Speaker of the House.

During the 1960s, Trustees debated about whether a police academy should be added to the WCC curriculum. "In those days, some people felt that the police were not friends of the ordinary citizens," Croake said. Faculty members were among them. Edith Croake remembers Dan Laursen, a Norwegian and WCC's first geology teacher, standing up at a faculty meeting and warning that schools had to be very, very careful when people with uniforms and guns become visible on campuses. "He was teaching in Norway when the Nazis came and he saw them shoot his students," she said. Mike Keresteszi, who became the College's second library director, told harrowing tales of political duress in Eastern Europe during World War II. "He escaped the Nazis with only the shirt on his back," Croake said. "Those stories echoed what was happening in our society at this time. There were many opportunities, formal and informal, to talk about what was happening to America."

■ ■ ■

In April of 1968, Martin Luther King Jr., was assassinated. The world was shocked, angry, and saddened. Faculty members opened up classes to discussions about racism. One of Edith Croake's students recommended a church janitor as a speaker. He was invited to campus and spoke convincingly about the Civil Rights Movement and the current unrest. Counselor Marguerite Eaglin visited classes, advising students about how they could become involved in helping to solve society's social problems.

The shock waves of upsetting events didn't cease. WCC's first graduation was held on the lawn in 1968, shortly after Robert Kennedy had been assassinated. Administrators changed the time of the ceremony so it wouldn't conflict with the time of his memorial service. The Commencement audience was asked to begin the ceremony by standing and singing "The Star-Spangled Banner." "I love to sing, but I was so moved by national events that my voice cracked and I could only hum," Croake remembered.

BLACK STUDENTS DEMAND "DECISIVE ACTION"

On August 28, 1969, as the end of school approached, members of the Black Student Union presented a list of demands to President Ponitz, who suggested that they meet again at 1:30 that afternoon to "take decisive action."

The demands called for:

1. Changing the name of all courses "dealing with the so-called Negro" to "Black."
2. Creating a Black Studies Program "immediately," with a black coordinator, review committee, and appropriate focus.
3. Discontinuing the use of the word "Negro."
4. Creating a Black Student Court immediately.
5. Launching a recruitment program "to find more Black students and instructors and to enroll all Blacks who want to go to WCC."
6. Naming three Black students to the Teacher Review Board.
7. Flying the Afro-American flag "with the other flag of this country."
8. Promising not to prosecute students "for any action taken regarding these demands."

The President called a meeting with Dean Jim Jones (an African-American), Instructor Ivan Hakeem (from India), Assistant to the

WCC Students Urge President To Find Good Negro Admin.

By THOMAS BALDWIN

An interacial group of WCC students met April 22 with College President David Pontiz and several other members of the administrative staff and faculty to express their insistence that the College make a special effort to appoint a qualified Negro to the vacated position of Executive Assistant to the President.

The students' leader, Robert Hunter, spoke for the group when he said, "I would like to see a Negro in one of the top six administrative positions so that Negro students can identify with him."

President Pontiz agreed with the problem of Negro identification, and noted, "We have the most integrated Junior College in Michigan. Negroes at WCC compose 22 percent of the student body and 17 percent of the faculty."

Throughout the 1960s, race was an issue that galvanized attention on campus.

President Dave Pollock, and Sociology Instructor Don Bylsma to review the demands. "A number of the demands were very reasonable and others could be modified, we agreed," Bylsma remembered.

When faculty, administrators, and students gathered that afternoon, the meeting grew heated and, to Bylsma's surprise, the administration took a tougher stance than had been discussed earlier. According to *The Voice*, nothing was resolved:

> James Jones, Dean of Student Personnel Services and meeting moderator, frustrated by the course the meeting was taking, announced in an emotion-charged moment that he would resign "if these things are not taken care of now!"

The newspaper went on to note that upon Jones words, "the entire College Hall Auditorium shook with wild applause commending Jones for his action." At the suggestion of student (and later faculty member) John Tigner, the audience emptied the hall, leaving only the administrators and "straggling observers."

Don Bylsma remembered getting a call later that Dave Ponitz had gone over to Jones' house and the two men had managed to come to a meeting of the minds. Another meeting was called for 7:30 that night in King Hall. Jim Jones introduced President Ponitz, who then concurred with all of the demands, "with reservations on items 6 and 7." A review committee was appointed to work out the details and the next day a flier informed the students of the progress. "The place was packed—people were hanging from the rafters," Bylsma said. "Bob Foreman, an excellent and well-intentioned member of the Board of

Trustees, told the students, 'We'll work with you.' That defused the tension."

John Tigner, who was president of the Black Student Union, later told Don Bylsma that a number of cars in the parking lot that night were stocked with molotov cocktails and shotguns. "Whether that was true or not, I'll never know," Bylsma said. "I never saw them."

After that confrontation, Bylsma was part of the committee that launched WCC's Black Studies Program. Several administrators suggested naming John Tigner the first director, but he didn't have an associate's degree, so Alvin Roberts headed the program and John served as his assistant.

The Black Action Movement continued to have a strong presence on WCC's campus. Several times when Bylsma was teaching a course in the library, a young man arrived armed with a rifle. "In those days, it was legal, if you can imagine that! I checked into it, as you can imagine," the sociology instructor said. "Fortunately, I was always on good terms with him. He was part of a Panthers group in Detroit who ended up in a shoot-out with the Detroit cops."

PROTESTS AND PICKETS

WCC students occupied the College Hall gym in the spring of 1969. In the midst of nationwide student protests and marches, the administration decided not to inflame students. The campus was briefly shut down. "Many nights, one or more administrators or faculty members would sleep in their offices to oversee things," Andy Ford said. "Those were violent times and we didn't know what to expect."

One night in the late 1960s, a fire bomb was thrown into the Registrar's Office. It smoked and fizzled, but didn't go off. "None of us was prepared for any of this," remembered Math Instructor Dennis Bila, whose office was in that building. "The only protests I'd seen at Central Michigan University happened when a football player was kicked off the team. Students marched to the president's house, he came out, explained the situation to us, and we all went home. That was hardly preparation for the antiwar and civil rights protests. Those had violent underpinnings, but I was involved in them myself, so it was hard to separate my role as a young person and my role as a professional. We were supporting students, so it was hard for us to realize that they saw us as establishment, not as one of them."

"We joked, tongue in cheek, that the bomb must have been thrown by a general studies student because if it had been built and thrown by one of our technical students, it would have burned the place down," Andy Ford said. "Besides the fire bomb, there was just a lot of noise here. Washtenaw Community College escaped most of the damage and rioting suffered by other institutions."

During these years, Washtenaw County Sheriff Doug Harvey was making a name for himself nationally for his handling of the occasional riots and frequent marches and demonstrations at Eastern Michigan University and the University of Michigan. He became notorious for his treatment of protestors. "Some of our students were involved in those demonstrations, but we never had anything of that magnitude here. Our goal was to keep Doug Harvey off our campus," Bylsma said.

On February 28, 1970, *The Voice* subsequently reported, "Rallies, uprisings, loud arguments, slapping a member of the 'Geyda' in the face, secret meetings, and visits to the President's suite are just a few of the recent happenings." Once again, Black student activists marched to the President's office and presented an updated version of the 1968 demands, with several additions. The Black Student Union asked that the Black Studies Program "be developed by competent people" and function as a legitimate department, that a Black Culture Center be established on campus, that a Black Review Committee be empowered to review the cases of African-American applicants who had been refused financial aid, that a nursery become a permanent facility on campus, and that a permanent office with a secretary be established for the Black Student Union. In addition, one other demand insisted, "No more uniformed police in the student bookstore or in any building relating to the campus community."

The Voice reported that "Oddly, the most discussed item during the rally was centered around the resurrection of the school's nursery." Different administrative proposals were offered—"but since the BSU has no certain leader (that we know about) the question was not clearly answered," the paper said. One African-American student was quoted as saying, "They (the white people) can interpret our demands any way they wish. All the black students in America are fighting for the same thing we are—and we ain't gonna run."

THE AFTERMATH OF KENT STATE

On May 4, 1970, National Guardsmen fired on a crowd of student protestors at Kent State University and four students were killed. Waves of protest shook the nation's campuses. By the end of the week, 227 college campuses were closed in protest. *The Voice* reported, "In the middle of this national awareness of, and reaction to these offenses to

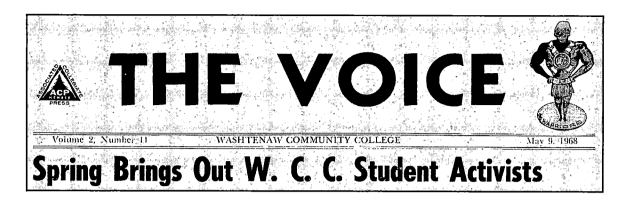

THE VOICE

Volume 2, Number 11   WASHTENAW COMMUNITY COLLEGE   May 9, 1968

Spring Brings Out W. C. C. Student Activists

"Those times were exciting, energizing, hectic, and sometimes even hazardous," recalled English Instructor Edith Croak.

humanity, Washtenaw Community College intended to carry on business as usual." The paper noted that on Wednesday, May 6, "a few students entered classes with instructors' permission and described the situation, asking students and teachers to strike. The effect of this maneuver was negligible."

A rally later in the day attracted two hundred students and faculty members. Afterwards, twenty or thirty students picked up placards and marched to College Hall with a "horn-honking escort of automobiles...picking up more students on the way." They declared a school strike, then ran through the halls shouting, kicking doors, squirting fire extinguishers, "and apparently having a good time." Students on their way to classes never got there.

President Ponitz fielded complaints from irritated students and instructors, then talked to a contingent of the striking students. He told them he refused to close the school. According to the newspaper, the same students next went to an emergency WCC Education Association meeting to advocate a strike, and the members passed a motion asking President Ponitz to declare the school closed for two days so that a teach-in about related issues could take place. Ponitz agreed and asked the students to help organize the teach-in. They refused. Later that night, WCC students joined students from the University of Michigan, Eastern Michigan University, and local high schools as they marched through Ann Arbor.

On May 7 and 8, while WCC was on strike, the Student–Faculty Assembly held a "Moral Action Conference" and passed several motions, asking President Ponitz to publicly denounce America's Indo-China policy, repression of African-Americans, students, "and other groups in this country," to break all ties with ROTC, to send the remainder of the College's Student Activities budget to the Bobby

Seale Defense Fund, and to boycott companies providing equipment to the war effort. *The Voice* article then went on to note:

> Some students from WCC were part of a group which occupied the U of M ROTC building on Thursday. The ROTC office was turned into a "community center" with a child care section and free dinners on Friday and Saturday. Saturday night at nine o'clock the people left the building "en masse" and unburnt for some unknown reason. Monday, May 11, WCC was back to "business as usual."

■ ■ ■

On Thursday, May 24, 1970, just two weeks after the Kent State killings, two African-American students were shot by state troopers at Jackson State College in Jackson, Mississippi. WCC protests began almost immediately after hearing the news. Students gathered around the flagpole at College Hall, "where the Red, White and Blue was lowered," *The Voice* reported. WCC was on strike again.

SPECIAL **The Voice** ISSUE

Vol. 4. No. 11   WASHTENAW COMMUNITY COLLEGE, ANN ARBOR, MICHIGAN   May 20, 1970

WCC students join nationwide strike; hold teach-in

When the U.S. flag was lowered and the flag of the Republic of New Africa was raised, Milton Poole rushed through the crowd to the flagpole. The chemistry teacher took the black nationalist flag down, hoisted the American flag to half-mast, and stood beneath it with folded arms, surrounded by 150 African-American students. "He had fought for our country during World War II, and he wasn't about to let anything happen to the American flag," Mehran Thomson said. "One of our counselors [Mel Anthony] was a former fullback for the University of Michigan; he came out with Jim Jones and took care of the situation."

"A few black students stopped him [Poole], but not without a struggle. No one was hurt," *The Voice* reported. Students then formed into two groups, the Political Action Committee and the Radical Action Committee, "in an attempt to utilize their energies constructively." Alvin Roberts, president of the Student-Faculty Assembly and director of the Black Studies Program, presided. The students voted to

College campuses around the nation witnessed strikes, marches, sit-ins, and teach-ins during the turbulent years of the 1960s and 1970s.

demonstrate their opposition to the Kent State and Jackson State killings by attending classes and discussing the issues there.

The pages of the same issue of *The Voice* resounded with warlike headlines: "The 'Revolution' has begun," "Campus tension and involvement," "Where do we go from here?" "Failure to communicate," "How important are WCC's bullshitters?" On the same pages, President Ponitz wrote a long explanation of the administration's position:

> Tensions are running high on many college campuses and college students are concerned over many social matters. I am writing this...as upwards of 60,000 people—mostly concerned students—are converging on Washington, D.C., to protest the increased United States involvement in Cambodia.
>
> My comments are further influenced by participation in the two-day Moral Action Conference of the Student-Faculty Assembly, on May 7 and 8.
>
> Neither Washtenaw Community College, nor any other college for that matter, can assume that it can solve all problems that create campus tensions. Alone we cannot stop war, eliminate poverty or stamp out racism. By the same token, this college cannot afford to be indifferent to these social ills.
>
> All members of the college community must take the time to discuss ideas on these and other issues...in a rational, reasoned manner without resorting to slander, libel, innuendo, filth, or demagoguery.
>
> Campus tension could be reduced by involving all members of the community college in decision making....
>
> At an early date the college must develop guidelines to have each member recognize and accept his responsibility and right to participate. If this is not accomplished, there will be less than full participation and the quality of decisions will not reflect the full concern of the total student body, the staff, and the public...
>
> There is much work that needs to be done...Now is the time to develop both the ideas and the ideals to make it work.

■ ■ ■

Because of the length of U.S. involvement in Indochina, war was a theme that ebbed and flowed throughout the first ten years of the College. Dave Ponitz remembered sitting in antiwar student demonstrations at the University of Michigan to hear President Robben Fleming talk—"hoping that would prepare me for what might happen at WCC," he explained. Interestingly, when Dave Ponitz was leaving one demonstration in Ann Arbor, he bumped into the vice president of Eastern Michigan University, who was there for the same reason.

"The University of Michigan has always been fortunate in picking the right president for the right time," Ponitz said. "Bob Fleming was the best mediator with students and he served as a role model for many of us. The classic story about him involves a confrontation with students where someone told him to go to hell. He responded, 'Well, that's a unique proposal. Would you be willing to share half the cost?'"

When the war in Vietnam began winding down, the women's movement began gearing up for action. "We had an interesting confrontation with the Women's Movement at WCC," President Ponitz said. "A group of women decided to picket us for two reasons which were inaccurate. They claimed that we had a policy of admitting a limited number of Jewish women and they claimed that we wouldn't let women into the automotive program. We told them they were wrong on both counts. In fact, we told them, we'd love to have them in the automotive program. 'Here's the application form,' we said, inviting them to sign up. They were students in French literature and they didn't take us up on our offer."

■ ■ ■

"Looking back on the 1960s, I think that faculty and administrators across the nation—and occasionally here on campus—probably overreacted—often," Dennis Bila said in retrospect. "Students need to be given nonconfrontational ways to express their feelings and thoughts. It never makes sense to stop students from their desire to protest and express themselves. We all need to be able to look back on something we stood up for in our youth and remind ourselves, 'Isn't that neat? I had my say. I took a stand.'"

Throughout its history, WCC has had a sense of social activism, Spanish Instructor Rosalyn Biederman observed. She took a leave from teaching at WCC in 1972, and lived in Chile for a year during the Salvador Allende administration. "I fine-tuned my Chilean Spanish listening to political debates on television in my room in Santiago," she said. "It was a very eye-opening experience to live in such a politically-charged place." The year in Chile sharpened her sense of social activism.

Since that time, she has encouraged her students to be informed, to take a position, and to vote. "I have never felt that I am teaching in a vacuum with no connection to that world," she said. "I always remember Chile and the other experiences that I have had in Spain and Latin America and I discuss them with my students as part of the whole language-learning package."

1969

- Fred Hampton, Black Panther leader, is killed in Chicago police raid.

- First draft lottery is held.

- Bobby Seale is bound and gagged by order of Judge Julius Hoffmann during the "Chicago 8" trial. Charged with violating the antiriot clause of the Civil Rights Act during the 1968 Democratic convention, the accused are found not guilty.

- First U.S. troops are withdrawn from Vietnam; by year's end, 75,000 leave.

- Vietnam: U.S. troop strength: 484,000; U.S. dead: 39,893; wounded: 250,000; missing: 1,400; enemy dead: 568,989.

History & Politics

- Academy Awards: Best picture: *Midnight Cowboy*. Best Actor: John Wayne (*True Grit*).

- Opening: *Butch Cassidy and the Sundance Kid; Hello, Dolly!; Alice's Restaurant; Bob and Carol and Ted and Alice; Easy Rider; Goodbye, Columbus; True Grit; They Shoot Horses, Don't They?*

Movies

- The first-year lineup for PBS includes *The Forsythe Saga* and *Sesame Street*.

Television

- Hit songs: "Good Morning Starshine," "Hair," "I've Got to Be Me," "Lay Lady Lay," "Get Back," "Oh Happy Day," "Honky Tonk Woman," "Crimson and Clover," "Love (Can Make You Happy)."

- Grammy Awards: *Aquarius/Let The Sun Shine In*, 5th Dimension (record); *Blood, Sweat and Tears* (album), *"Games People Play"* (song).

- Rock concerts proliferate; the Rolling Stones, Who, Joan Baez, Ravi Shankar, Jimi Hendrix, and the Jefferson Airplane draw record audiences: 100,000 in Atlanta; 150,000 in Dallas; and 500,000 at Woodstock.

Music

- Broadway musicals: *1776, Oh! Calcutta, Coco, Dear World*.

Theater

Literature

- Best-sellers include *Portnoy's Complaint* (Philip Roth), *The Godfather* (Mario Puzo), *The Inheritors* (Jerome Robbins), *The Andromeda Strain* (Michael Crichton), *Naked Came the Stranger* (Penelope Ashe), *The Making of the President: 1968* (Theodore H. White), *The Burden of Southern History* (C. Vann Woodward), *I Know Why the Caged Bird Sings* (Maya Angelou), *The Establishment Is Alive and Well in Washington* (Art Buchwald).

- Dean Acheson wins Pulitzer Prize for History for *Present at the Creation: My Years at the State Department.*

Education

- Police remove 400 Harvard students in sit-in.

- A total of 448 universities have strikes or are forced to close; student demands broaden to include revision of admissions policies and reorganization of entire academic programs.

- Many universities make ROTC voluntary or abolish it; Defense Department contracts with universities drop from 400 to 200.

- A group of black students armed with machine guns take over a building at Cornell University; they leave after negotiations with administration.

New Words

- Downers, uppers, command module, lunar module, mini beard, headhunter, noise pollution, hunk, total.

Quotes

- "Houston, Tranquillity Base here. The Eagle has landed....That's one small step for man, one giant leap for mankind." —Neil Armstrong, landing on the moon.

- "The Youth International Revolution will begin with a massive breakdown of authority....Tribes of long hairs, blacks, armed women, workers, peasants and students will take over....The White House will become one big commune....The Pentagon will be replaced with an LSD experimental farm....To steal from the rich is a sacred and religious act." —Jerry Rubin, *Do It.*

- "(The protesters are) a vocal minority. The great silent majority support us."—Richard Nixon

- "Drugs, crime, campus revolution, racial discord, draft resistance...on every hand we find old standards violated, old values discarded, old principles ignored. (This threatens) the fundamental values, the process by which a civilization maintains its continuity." —Richard Nixon

- "A spirit of national masochism prevails, encouraged by an effete core of impudent snobs who characterize themselves as intellectuals."—Spiro Agnew

---

The Voice chronicles the year's highlights:

- On March 17, *Voice* editor R. F. Bodnar writes: "*The Voice* has been asked to support 'the (student) movement' by printing hate articles and calling upon the student body to boycott classes, disrupt College activities and seize College buildings. Those who have made this request were unable to understand our refusal....Let violence and destruction be the reference to past generations; this generation and those to come are born to better things."

- A "dope-pushing ring" on campus is alerted that narcotics agents are aware of their activities. "The student who related this information to *The Voice* has recently said that he has ceased all activity and use in the drug traffic (also unconfirmed)."

- Black students confront President Ponitz with a list of demands. As a result, a Black Student Union is formed and a Black Studies Program is created, headed by Al Roberts.

- WCCEA casts a vote of no confidence in President Ponitz, citing problems of black students in achieving their rightful place in the academic community.

- WCC offers 41 occupational programs involving 70 different skill areas; 500 WCC students have been placed in 42 local manufacturing plants.

- On June 7, 165 graduates receive degrees during Commencement held at the new Huron River campus.

- Student Joe Tiboni, a member of the "New Mobe," urges WCC students to join the nationwide boycott of classes on October 15; he asks Dean of Students Jim Jones for a table so that he can publicize the boycott.

- English instructor Woody McClellan launches the American Studies Program.

Chapter 4:

The Students

REGISTRATION:
"WE HAD NO IDEA WHAT TO EXPECT"

After one hundred frantic days of advertising, hiring, promoting, organizing, painting, preparing, planning, purchasing, printing, and publicizing, came the day all of Washtenaw Community College had been working towards: September 12, 1966. The first day of Registration.

As Registrar, Douglas Woolley's job was to interact with the Selective Service and veterans on the G.I. Bill, register students, keep student records, schedule classes, allocate their time slots, and coordinate classes for students who had to travel to different campus and off-campus locations—even before appropriate faculty members had been hired. "We were shooting to have five hundred students as a minimum, though we really didn't know what to expect," Pollock said. "We had to hire faculty and staff to accommodate that number of students."

Throughout the summer, *The Ann Arbor News* had monitored the early interest in WCC and its registration levels. By August 1, the paper reported that four hundred students had filled out the College application. "We had been expecting—or, I should say, hoping for—a total of seven hundred students, but none of us really knew what to expect," Andy Ford remembered. "Part of the advantage we had in hiring administrators with previous administrative experience was that someone would know what to do in every area if we were underwhelmed or overwhelmed."

WCC administrators and faculty members were overwhelmed.

When the doors opened early September 12, all the faculty members were present in the College Hall gym. Three or four sat at each

When WCC opened, only one in four students was a woman, but by the end of the decade, women made up almost half the student body.

department table, two to answer questions and provide some on-the-spot counseling, one or two to enroll students. They had cards to distribute for each class, to keep track of the enrollment. Technically, once they ran out of cards, the class would be considered full and closed. But it didn't work that way.

Students came in surges throughout the three days. Evening hours were particularly busy because of the large number of working adults interested in enrolling. The stacks of cards disappeared very quickly. "When we ran out of cards, we punted, added more students to our classes until they just couldn't hold any more, and we then created new classes on the spot," Don Bylsma said. "When we saw the way the wind was blowing, and how many people had turned out to enroll, we started adding course sections, scrambling to arrange overloads for full-time faculty and to locate part-time faculty. Then we scrambled to get enough spaces for classes."

To expedite the process, Registrar Douglas Woolley had wisely decided to require only a single-page document—"otherwise, we'd still be there in Willow Run signing students in today," he said with a grin.

Student John Phibbs compared that first Registration to an open bullpen. "Faculty, counselors, students, and parents were all crowded together and milling around the gym in College Hall, carrying Registration cards and talking, conferring, asking and answering questions."

The crowd that turned out amazed everyone. "It was apparent the community was ready for what we could offer," Roger Bertoia said.

"We took people the way they came to us and worked with them to help them get to the point they aimed to reach. Our job was to remove hurdles, not put hurdles in the way of anyone."

For three days, the College registered students and collected tuition in the old meat-market-turned-administration-building until 10 p.m. One of the bookkeepers later told History Instructor Flavia Reps that until closing time she would sit on a pillow filled with the tuition money. When the last student had left, she would put the money in the meat market freezer, which locked. In the morning, she unlocked the freezer and brought the money to the bank.

Woolley had ordered IBM accounting machines to help with Registration—in those days WCC used punch cards—but neither the reproducing machine nor the interpreter arrived in time. Woolley made urgent phone calls to local businesses. One agreed to allow him to bring his nine trays of punch cards at night for processing. "I couldn't stay any longer than their opening hour. That meant that I had time to process the cards, but not to interpret them," Woolley said. "I had to go back later to finish the job. That was an interesting—and very nerve-wracking—week."

When Registration ended, Douglas Woolley added up the numbers and announced that Washtenaw Community College would start its first year with 1,211 students.

"I was overwhelmed at the numbers who appeared at our first Registration," President Ponitz said. He was also caught by surprise at the number of students who said that they planned to transfer to four-year colleges. Fortunately, Dave Pollock had already approached

Counseling was a vital service WCC offered its students. Cal Williams was one of the early members of the Counseling Office. He eventually became Associate Vice President, Student Services.

Eastern Michigan University and the University of Michigan to see if they would accept WCC's best students and their academic credits. "They turned out to be the easiest institutions to deal with. They understood our mission," Ponitz said. "Bob Fleming, president of the U of M in those years, was particularly helpful. He worked very closely with us and was one of our biggest supporters. It was the smaller, lesser known colleges who gave us a hard time about transferring credits."

Pomp and ceremony, caps and gowns, marked the early Commencement exercises, which were always held outdoors.

   The decision to offer enrollment to anyone who wanted an education had a great impact on the College's enrollment and on its future, Andy Ford believed. "We had a 'y'all come' attitude. We had committed ourselves to accepting students regardless of their previous academic record and regardless of whether or not they had taken college boards. We decided to take people as they were, not as we wished they were. We wouldn't guarantee a graduation at the end of two years—unless the student met all of our requirements—but we would guarantee that every student would be given a fair shake and a chance to move ahead."

Also significant was the decision that there would be no distinction made between disciplines at the associate degree level. WCC offered only one associate degree, both for General and Occupational Studies students. (That would later change.)

Over the years, Washtenaw Community College has served as a barometer for the state of the economy. The worse the economy, the higher the College's enrollment. The diversity in the student body has always remained constant, however.

STUDENT FINANCES: "CAN YOU SPARE SOME CHANGE?"

By the time Registration ended, Dave Pollock had realized that WCC was making history with many of its policies and decisions. He was responsible for some of those new, made-on-the-spot policies.

The Board of Trustees had established one hundred dollars as the semester's full-time student tuition, or nine dollars per credit hour for part-time students. Non-Washtenaw residents paid two hundred dollars per semester; non-Michigan residents paid three hundred dollars per semester. The Trustees realized, however, that despite the reasonable tuition fees, not all the students they hoped to reach would be able to pay the full amount. Some wouldn't be able to pay anything at all. They authorized Dave Pollock (whose job title had changed from Executive Assistant to the President to Dean of Students) to grant "an indeterminate number of Trustees' Awards," which essentially waived tuition.

On the first Registration day, Pollock taped a sign saying "Financial Aid" on one of the classroom doors and set up shop. One of the first to come through the door was an older woman who told him she couldn't pay the tuition immediately, but she could pay it month by month, like rent. "I didn't have time to ask the board for its approval of a pay-as-you-go program, but I remembered reading an article saying that Yale had begun to accept credit cards," Pollock said. "I thought to myself, 'If it's OK for Yale to let people pay as they go, it should be OK for Washtenaw.'" He agreed to the woman's suggestion. "We felt strongly that this was the only way for an open-door institution to operate. It was not my intention to give the place away, but to give everyone who wanted a chance the opportunity to take that chance."

One curious challenge during Registration was posed by the federal government, which required WCC to count the number of African-American students, but refused to allow a place on the form for students to state their ethnic backgrounds. Finally, someone in the

Registrar's Office offered to look at all the addresses and make a guess about the students' ethnic background. According to his calculations, twenty-four percent of the students were African-American, about twice the proportion of African-Americans in the city of Ann Arbor.

WELCOME!

In the inaugural issue of the brand new WCC student newspaper *The Voice*, published in October 1966, President Ponitz launched the new school with a message full of optimism and advice:

> As the first enrollees at Washtenaw Community College, you have a magnificent opportunity to contribute to the lasting quality of this institution. There are many decisions that the first class will make which will become tradition over the years. The quality and maturity of these decisions will shape the destiny of the college for many years to come. We are confident that each of you will be eager and ready to meet these challenges to make Washtenaw Community College an outstanding institution. We look forward to meeting you personally throughout the college year.

"WE TOOK EVERYONE WHO KNOCKED ON OUR DOOR"

When the College opened its doors in the fall of 1966, enrollment was more than double what administrators had predicted for the first year, grew to 1,506 within six months, and 2,394 the second year. WCC faculty and administrators had to scramble for additional classrooms and laboratories—and gratefully accepted whatever they could find. Classes were held at the Ann Arbor Public Library, the YMCA, and several churches. Don Bylsma taught a criminology class in the Ann Arbor Council Chambers. X-ray Technology classes occupied a church basement in Ann Arbor. The Technical & Industrial Program moved to a former shopping center near the Willow Run bomber plant. Trailers were hauled onto campus.

Parking was a persistent problem, particularly as the student body and faculty grew. Ron Zeeb remembered that President Ponitz often met challenges with a smile, a grimace, a joke, or a laugh. As WCC's night program caught on, the parking lots seemed jammed around the clock. Once, when faculty and staff members were complaining, someone suggested, "All those cars can't be from students attending classes. They might just be parking here." The president winked and said, "Really? I didn't know there is that much going on here!" One

Faculty member Paul Niehaus oversees his science class in the early 1970s. WCC has always maintained a diverse student body.

muddy day, Edith Croake's car became mired in mud outside the old bowling alley, which by then had been named Martin Luther King Hall. Chemistry Teacher George Griswold pushed it out.

To the administrators' relief, students accepted without question or complaint the challenges of attending a brand-new college on a formerly deserted and dilapidated site. Betty Brayton, a student in the Dental Assistant Program, hadn't seen the campus before the day she enrolled there. She remembered thinking how big it was—"Now, remember, I was coming from Manchester," she said, laughing. "Despite the fact that the campus looked like a bomb shelter, there was a sense of excitement about it. We had the feeling that everyone was determined to help this college grow and we felt like adventurers."

John Phibbs remembers coming to campus in 1966 as an eighteen-year-old without any preconceived notions of what a college campus—or a community college campus, in particular—would be like. "I understood that the place was new," he said. "Everything was very spartan. Furniture and equipment were appearing throughout the first semester. The buildings were old, but clean and freshly painted. All the tables, chairs, and lab equipment were new. This college was starting from scratch, and it showed. I remember those days as being a very enjoyable time in my life."

"We knew absolutely everyone who worked on campus. It was a real exciting time," Judy Hicks agreed. "Everyone was working together

for the same reason: to make the college a success. Everyone gave 110 percent."

The College was founded with a goal of training people for job entry and for life. A secondary mission was to offer a second chance to students who hadn't excelled in high school. In its second year, the College surveyed its students to determine its effectiveness. "Ninety-nine percent of them said they thought they would be going on to a four-year college," Mehran Thomson said. "That was an interesting expectation level among students, but it said something about WCC's ability to impress the value of education on its students."

"One of the best policies President Ponitz instituted was the drive for a diverse faculty, staff, and student body—long before the word 'diverse' was cool," Don Bylsma said. "We took everyone who knocked on our door. All the teachers served as counselors, too, and they took those responsibilities seriously. I remember a real estate salesman dressed in a seersucker suit with white patent leather belt and shoes who walked through our doors at the beginning of our first semester. I asked him what he wanted to do and he said, 'I want to be a doctor—and I don't care if it takes all two years to do it!' Some of these students needed more counseling than others!"

As he talked with potential students, Douglas Woolley discovered that the students enrolling were as dedicated to their education as WCC's faculty, staff, and administrators were. Students were fairly evenly divided between General Studies and Occupational Studies,

Instructors were impressed with the caliber of their first students. They had one thing in common: the goal of bettering themselves.

despite the administrators' expectations that Occupational Education would be the College's primary focus.

Staff and faculty all felt that the new students seemed as excited about the College as they were, Judy Hicks said. "It was apparent to us all that they had goals they were hoping to reach, and they were serious about getting an education."

Many of WCC's new students were the first in their families to go to college. Many came from farms, others from city neighborhoods in Ann Arbor, Ypsilanti, and Willow Run. Speech Instructor Char Hanson suggested, "They probably wouldn't have ventured to Eastern, almost certainly wouldn't have enrolled in Michigan, but when the school came to them, they knocked on its doors. And WCC changed the course of many lives."

The College also enrolled dropouts from Eastern, Western, and Central Michigan universities. Vietnam veterans. A few University of Michigan students catching up on required classes. Employees who wanted to upgrade their job levels. High school dropouts who hoped for a second chance. Mothers of small children. Factory workers who wanted to learn new trades. A University of Southern California graduate who wanted to pick up a few summer credits. A seventy-one-year-old widow named Elsie.

"WCC students are—and always have been—very special. No two students are alike," Betty Finkbeiner said. "Many work or have family commitments, so attending school isn't easy for them. There are always students with special problems or challenges. We try hard to help each one."

Roger Bertoia left University High School to come to WCC. He was surprised at the difference in the maturity level between the two student bodies. "WCC's students were extraordinarily demanding and challenging," he said. "They were in our classes because they wanted to be there, because they wanted to get an education in order to get ahead. They weren't dealing with hormones or social issues. They had no interest in fooling around. They were serious about getting down to work. For these reasons, they were very easy to teach."

Student populations varied widely from program to program. Many of the early Occupational Education programs were filled with men, although Betty Finkbeiner's Dental Assistant classes had only women. Dennis Bila taught calculus for ten years before having his first woman student. Morris Lawrence's music classes were packed with African-American students. Fred Horowitz's art students were generally white and planning to go on in the field. Ron Zeeb's busi-

History was made June 8, 1968, when the College's Charter Commencement took place. Attending dignitaries included members of the Board of Trustees, the President, deans, and directors.

ness students during the day were sixty percent female—unusual in the 1960s—but students in the evening classes held in outlying areas were males between twenty-five and thirty-five years of age applying what they had learned in their job situations.

By the end of the 1960s, WCC also had students from the Federal Correctional Institution in Milan and the women's prison in Ypsilanti. Roger Bertoia remembered one male inmate who later went into politics. "He had been sent to jail for bank robberies and he spoke often of his desire to go straight. He was a terrific success story." Several years after the school was established, one female inmate arrived at Commencement accompanied by her guard, in order to receive her diploma. "We had adults coming to us in various stages of their lives, with very different work and life experiences,"

Bertoia said. "Our role as a college was to take them wherever they were and place them in classes and programs where they could develop and grow. Unlike the four-year institutions, we could give them credit for their life experiences. There was a tremendous excitement about being the only educational program in the community that would take everyone, just as they were."

Bill Moy was very impressed with the first crop of students. "Most could have gone to Michigan or Eastern if not for their cultural or economic deprivation," he said. "Many were older students, unable to afford college before this opportunity appeared. In my experience, they were racially diverse, academically strong, extremely motivated, disciplined, and capable. There were a few middle-class students, but they weren't predominant. At its inception, WCC had a very diverse student body, yet there was also great homogeneity in that most of our students were from backgrounds culturally or economically deprived." Gary Owen agreed. "I believe that a significant factor in the College's early success was the fact that race wasn't an issue here," he suggested. "In part, I think that was because there were significant numbers of African-Americans working as well as studying in every area. The African-American students were like me. They couldn't afford to go anywhere else, either. For them, WCC was an economic decision. For me, it was an academic decision. With the veterans' assistance programs, I could afford higher education, but I didn't have the academic skills to go anywhere else."

Because Speech was required by many majors, Char Hanson's classes often had interesting mixtures of people. Men from the Automotive Program arrived in pick-up trucks sporting gun racks—"and they weren't entirely sure that a woman was capable of teaching them anything," she realized. Sharing the class with them were long-haired youngsters wearing flip-flops. On the first class day, she watched the two groups look each other over, sure that the others would have nothing to say worth listening to. "By the end of the semester, they were at least listening to—if not completely understanding—each other," she said. "That was very gratifying."

"Our students were so motivated that they made WCC a really exciting place," Bertoia said.

WHO WERE THESE STUDENTS?

Gary Owen: *"I learned that if I really applied myself, I could accomplish anything."*

Recently, the Michigan Historical Society published a list of Michigan's most outstanding statesmen. Gary Owen was ranked second on the list of the best Democratic legislators to hold office in the last fifty years. Now retired from politics, he owns a lobbying firm whose clients include Washtenaw Community College. On days when he can work at home, he retreats to his office in a restored barn outside Ann Arbor, surrounded by mementos from his days in office. A southerner, he has a gift for storytelling and the story he tells is extraordinary.

"I grew up in a housing project in Montgomery, Alabama, while my father was serving time in prison for murder," he begins, as he settles into a chair. "After my father was sentenced, my mother loaded four small children onto a bus and moved us from our home in the country to Montgomery—with fifteen dollars in her pocket. She worked very hard to take care of her children."

The family struggled to stay intact. Gary struggled in school until he dropped out in the eleventh grade and enlisted in the Army. "It was while I was in the Army that I discovered the value of education," he

Former WCC student now WCC Dance Instructor Gayle Martin (right) shares the stage with a talented student at one of the College's community picnics.

Under Betty Finkbeiner's supervision, the Dental Assistant Program has become a leader in the field.

said. "The enlisted men did all the hard and dirty work. We used to look at the officers and realize that they had it made. I made the connection that the difference in our status was due to education. I wanted what they had. I realized that I wanted something better for myself."

After his discharge, Owen and his younger brother hopped on a bus and moved to southeastern Michigan, where their father had been paroled. His first job was working on a construction crew shoveling concrete. He soon decided that he wanted to become a carpenter "because they had a better deal." He was learning the trade in 1966, when he read about WCC and its open enrollment policy. "That day, I realized that I might be able to get an education and make more out of my life," he said.

He visited the new Community College's campus that summer, and saw someone sweeping the steps of the new College Hall. That man turned out to be Dave Ponitz. The young carpenter told the College President that he wanted more education, but he wasn't sure if he could do it. The President told him that he'd come to the right place.

"At first, I wasn't sure I had the confidence to go to college," Owen said. "I was basically illiterate, and I didn't think I was smart enough. After all, I hadn't been successful in my education in the past." But faculty members encouraged him. "I had realized by then that if someone has a higher ambition, the only option is college," he said. "When you come from the environment I grew up in, that seems so impossible. I can count on one hand all the kids I was raised with in that large public housing project who ended up going to college—and two of them are my brothers."

The College's proximity to his home was also encouraging. "I needed a comfort zone and the fact that the College was starting in my neighborhood in an old beat-up school made higher education seem a lot less intimidating to me." At the age of twenty-two, he enrolled. "He was older than the traditional student starting college, and had no high school diploma, but he discovered many of his classmates were like him in the fact that most of us had not been participants in high school," Owen said. "There were no presidents of their high school class or editors of high school newspapers in our ranks. Washtenaw Community College offered a second opportunity for us all. We offered the College a chance to test its resources and brand-new program."

After remedial reading, writing, and math classes, Owen signed up for the coursework required to earn an associate's degree in General Studies. "I basically couldn't read or write when I came here, but I ended up being editor of the student newspaper," he said. "I give the credit to those early faculty members; they were so dedicated to working with me and all the others like me." Owen was chosen by his classmates to give the Commencement address. After graduation, he transferred to the University of Michigan, where he earned a bachelor's degree in education. "I didn't want to waste any time," he said. He became a part-time instructor in political science while finishing his master's degree in urban planning. In 1970, he ran for the Ypsilanti Township board and won. Encouraged by President Ponitz, Owen ran for State Representative and won his seat in 1972. As a legislator, he would work with Dave Ponitz on funding new College buildings. Washtenaw Community College was proud to have a graduate in the state legislature, particularly so soon after the College was established.

"I am very committed to the role of education in our society. I carried a consciousness of the plight of African-Americans with me when I went to Lansing," Owen said. "I know what it's like to be stuck on the bottom rung of the social structure. I understand what it's like to be prejudiced against. That knowledge makes you a very, very good politician! It makes you hard to beat because you understand them. I have always had a tremendous motivation to make life better for myself and for others."

The WCC graduate was sworn in as the first Democratic Speaker of the House in modern times in 1983, and served in that position until 1988.

When he first arrived in Michigan as an unemployed, uneducated eighteen-year-old, Gary Owen climbed off the Greyhound bus in Ypsilanti. Now, on that spot stands the Gary Owen School of Business at Eastern Michigan University.

"Education has made all the difference in my life," he said.

Bill Figg: *Moving to the beat of his own drum*

The December 15, 1966 issue of *The Voice* profiled WCC student and future faculty member Bill Figg:

> Walking the halls of Washtenaw Community College is a great celebrity, a man of 18, who certainly has made a name for himself and his fellow musicians. His name is Bill Figg and he is the

drummer for "The Rationals." Ever since the day when Bill was watching a Michigan Homecoming parade and a brass drum went past, the sound he says, "just went through me and turned me on…" He first started playing six years ago in junior high, then in ninth grade he met Steve Correll (lead guitar), Scott Morgan (lead singer), and Terry Trabant (bass guitar); together they became "The Rationals." The other three are seventeen and are attending Ann Arbor High School. Bill is a full time student at WCC and is carrying sixteen hours…(in) pursuit of an Auto Mechanic's Teacher Certificate.

Bill and the other members of the band play rhythm and blues, not rock n' roll. Their latest record "Respect" has sold 100,000 copies in the Detroit area alone….

When asked why do you wear your hair so long? Bill answered, "Because it distinguishes me from a person in the crowd and (identifies) myself as a professional musician."

■ ■ ■

Bill Figg enrolled with WCC's first class of students in September 1966. "The whole thing started as a mistake, really," he said. While riding his motorcycle along Washtenaw Road he saw Bruce Welch, who had taught him in high school. Welch was standing in front of WCC's new automotive center on Carpenter Road. He recruited Figg, who was eighteen. "I'd just graduated from Pioneer High School and I had no plan," he said. "School was actually the farthest thing from my mind. I'd spent all summer in an electronics program in Detroit and I didn't like it, so I was between ideas." Through the summer, he had been devoting his attention to his motorcycle and his band, The Rationals. They were the first group to record "Respect." "Aretha Franklin picked up the song after us. We made it to the top of the charts by mistake; we were really just kids who liked to play together and were happy to play for others and earn a few dollars," Figg said.

Bill Figg (left) has taught generations of WCC students.

Soon, Figg and his band were flying from city to city and appearing on television. Schoolwork fell by the wayside. "Too often I'd fly into Detroit Metro Airport at 8 a.m., and remember that I had a paper due or a speech to give for Char Hanson," he said. "Char was great; she told me that she'd had Bob Seger in her high school class and she appreciated the music business, but she also told me that

I wasn't doing too well in her class." So, he quit school and pursued his music until 1972, when the group realized they were getting older and needed to settle down. That was when Figg returned to WCC and started applying himself.

One day, Dan Gray called to tell him that he had a part-time job in the welding program for his father and a full-time job for him. Figg returned to WCC in 1972, to work as a "lab coach/assistant" and to finish his schooling. In 1979, WCC told him he was instructor material.

"WCC has always been a coincidence—a very fortunate coincidence—in my life," Bill Figg said.

Frances Spelman & Ana Tomas: *"unconventional students"*

The new Community College attracted an interesting and varied group of students, with a strong contingent of "older" women and working mothers. In the April 1967 issue of *The Voice*, Mrs. Grace Davis wrote:

> It is very apparent that all of the students going to WCC are not in their late teens and early twenties. Many of the students that you notice carrying books up and down the halls are the very young middle age group....
>
> One such student that finds school a very gratifying adventure is Mrs. Frances Spelman, homemaker and mother of three teen-agers. Her husband is employed with the Park Davis Co. in Ann Arbor where the family lives. Mrs. Spelman bowls, plays bridge and enjoys dancing....
>
> Like many of her generation, Mrs. Spelman has wanted to go to school for the last three or four years but didn't think she was ready for Eastern or U of M. When WCC came into being, Mrs. Spelman was delighted as this was her chance to go to school. She enrolled in September of 1966 and hopes to obtain a degree in Business Education. Eastern will be her next step....
>
> One of her classmates is Mrs. Ana Tomas.
>
> Mrs. Tomas came to this country with her husband Juan in 1962 from Cuba. They were teachers under the Castro government and found it difficult to do their teaching in the manner they were familiar with. They were allowed to leave....
>
> Mrs. Tomas went to work at the Public Health Department and at the same time attended the English Language Institute for Foreign Students at the U of M....
>
> It is hoped that the story of Mrs. Spelman and Mrs. Tomas will give others the courage to follow the growing trend of middle ages returning to school.

Betty Brayton: *"The first in my family to go to college"*

A 1968 graduate of Manchester High School, Betty Brayton enrolled in WCC's brand new Dental Assistant Program that fall. "My father had died in a farm accident when I was fourteen and my family was very poor, but a friend of our family, who had heard President Ponitz speak at my high school graduation, offered to send me to school if I wanted to go," she said. She spent the summer studying the WCC catalogue and debating about what to do with her life. Eventually she decided to become a dental assistant. "It sounded interesting and something different from what my friends would be doing," she said.

Classes were held in College Hall. The eight women in the program would walk through a social studies class to enter their classroom; every day Mr. Glusac would wave to them without interrupting what he was saying as they marched through. "By today's standards, that classroom was fairly primitive, but we didn't know any better. It seemed state-of-the-art to us," Brayton said. The students in her program became fast friends after two years of classes together.

During their first year, they were taught by Gerry Patton and Dr. Carl Woolley. The second year, Betty Finkbeiner and Dr. Joe Chasteen replaced them. "We worked hard. Betty and Joe were sticklers about ethical and cleanliness standards, but they made things interesting and fun," she remembered. Finkbeiner and Chasteen established a rotational program, where second-year students worked in a variety of dental offices, one of them at the University of Michigan Dental School. Their education was more than just working on dental matters, however. They were required to take general education courses, attend the Earth Day rally at Crisler Arena, and apply themselves. "WCC introduced me to new philosophies and ideas—and that was a major part of my education," Brayton said.

So was the opportunity to meet new people. "There were no blacks in my rural high school, and I had no previous experience with people who didn't look or sound like me," she said. At WCC she had one teacher from India (Gargi French), several teachers who were African-American, one teacher (Woody McClellan) who was blind. She also made life-long friends among her classmates; one of them, Dianna Hale Roberts, still calls to chat every night. "Those two years introduced me to a much bigger and more exciting world," Brayton said. "WCC equipped and trained me very well for my vocation and for my life."

Looking back on it, she said, the dental program seems like such a small world—"but to a girl coming from a sheltered home life and a rural community, it was different and big and exciting and wonderful. I felt like I was a pioneer, between enrolling in the first class of the Dental Assistant Program and being the first in my family to go to college."

Dianna Hale Roberts: *"A lifelong friend"*

The same week in which Betty Brayton graduated from Manchester High School, Dianna Hale Roberts graduated from Chelsea High. Her senior year, a counselor talked to her about her future and recommended the Dental Assistant Program at the new community college. She realized that she could probably manage the one hundred dollar tuition by cleaning houses and babysitting. "During those two years, it seemed as if all I did was go to school, work, go home, do homework, then start all over again," she said.

Her first glimpse of Willow Run was on Registration Day. "Willow Run certainly wasn't an exciting campus. It just consisted of a few old buildings—after all, it had been built in a hurry for the people working at the bomber plant. In that sense, though, it was unique. My Dad and my uncles had been in the Armed Forces during World War II, so I had an interest in its war-time heritage, but it was by no means a beautiful college campus," she recalled.

In one regard only, the Community College reminded Dianna Hale Roberts of high school. "The faculty truly cared about us as a person. They even wanted to know what was going on in our homes if some situation was affecting our schooling." The women in the program were required to wear a nurse's uniform, cap with a green ribbon, white nylons, and white shoes. Pants were unacceptable. "Betty and

The capping ceremony was the reward for two successful years of study in the Dental Assistant Program. Early students remember with humor the lack of success Dr. Joe Chasteen showed in securing caps to heads; Director Betty Finkbeiner soon took over the responsibilities.

Joe Chasteen brought the Dental Assistant Program up to speed fast in the second year," Roberts said. "Betty meant business. She was strict in class; she wanted to make big changes in the program so we would be well qualified in every way and very professional." Finkbeiner insisted that fingernails be kept short and without polish, hair kept up and off faces, and no perfume worn. "Those habits she instilled have stuck with me all though the years," Roberts said. "Thanks to Betty, I became a stickler about cleanliness and orderliness."

"When I was here as a student, most of us were aware that we were part of something new, witnesses to a creation," **John Phibbs recalled.**

During the second year, students did clinical work in a variety of dental offices, working with real patients and learning how different dentists worked and the different procedures they used. They also worked at the dental school and in specialty offices.

The eight classmates received their caps in a ceremony held in St. Alexis Church on the campus. Roberts still remembers how Dr. Chasteen plunked their caps on their heads. "We looked ridiculous!" she said with a smile. "In his defense, putting caps on heads is not an easy thing to do." Shortly afterwards, the class graduated in a Commencement held in the apple orchard on the new campus.

"I have always been very glad I went to WCC," she said. "It was a good educational experience and it prepared me well for my profession."

John Phibbs: *"I was attracted by the idea of trying something entirely new"*

John Phibbs graduated from Pioneer High School with honors in 1966, then decided to investigate the new Community College. "I'd been considering the U of M business school and various other places, but I'd done some procrastinating about getting applications mailed," he remembered. "I decided to see what the new College could do for me."

He was among the earliest students to sign up, filling out the one-page application form in the Huron Street office. The Community College was attractive from the financial standpoint, he discovered. He could take a full semester load of classes for one hundred dollars, work fifteen or twenty hours at Ann Arbor Publishers, and somehow still find the time to participate in Arbor Day plantings, help with the Miss Washtenaw Pageant, work at car rallies, and participate in the

Student Senate and Ski Club. After two years, he transferred to Eastern Michigan and majored in business. EMU accepted sixty of his credits. His brothers and later his nephews followed in his footsteps and enrolled at WCC. Phibbs returned to WCC in 1969, and has remained ever since. In 2002, he was named manager of Archives and Records Management; by that time he had taken ninety more credits in everything from physics to calculus, secretarial skills,and gardening.

"When I was here as a student in the first class, most of us were aware that we were part of something new, witnesses to a creation," he said.

Phyllis Grzegorczyk: *Balancing work, family, and school*

In 1978, Phyllis Grzegorczyk became a faculty member in the nursing program at WCC, but her history with the College began six years earlier, when she enrolled after earning a diploma from Mercy School of Nursing in Ann Arbor. She attended classes by day and worked the evening shift, so her husband could stay home with their four daughters. "I enjoy learning and I was determined to advance in my career and learn everything I could that would help me in my job," she said.

Phyllis Grzegorczyk worked full-time while raising four daughters and attending classes at WCC during the early 1970s.

The cost and convenience convinced her to start at WCC. With Hal Weidner for English composition, Don Bylsma for sociology, and Bill Moy for psychology, she found the academics challenging—"but after taking George Griswold's chemistry class, I knew I could go on and get my Ph.D." she said. "That class was rigorous and demanding—as were the others."

Her two- and four-year-old daughters accompanied her to WCC. When their mother went to class, they went to the Children's Center, which became Grzegorczyk's only extracurricular activity. "This was during the era when newspaper headlines talked about student marches and riots and demonstrations, but I believe that WCC's student body was much like me: older, with many family and career commitments," she said.

Student parents were asked to pay for one credit of tuition to cover childcare costs; Grzegorczyk paid fourteen dollars a semester, and she credits Shirley Roberts with running a program the little girls couldn't wait to attend.

In the early 1970s, the new campus consisted of three buildings (Power House, Liberal Arts, and the Technical & Industrial buildings), several temporaries, and many apple trees. Both the food service and bookstore were located in portables. At the time, students thought the facilities were terrific—"even the trailers," she said. "This

While their parents were away at classes, children could play— and play they did. Former student (later Dean of Nursing at WCC) Phyllis Grzegorczyk brought her young daughters to the daycare center and remembered how much they enjoyed the center's activities.

campus worked. It reflected the concerns of its student body. We didn't need a lot of frills. We were here to do a job and WCC provided us with the means of getting that job done so we could go on with our lives and better ourselves."

After earning her associate degree, she transferred to the University of Michigan, where she earned her bachelor's and master's degrees in nursing. Grzegorczyk served as WCC's Health and Public Service Division Dean while working on her doctorate in higher education.

STUDENT LIFE ON THE WILLOW RUN CAMPUS
"Something for everyone"

Of the 1,211 students who enrolled in the brand new Community College in the fall of 1966, 765 were part-time students, 446 were full-time. Their average age was thirty-two. About half attended the College at night; many of them had families and job responsibilities, so they had little time to get involved in extracurricular activities, political movements, or protests. In contrast, day students tended to be younger and often didn't have major commitments, so most student activities revolved around them.

"I was in the first class to enter the college, so there was nothing in place for extracurricular activities, but things started happening quickly," Gary Owen remembered. "This was a terrific opportunity for all of us to help start whatever we wanted."

Baseball was a game of prowess, athleticism, and, occasionally, disagreements. Coach Larry Slepsky challenged one umpire about a call.

Owen joined the staff of the new student newspaper, *The Voice,* helped launch the Student Senate, organized an international relations discussion group, and played on the basketball team. "Between the academics and the opportunities to work with student organizations, I gained a lot of confidence at WCC," he said. "The College instilled in me a stronger sense of self-respect. I learned that if I really applied myself, I could accomplish anything. The College offered that opportunity to a lot of people."

The Ski Club and Model U.N. were the first two clubs organized. They were soon followed by many others.

The Voice

The Voice was produced by students taking English classes with Fred Wolven, who had agreed to serve as the newspaper's advisor. Students Gerald Ulmer and Pete Toggerson suggested the winning name for the new student newspaper, then students were free to follow their reportorial interests. "We ran into lots of editorial controversies, thanks to the new campus: questions about student input, race relations at WCC, the war in Southeast Asia, and the normal conflicts between students and administrators over issues like sports," Gary Owen said, adding, "Probably many of the issues we addressed are the same issues students are still addressing."

Sports

Basketball was the first sport organized at WCC. Gary Owen and his teammates Jim Allen, Charles Schmunk, Fred Shure, John Tigner, Paul DeShano, Mike Mayhew, Zonnie Askew, Gerald Ulmer, Dave Biggers, Walt Johnson, Bill Boatwright, and Jerry Hayes practiced and played in the gym of a nearby junior high school under the experienced direction of Coach Bill Perigo, a member of the University of Michigan staff and a former teammate of John Wooden.

"We were very competitive. We even had some All-State players on our team," Owen said, adding with a grin, "I remember Bill Perigo looking me over the first time I met him. He noticed I was a little out of shape. 'This isn't going to be a beer league, you know,' he told me. I worked hard to get into shape."

WCC drubbed Cleary College's hoopsters in its first game. Led by the scoring of Jim "Tweet" Allen (22 points) and the outstanding floor play of John Tigner (14 points), the soon-to-be Warriors outscored Cleary's team 72-42. After describing the victory, *The Voice* announced,

> Plans are underway for more games and the team would appreci-
> ate student support. Jack Miller, student activities, said that
> plans are being made for Washtenaw's entry into league competi-
> tion consisting of other Michigan Junior Colleges.

■ ■ ■

The first Warriors baseball team was fielded in 1967, with a 27–game schedule. The ballplayers practiced at 9 p.m., every night, on Eastern Michigan University's ball fields.

In May 1967, the WCC Bowling Team won its first Tri-State Collegiate Bowling Championship against nine other schools. The team of Paul DeShanno, Emmett Byrne, Dave Elchuck, Gary Mortinson, and Tom Baldwin had been formed after a roll-off at the Ypsi-Arbor Bowling Lanes.

Later, in the fall, the league was officially organized by Lee Comstock, Bob Brakken, Bob Bowen, Willie Hawkins, Mike Real, Steve Wilson, Larry Sanderson, Oklin Wilder, and Tom Baldwin. There were "many more people" at the first tournament, *The Voice*

noted, "but they were so busy bowling that they forgot to put down their last names." Tom Baldwin and Oklin Wilder were the first officers.

Shortly afterwards, a *Voice* article headlined "Bowling Club Is Hip to the Female Student" pointed out, "The amount of students showing up for the bowling league is a clear indication that WCC coeds are one reason for its success." The coeds served as cheerleaders.

■ ■ ■

WCC Athletic Director and Coach Larry Slepsky fielded a baseball club with a twenty-seven-game schedule in 1967. The ballplayers had to wait until 9 p.m., every weekday night, and 7 p.m., on Sundays to practice because they were obliged to borrow Eastern Michigan University's practice fields. Two of WCC's early players, Art Russeau and Rick Berry, signed with the Pittsburgh Pirates. In 1973, Larry Graves signed with the Detroit Tigers Minor League.

■ ■ ■

WCC sponsored a cross-country team in 1968, with Cliff Bellers as coach and former Ypsilanti High School track star John Hill as the Warriors' star runner.

■ ■ ■

By the fall of 1971, WCC offered golf, bowling, archery, and weight-lifting classes, as well as three related academic courses: "Principles of Safety," "Healthful Living," and "Red Cross First Aid." In order to play college sports (basketball, baseball, cross-country, track, and golf), students had to carry at least ten hours of classes and hold at least a 1.5 grade point average.

In 1976, WCC took another look at sports. Student Activities Director Guy Hower and Dean of Students Jim Jones decided that the College would offer two sports programs: an intramural program for the entire student body and an intercollegiate program ("basically for male students with a grade point average of at least 2.0") in basketball, baseball, bowling, track, and golf.

Basketball flourished during the early College days, even sending several players onto professional teams, but President Ponitz was forced to cut the program in 1971, when state budget cuts called for rigorous action.

Music

On December 15, 1966, *The Voice* announced the first choral concert, which would highlight the talents of the group's forty-two registered members. When Morris Lawrence arrived on campus, the place began jumping, with jazz bands, ensembles, and a variety of other musical guests filling a year-round schedule.

Student Senate

The faculty was responsible for the formation of a Student Senate, but the students ran the organization. On January 5, 1967, the Senate, led by President Jerry Morgan, unanimously chose green and white as the student colors and formed committees on finance, major construction, special activities, student organizations, elections, Student Court, research, hospitality, and administration policy. Several weeks later, the Senate christened WCC's student body "The Warriors."

The Jestettes

"Listen to the trumpets! Can you feel the trumpets?... Now listen to those drums!," Morris J. Lawrence urged his students.

"A group of girls at WCC who really have a ball together," the Jestettes met Tuesday evenings at members' homes. The first slate of officers included Brenda Edwards, Anna Henderson, Edith DuHart, and Jackie Smith. They sponsored dances and other social functions to raise money for a trip to Expo 67 in Canada and New York City. Membership was open to any WCC coed who would submit an appli-

cation, provided members agreed to accept the applicant. The group's motto: "Dignity, Honesty, and Finesse."

Interest Groups

The Ski Club, Math Club, Future Secretaries Association, Future Teachers' Club, WCC Pinochle and Bid Whist Club, Model U.N., and literary magazines were all started by students.

AND THEN WHAT HAPPENED?

Some say that the WCC students have changed over time, but Dennis Bila doesn't think so. "We've always been watchful to maintain a diverse student body," he said. "From our earliest days, Dave Ponitz was very, very aware of that. Long before diversity was a trend, he worked hard to achieve diversity here on campus and he should get a lot of credit for that. He strongly believed in achieving a great mix of people."

Guy Hower, who has held a variety of positions related to students over the years, has seen the percentage of women grow dramatically while the interesting mixture of students has been maintained. "Blacks have always made up seventeen or eighteen percent of our students, but we go through periods where we have an influx of people of different nationalities," he said. In the late 1970s and 1980s, WCC had a large Vietnamese population learning English as a Second Language. Now the big ESL population is Russian. The College has always enjoyed sizable Middle Eastern and Asian popu-

As the decade went on, increasingly more women enrolled in WCC's classes.

lations. WCC strove to make education available to everyone, Hower said. "We worked hard to serve the inner-city and disadvantaged population. We have a large GED program and our hope is that once people complete their GED, they'll continue on here."

Douglas Woolley joined the administration at Washtenaw Community College because he believed strongly in its philosophy of helping and serving students—"I still do," he said. Throughout the early years, administrators were concerned about the effects of the school's huge and rapid growth on the College's quality. President Ponitz remembered, "I didn't worry much about the elite student who would eventually go on to earn

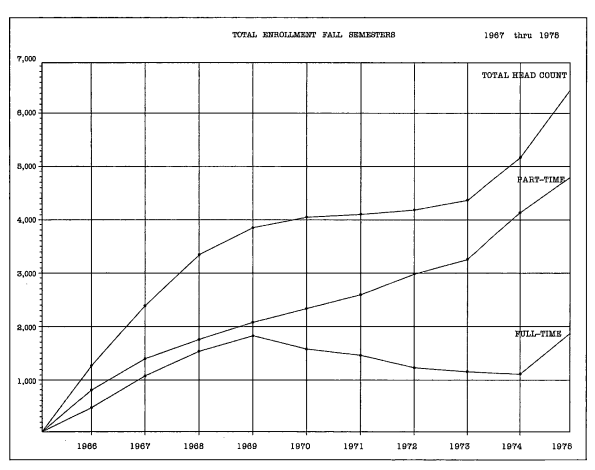

TOTAL ENROLLMENT FALL SEMESTERS   1967 thru 1975

TOTAL HEAD COUNT

PART-TIME

FULL-TIME

7,000

6,000

5,000

4,000

3,000

2,000

1,000

1966   1967   1968   1969   1970   1971   1972   1973   1974   1975

Washtenaw Community College has traditionally experienced its greatest growth in the years when the local and national economies have seen downturns.

a Ph.D.; I worried about the guy or gal who would either get their start at WCC or go on Welfare for the rest of their lives."

Despite strong faculty involvement and caring, during the College's early years, dropout rates were tremendously high and attendance was often erratic. "Most WCC students were working as well as taking classes and many also had families," Don Bylsma pointed out. "And remember, a lot of our students had been mediocre students in high school and never developed good study habits. If, on top of that, they were working thirty or forty hours a week, they often found they just couldn't cope."

Shortly after the first semester started, one of Bylsma's students asked for a drop slip. When he asked why, she told him that her husband had threatened to divorce her if she didn't. He urged her to take an incomplete in the class, so if she ever wanted to return, she wouldn't have to pay. That scenario was repeated several times every semester over the next few years, Bylsma said. Sometimes the wife would report that her husband worried that college would make her

*WCC students
Sherman Smith and
John Stein were
second-place winners
in the 1969 Plymouth
Trouble-shooting
Contest held at
Western Michigan
University.*

smarter than he was, sometimes husbands worried that wives would "get crazy ideas" or that the people at that college were "too liberal." "This was right around the time when the women's movement was starting and most of us were proponents of it," Bylsma said. "I suppose we were pretty radical for the times."

Early in his tenure as Dean of Students, Dave Pollock told students, "You have the opportunity to fail." "We'd decided early on that if a student failed one or two classes, we wouldn't kick him out. We'd stick in there and help him find a place where he could succeed," he said. "That was part of our sense of fierce commitment." Many times, students would come to WCC right out of high school, drop out after a semester or two, then return six, eight, or ten years later, when they realized that they needed further education in order to make their way in the world. "Often they had been poor students their first time here, but when they returned, they became our most motivated students," Bylsma said.

Vietnam veterans enrolled in great numbers, but many would disappear for days or weeks on end as they struggled to readjust to civilian life. Other young men enrolled in order to maintain their student deferment status with the Draft Board; quite a few of those never appeared in classes, either.

In many cases, WCC faculty have taught the children, and even the grandchildren, of former students. Bylsma has taught mother-daughter and husband-wife combinations. John Mann was a student

Only one Commencement–WCC's first, held in 1968–was located on the Willow Run campus. President David Ponitz addressed the students, as did future Speaker of the Michigan House of Representatives, Gary Owen (above).

who met his wife in Bylsma's class, then went on to become a faculty member in the automotive program. Years later, Bylsma taught the couple's daughter. Occasionally, instructors married former students. "Remember, this was an older student body, so it wasn't a forty-year-old instructor marrying a twenty-year-old, but a forty-year-old instructor marrying someone thirty or forty," Bylsma said.

Every teacher remembers outstanding and memorable students. Char Hanson recalled the beautiful poetry one older gentleman in her speech class would read. Fred Horowitz taught Nicole Cattell in the late 1980s. She later won a Fulbright Award for her work in film-making. Over the years, many art students have been accepted to the finest art departments in the country, including the Rhode Island School of Design, the Art Institute of Chicago, and the Cleveland Institute of Art. Others have transferred to the University of Michigan. "One associate dean at Michigan told me that our students are the best-prepared of his transfer students," Horowitz said. "I'm proud of that fact." Don Bylsma spoke fondly about an elderly lady named Elsie, who first enrolled at WCC at the age of seventy-one, a semester after her husband died. After she graduated, she earned a degree in gerontology from the University of Michigan, then returned to WCC for more classes. "She told me that the day she quit learning

was the day she'd die," Bylsma said. "She would drive herself to campus in her Ford Escort, going ten miles an hour. When she couldn't drive any longer, she'd take the bus to campus." Betty Finkbeiner is one of many faculty members who looks forward to updates about graduates' jobs. "It is always fun to see their satisfaction when they land a good job," she said.

Often the day-to-day success stories are shared on campus. Roger Bertoia remembered one student in the middle 1960s who had good credentials but couldn't seem to get a job. He came to Bertoia for advice, and the teacher asked what he'd worn to the interviews. When he described his wardrobe choice, Bertoia blinked several times, then suggested, "Let's think about that." "The best way I could describe his mode of dress was 'hip,'" he explained thirty years later with a smile. "After our talk, he went out and bought himself his first real suit. At the next interview, he got the job."

Over the years, it has become increasingly difficult to go anywhere in southeast Michigan without meeting a Washtenaw Community College graduate, whether that person is a nurse, auto mechanic, banker, dental assistant, or builder, Bertoia pointed out. "It has been very satisfying for us all to see how they have moved up in their professions. The individual stories are the highlights at WCC. This College is proud to be a part of so many lives."

- First Earth Day is celebrated on April 22.

- On April 24, President Nixon announces his decision to carry the Vietnam War into Cambodia. Yale students strike.

- For the first time in American history, no deaths from polio are reported this year.

- Inflation grows, U.S. economy falters, recession is anticipated.

- Apollo 13 Astronauts James Lovell, Fred Haise, and John Swigert splash down safely in their crippled spacecraft.

- A Greenwich Village townhouse is destroyed by an explosion in what is believed to be a "bomb factory" of a radical group known as the Weathermen.

- Vietnam: U.S. troop strength: 343,000 (down from a peak of more than 500,000). U.S. dead: 44,241; Wounded: 293,529; Enemy dead: 687,648.

History & Politics

- Four Kent State University students are killed by National Guardsmen during an antiwar protest. Two weeks later, two students are killed in a Jackson State University demonstration.

- After Kent State and Jackson State student deaths, 227 college campuses are closed in protest.

- Senate curbs de facto school segregation. Whites in South Carolina storm buses to prevent integration.

- The Scranton Report on the Kent State shootings calls them "unnecessary, unwarranted, inexcusable." Vice President Spiro Agnew calls the Scranton Report "Pablum for the permissivists."

- A bomb is planted in the math building at the University of Wisconsin as a protest against war research; a student working late is killed.

- Nearly 100,000 students demonstrate in Washington D.C. President Nixon, unable to sleep, goes to the Lincoln Memorial before dawn to address them.

- Six construction workers are arrested after they attack 70 students carrying antiwar posters at Pace College in New York.

Education

Movies

- Americans are flocking to theaters to see *Patton, M*A*S*H, Ryan's Daughter, Airport, Love Story, Lovers and Other Strangers, Five Easy Pieces, Little Big Man*.

Television

- Viewers tune in to watch the premieres of *Monday Night Football, The Mary Tyler Moore Show, The Odd Couple, The Flip Wilson Show, The Partridge Family, All My Children, Flipper*. Top ten shows include *Marcus Welby, M.D.; The Flip Wilson Show; Here's Lucy; Ironside; Gunsmoke; The ABC Movie of the Week; Hawaii Five-O; Medical Center; Bonanza; The F.B.I.*

Music

- Hit songs: "Bridge Over Troubled Water," "For All We Know," "Rubber Duckie," "Candy Man," "Let It Be," "We've Only Just Begun," "Band of Gold," "He Loves Me All the Way."

Books

- Americans are reading *Love Story* (Erich Segal), *The French Lieutenant's Woman* (John Fowles), *Deliverance* (James Dickey), *The Crystal Cave* (Mary Stewart), *Travels with My Aunt* (Graham Greene), *Sexual Politics* (Kate Millett), *Future Shock* (Alvin Toffler), *Nixon Agonistes* (Garry Wills), *My Lai 4* (Seymour M. Hersh), *The Greening of America* (Charles Reich), *Everything You Always Wanted to Know about Sex but Were Afraid to Ask* (David Reuben), *Body Language* (Julius Fast), *Human Sexual Inadequacy* (William Masters, Virginia E. Johnson).

New Words

- Ergonomics, blahs, psycho-technology, fast food, head shop, hype, Oreo, plastic (credit card), ripoff, sexploitation, sensitivity training, encounter group, Jesus People, hassle, putdown, preppie, radical chic.

Quotes

- "I know that probably most of you think I'm an S.O.B., but I want you to know I understand how you feel."—President Nixon to student demonstrators
- "Youth in its protest must be heard."—Secretary of the Interior Walter Hickel

- "The issue of race has been too much talked about....We may need a period in which Negro progress continues and racial rhetoric fades."—Senator Daniel P. Moynihan

- "This is not a bedroom war. This is a political movement."—Betty Friedan, on women's rights

The Voice chronicled the year's highlights:

- The Trustees are forced to slash $140,000 from the budget. The Learning Materials Center and the sports program suffer the greatest losses.

- The revised summer program reduces the number of courses offered from 66 to 40.

- The Black Student Union receives its official recognition. In King Hall, two BSU spokesmen present a list of demands before a "jam-packed crowd" on an "either-or basis:" "Either the demands be met or a declaration of war will be made between the white and black communities of Washtenaw County."

- In February, several classes move to the new T&I Building. Others will follow in the fall.

- WCC holds its first Teach-in. State Senator Gilbert Bursley joins Urban Technology Instructor Vern Albright and two University of Michigan professors to discuss critical environmental concerns.

- WCC athletes have "a great spring season." The Warrior baseball team claims two championships, boasts a 29-10 record, and battles for the Michigan Community Junior College Athletic Conference Region 12 title. Students Pete Hill and Terry Boldon set school records in the long jump and high jump, respectively, at the MCJAC track and field championships, then travel to Garden City, Kansas, for the National Junior College meet. Hill leaps 23', 2", breaking his own record of 22', 8", winning second place. Boldon betters his record by three inches.

- June 6 Commencement graduates 260 students.

Chapter 5:

The People of Washtenaw Community College

Several years after he assisted in the creation of the College, Ann Arbor Chamber of Commerce Director Bill Bott ran for election to the College's Board of Trustees.

"In every way they could, the President and Board sought out and welcomed newcomers," Edith Croake said. In a city like Ann Arbor, the College could have hired a complete faculty without leaving the city limits, but Dave Ponitz made the decision to get the very best— and to do this, he launched a nationwide advertising campaign. WCC ran ads in the *New York Times, Miami Herald,* and *Chicago Tribune.*

THE FACULTY: "WE WERE SHOOT-FROM-THE-HIP PEOPLE"

Fifty faculty members had been hired by the time the first Registration took place; when the enrollment soared higher than even dreamed of, another fifteen full-time faculty members were hired and department heads began scrambling to recruit part-time help. "One of the things that strikes me about the beginning of the College was that it never occurred to us that we couldn't make it work, even though none of us had ever done this before," Edith Croake said.

"We had two very important criteria for hiring," Andy Ford said. "Regardless of one's area of responsibility for teaching, every instructor had to be able to communicate well with students and they had to have experience outside the classroom. We weren't interested in the traditional post-secondary faculty person, although many teaching faculty actually came from universities. We were looking for people with teaching or administrative experience."

President Ponitz and the Board of Trustees wanted "role models for success," people who could show all students that there is a way to

succeed no matter who they were, no matter what their background, Roger Bertoia explained.

Before coming to the College, Andy Ford had been working for the state on a program for identifying and evaluating industrial education instructors and administrators. As soon as he arrived, he became involved in WCC's hiring process, contacting professional organizations and advertising in their publications. WCC administrators visited high schools, businesses, and industries to identify the finest teachers—and then tried to convince them to come to WCC. "Our feeling was that we could be very parochial—but that was the one thing we didn't want to be," Dave Pollock said. "We aimed for top-drawer people and we had foot-high stacks of applications," Ford remembered. "It was exciting to be on the ground floor and witness the start of this new College." Lured by attractive salaries, benefits, and the opportunity to help launch a brand new College, faculty members came from Lansing, Detroit, New York, Washington, and Chicago.

Charter members of the College posed for their tenth-year anniversary celebration in 1976: Front row: Richard Mallory, Gwen Arnold, Judy Hicks, Kenneth Wheeler, Guy Hower. Back row: David Pollock, Mehran Thomson Jr., Robert L. Jackson, Roger Bertoia, Ivan Glusac.

"I modestly say that I am one of the best hirers anyone has ever seen," retired Dean (and former Divisional Director) Mehran Thomson said with a grin. "It takes guts to make a decision and it takes guts to fire people if they don't work out. The easy wrong way is just to look at credentials. My hiring was based on the old boy network, personal interests, and watching people teach." Like other division and department heads, Thomson brought former colleagues to the College. When Livonia's schools were forced to lay off many fine teachers, Thomson snagged some of them. "That episode led me to a revulsion against seniority-based retention policies," he said.

Years before affirmative action legislation, the College actively sought women and minority members for faculty, administrative, and staff jobs. "It sounds archaic now, but in those days one of our selling points was that WCC had just one pay scale; women were paid the same as men," Pollock said. "That wasn't the case in public schools." WCC didn't reach its goal of fifty percent women faculty members, but nearly one-third of the faculty members were women by the time the College's doors opened. There was also a strong African-American contingent.

In the Technical and Industrial Division, three out of ten faculty members were African-American—"and I would say that that statistic was true throughout the WCC faculty," Bertoia said. "Qualified women were harder to come by in occupational programs; there were more women faculty members in general studies." Some years after WCC was founded, the College located and hired the first part-time women in occupational education, one to teach drafting and the other for the machine shop. "In many respects, we raised our own faculty members; several of our students went into industry, earned higher degrees, then returned to WCC to teach," he said.

Initially, instructors in occupational education weren't required to have a degree. As a result, there was no uniform criteria for hiring; the criteria depended on the field. "If people were teaching social science, they had to have a more formal background than someone teaching welding, for example," Ford explained.

When the dust settled after the first Registration, administrators and Trustees were pleased with the people they saw in front of classes. "We assembled a high-powered collection of people," Ford said. "There were no rookies. Everyone had been in the trenches at least once or twice."

■■■

"Our nightmare was seeing a room full of students and no teacher in front of the class," Douglas Woolley said of the days during and immediately following Registration. "Everyone helped wherever they could to make the College a success." The auto body program needed nine students to open, but only eight had registered, so Woolley signed up as a student. He took auto body for two semesters, until the program no longer needed him. He also taught IBM tabulating (now called data processing) on Saturdays. He had been offered the position with the promise that he would have twenty-four students, but the number climbed to forty-eight. "I enjoyed the teaching, although I hadn't anticipated doing it when I was hired," he said.

Woolley's enthusiasm was representative of the faculty Dr. Ponitz assembled, Roger Bertoia said. "Everyone was idealistic, gung-ho. We had a sense of mission and that was exciting." John Phibbs remembered his teachers as idealists, enthusiastic about starting something new. WCC's faculty was politically active, Edith Croake observed. "If you lived through the 1960s as a young person, you had the sense that you needed to help your country move forward. We listened when President John Kennedy said, 'Ask not what your country can do for you; ask what you can do for your country.' We were determined to do just that." Early faculty members had been members of labor unions, the Peace Corps (among them, Ernie Zaremba), and CORE, a civil rights organization. Others (including Bill Moy) had worked at the University of Michigan's Fresh Air Camp, which served underprivileged children. "We had a sense of participation in great causes: Civil Rights, the Vietnam War, the Peace Corps, the Great Society," Bill Moy said. "We believed that we were doing something important, something that validated our entire lives. We all believed that public service ennobled our lives. We were all caught up in the excitement. The temporary, make-shift nature of the old campus symbolized the creation of opportunity, the opening of education to another—and a deserving—side of society."

Don Bylsma discovered that this was "by far the sharpest group of people I had ever worked with—and the most dedicated people when it came to the students. Like every job, there were a few bad apples, but on the scale of one to ten, our faculty definitely scored an eight or nine. In a community college, the emphasis must be on teaching, and we had outstanding teachers. Yet everyone went far beyond their teaching responsibilities. We were involved in everything. We were totally committed to this institution, totally committed to making it work."

At the suggestion of Lee Luchsinger, faculty members' offices were jumbled together rather than organized by departments. This was known as "the mix." Many look back on those days fondly. In the bowling alley the first year, Croake shared office space with Floyd Belkola, an instructor in the Auto Center. Nearby were Gus Amaru (Political Science), Jim Jones (Psychology), Don Bylsma (Sociology), and Herb Martin (Psychology). In those days, English teachers taught four courses and had eight office hours for grading compositions. (Other teachers taught five classes and had five office hours.) Late one afternoon, when Croake was grading papers, she overheard the social scientists discussing their wives. "I remember Gus Amaru saying his pet peeve was getting a call in the grocery store asking him to get several additional items. (This was long before the days of cell phones.) I was a newlywed and I resolved never to call my husband while he was at the grocery!" she said with a smile.

"We knew everyone on campus in the Willow Run days, and the faculty members were close," Dennis Bila said. "With a few exceptions, we were all in our twenties and early thirties, so you might say that we grew up together. We taught together, partied together, and worked together closely." "There was a great sense of camaraderie," Croake agreed, remembering a long-ago conversation with one of her colleagues, Dave Byrd, an African-American architect who came to WCC via Washington, D.C. "I remember asking how he could be sensitive to the social unrest and still be a Republican," she said. "He laughed and explained, punctuating his remarks with funny anecdotes. I learned so much by hearing the stories of my colleagues." One social evening among faculty friends ended tragically, however. A forgotten cigarette was left burning in a sofa at John Wooden's house. Late in the night, the home caught fire, and Wooden suffered severe lung damage.

■ ■ ■

Often the success or failure of a new program depended on the individual at the head of the class. "In the early days, particularly, faculty members needed a spark, an emotional drive and commitment to see a program take off," Andy Ford said. "Some people made a lot out of nothing, others couldn't seem to do much with a good beginning." The economy also helped dictate what programs would fly and what programs would crash. Over the years, WCC administrators learned that they could predict the economy by the enrollment numbers.

"When the economy started to drop, our enrollment would rise—and vice-versa," Guy Hower pointed out. In the late 1960s and early 1970s, when the steel industry collapsed and Michigan became the "Rust Belt," the metallurgical program languished. In contrast, the Nursing Program flourished right from the start. At one time, the program had so many applicants that the administration had to resort to a lottery system for accepting candidates. For the most part, however, programs accepted all the students who wanted to enroll. The faculty and number of classes were expanded or contracted to absorb the enrollment. Some department and division heads were never able to hire a full faculty complement because of the unpredictable ups and downs in enrollment.

Shirley Roberts welcomed countless infants and toddlers to the College's daycare center and countless parents to the College's Family Education Program.

There was little academic snobbery between the instructors about who had degrees and those who didn't, but Fred Horowitz remembers some conflict between occupational and general studies faculty. "It may be that some vocational faculty thought the school was about them and we [general studies faculty and courses] were ancillary," he suggested. "The year I was hired, a graphic arts instructor made a taunting remark, something like 'We teach students the important things.' Another faculty member would regularly put down the people teaching history and English. Never had I expected that sort of thing."

Occasionally, jealousy existed between faculty members at the nearby universities and those at the College. "In the early days, the U of M academics looked down their noses at those of us teaching at the local community college—until the newspaper started publishing salaries," Char Hanson said. "I discovered that I was making more money than the chairman of the speech department at the university."

Because the Community College was neither a glorified high school nor a university, faculty members occasionally struggled to determine their roles. Some took on the role of a parent, uncle, aunt, brother, or friend with students. "Consequently, they couldn't hold the standards as high," Horowitz observed. Some saw their role as empowering students, while holding up high standards. He added, "There hasn't been a day since I arrived when I didn't look at students working and ask myself, "Should I push this student or should I just relax and work with the whole person?"

■ ■ ■

WCC reinvented itself after every Registration. Until the last minute, no one would know—or even be able to predict accurately—how many

Like many of her contemporaries, Lola Jones wore several different hats on campus over the years. Hired in 1966 as a counselor, she worked on campus for several years, then left to tend to her family. Upon her return, she worked in the Student Activities Office.

students to expect. "That's because we experienced such a meteoric rise in our student body during the first ten years," Roger Bertoia recalled. "Once we saw the way Registration was heading, we would have to scramble to find full- and part-time faculty, as well as classroom space." President Ponitz remembered trying for years to predict how many students would register for certain courses and often found that the administration was still surprised.

Washtenaw's faculty has been notable for its energy, enthusiasm, and the willingness and ability to adapt quickly to changing circumstances. "The first group of faculty members faced unbelievable challenges," Guy Hower said. "They were teaching in a brand-new institution, on a temporary campus, with few resources, and no established curriculum. We had people who were comfortable in that kind of unstructured environment. They had to pull together their programs and curriculum within a very, very short time frame. They were the types of people who are driven, highly motivated, and highly motivating." Gradually, the College arrived at a single hiring standard with a stronger emphasis on academic requirements for vocational teachers—"which I think has cost the College some very valuable people," Andy Ford suggested. "In fact, some of the people who created some of our strongest instructional programs wouldn't even merit an interview according to present-day criteria."

Bill Moy compares early faculty members to "cowboys in the best sense of the word." "There was a sense of 'have-gun-will-travel,' a sense of 'can-do,'" he said. "If we needed something, somehow we knew we could get it. The answer to every request was always yes, never no. Nowadays, procedures are more formalized. There are more faculty members, more layers of leadership, more buildings, more departments, more processes. Back then, we were in a hurry to get established, to get the equipment we needed to provide quality education. We found—or invented—ways to get what we needed and to do what we needed to do."

Through the years, however, WCC's faculty has always worked closely with students, with or without the official titles of "instructor-counselor." Gary Owen said, "Never before or since have I encountered so many committed people in one place. Everyone I met was dedicated to helping students with learning problems or students who for whatever reasons hadn't been able to focus in high school. The indi-

The Link-Up Staff paused for some reflection and a photograph in the mid–1970s: (l-r) John Phibbs, Donna Russell, Diana Glushyn, Sue Miller, Vivian Rowland, and Catherine Arcure. Phibbs was a member of the first incoming class of students and returned to campus after graduating from EMU to become Reprographics Manager, and later Manager of Archives and Record Management.

vidual attention and understanding directed towards the students was absolutely amazing. I would be very, very surprised if you could find another faculty anywhere that could match up to the people at WCC in those early days. You could feel their commitment to making the College a success."

Faculty and students socialized in the Student Union. "I can probably name every one of the General Studies faculty members even today," Owen suggested. "I could go on and on talking about the teachers who made a difference in my life: Chuck Belknap in math, Bill Alexander in biology, Fred Wolven in the English Department (he also served as advisor for the student newspaper), Don Bylsma in sociology, Ivan Glusac in economics, Steve Vass in economics, and Counselor Marguerite Eaglin. Edith Croake was one of the finest teachers I have ever had, bar none. I really respected Jim Creagar, a political science instructor; I even worked with him on his political campaign. Chuck Belknap ran a Math Lab that I visited often. The lab didn't offer credits, but he was there to answer our questions. That could be said of everyone on the faculty."

Looking back at the times, Edith Croake remembered the facility challenges at Willow Run, the students, and the times—"but I first think of the great camaraderie and the sense of mission we all shared," she said.

"We had a sense of making history," Bertoia said. "Our pet phrase in those days was 'A Fierce Commitment'—and that's how we all operated."

WHO WAS WHO: 1966–76

THE CLERICAL STAFF

Sometimes the people who have the greatest impact on faculty and students are the people who made everything on campus work smoothly on an hour-by-hour basis. "WCC had a core of administrative assistants who worked very hard and were very dedicated to the students and the success of the community college," Rosalyn Biederman said, citing Dave Pollock's secretary, Gwen Arnold ("who later received her master's degree, taught in and eventually chaired in the business program") and John Wooden's secretary, Phyllis Bostwick ("She moved up the ladder, starting in the Registrar's Office, to become the administrator in charge of the secretarial support services." "She worked from 6 a.m. to 10 p.m.," Betty Finkbeiner remembered.) They appreciated Mary Sabada (who eventually supervised Personnel, now Human Resource Management), as well as Joyce Wiley and Theresa Fleszar, both of them familiar and friendly faces in the Registrar's Office ("They were always available to help students"). Trustee Richard W. Bailey fondly remembered Gerry Brengle as "a nurturing person who made it easier for people to gather their confidence before going into the President's office."

The first Commencement was a time of celebration and reflection.

Ezell Agnew
Buildings & Grounds

"WCC wouldn't be the same without Ezell Agnew," Mehran Thomson said. "He has an absolutely cheery grin and a welcome for everyone who passes him. He loves people and he loves running big machinery."

"At some point, Ezell Agnew became the official campus greeter," Don Bylsma added. "I never met a man who worked harder or talked more. On his own initiative, when he wasn't working at WCC, he started cleaning downtown Ypsilanti because it was dirty. The city finally hired him part-time. He has a heart as big as Ypsilanti. It seems to me that he was illiterate when he was hired and he learned to read here. Whether that's true or not, I'm not sure, but over the years he has become part of our campus mythology."

Ezell Agnew has been one of the WCC landmarks, greeting visitors and students on campus daily.

Gwen Arnold
Clerical Staff, Business

"Gwen Arnold was an outstanding example of the way WCC offered a new life to people," Betty Finkbeiner said. "A single mother with two boys, she was the first secretary to the vice president on the old campus; she managed to juggle her schedule so she could work full-time, raise her boys, and go to school. She earned her associate's degree, then her bachelor's and master's degrees—and then she applied for a teaching job here. She became chair of the Business Department and launched the dream of the Business Education Building. People like these made WCC a special, warmly validating educational institution."

Richard W. Bailey
Board of Trustees

A University of Michigan professor, Richard W. Bailey has served on the Board of Trustees more years than any other Trustee.

Born in Pontiac, Michigan, he graduated from Dartmouth in 1961, with a degree in English, then earned his doctorate from the University of Connecticut four years later. He came to Michigan the day after his University of Connecticut graduation and has been a member of the University of Michigan Department of English ever since.

Bailey became involved with the University of Michigan's Doctor of Arts Program, which prepared people for teaching the first two years of post-secondary education. Two WCC instructors, Edith Croake and W. Bede Mitchell, were among the first group of students in the pro-

Many WCC veterans remembered the kindness and dedication of Gwen Arnold, who rose from secretary to chair the Business Program.

Coy Fulbright delivered the mail for forty-some years.

Tomie O'Banner has been a familiar face in the mail room since WCC's infancy.

gram, which began in 1971. WCC instructors Ruth Hatcher and Barbara Hunt later participated. That program put Bailey in touch with community college people around the country and with Washtenaw Community College in particular. So did the 1972 election, when he closely followed James Walter's unsuccessful campaign for the Board.

In 1974, he decided to run for the Board himself. "I thought—and I still think—that I could affect students who were not likely to get into the University of Michigan, students who did not come from an elite background," he said. "I wanted to have some connection to students who were working hard to upgrade their past and their present situation."

When he joined the Board, WCC had four thousand students and a budget of seven million dollars, a fraction of the present population and budget. "There was a very strong family atmosphere here," Bailey observed. "Everyone had been hired at the same time and had shared similar experiences in getting the College off the ground. There was a sense of shared mission."

Shortly after Bailey joined the Board in January 1975, Dave Ponitz announced his resignation. "By that time, the lore of the College had been established: stories of the early days in a bowling alley, meat market, firehouse, and abandoned elementary school," Bailey said.

Cliff Bellers
Physical Education

Cliff Bellers is remembered for being "extraordinarily dedicated to offering our students a well-rounded college experience." Responding to student concerns and suggestions, he helped launch the College's sports programs, beginning with baseball and bowling. He conscientiously presented the case for budgetary allocations to the teams and throughout the first decade, WCC attracted strong athletes and fielded strong teams.

Roger Bertoia
Industrial Drafting

A Detroit native and graduate of Cass Technical High School, Roger Bertoia earned his bachelor's and master's degrees in industrial education from the University of Michigan. He was teaching at the University High School when he heard about WCC.

"I well remember the campaign in 1965 to establish and create the community college," he said. "Tony Procassini's Education Committee was doing the research and spearheading the campaign, and the newspapers covered the activities very thoroughly."

Bertoia applied to WCC and was hired in the spring of 1966. He was elected to the Ann Arbor City Council during his teaching years at the College. "WCC has been proud of our faculty's community involvement," Trustee Richard W. Bailey said.

Robert Bickner
Counseling

A Vietnam veteran who could speak the Hmong language, Robert Bickner came to WCC from the University of Michigan. When Catholic Social Services settled a large community of Hmong in Washtenaw, Bickner was instrumental in helping them get established. "WCC acted in loco parentis and started a training program for them," Mehran Thomson said. "These people were in enormous demand as workers. They had a tremendous work ethic and they were very faithful in the execution of their jobs. I remember that we had a Tet (Vietnamese New Year) celebration on campus, thanks to Robert. The entire Vietnamese and Hmong community showed up. Every family brought food. Gunder Myran gave a speech. I will never forget the smell of oranges and the hoards of kids everywhere."

Rosalyn Biederman
Spanish

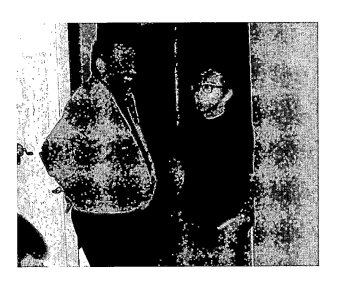

Rosalyn Biederman was the second member of the Language Department.

After earning her bachelor's degree in Spanish at Ohio State University, Rosalyn Biederman taught in the Romance Language Department at OSU while working on her master's degree. After graduation, she lived in Spain for a year, working as an interpreter and translator for a large automotive firm in Madrid. She became a College faculty member in 1967, when the large student enrollment caused programs and departments to expand.

At that time, WCC's French/Spanish instructor was Larry Radick, a very talented linguistics student from the University of Michigan who spoke the Romance and Slavic languages. He preferred teaching French, German, and Russian, so after interviewing Biederman, he recommended her for the Spanish position. She was hired on the spot at the age of twenty-four, and quickly felt accepted into a family-like atmosphere. "In the first ten years, the faculty grew up together and often socialized," she said. "I am still on the job, so you might say that I have given WCC the best years of my life!"

Dennis Bila
Math

Math Instructors Percy Mealing and Dennis Bila shared a joke as well as a strong commitment to their field.

Dennis Bila was raised on a three hundred acre farm on the banks of the Shaiwassee River in the Saginaw Valley. The American government had purchased the land from the Chippewa nation in the 1820s, then Bila's German ancestors paid $1.25 an acre for their farm, and raised corn and soybeans there. His mother's family owned the adjacent farm; they had emigrated from Czechoslovakia.

Bila attended a one-room country school with twenty students in eight grades. He learned early that he was very, very good at math; he watched the older students do their math and by the third or fourth grade he was helping them. In high school, Bila spent three years helping his math teacher teach. Bila married his childhood sweetheart at the age of nineteen and became one of only three or four in his graduating class of one hundred to go on to college. Most others either went back to farms or to

auto factories; he went to Central Michigan University. "My parents gave me no encouragement to go to college, but my Czechoslovakian grandfather did," Bila said. "He gave me ten acres of land to grow navy beans, which are hard to raise, and he taught me the secrets. Fortunately, the price of beans tripled that year." The money Bila made from that bean crop lasted him through nearly three years of college.

"The best thing that ever happened to me was Sputnik," the math teacher said, explaining, "When the Russians launched the space race, the U.S. government began to focus on education. The government provided money for college students studying math and physics, so my college education was virtually free. So were my master's and doctorate programs at Wayne State."

After teaching at Flint High School, Bila went to General Motors for the salary, but found that he was unhappy at his work. He remembered his grandfather's advice: "Find out what you want to do with your life. Don't complain about it. *Change* it." So, he returned to graduate school and got a job teaching math at Redford High School. The government matched his salary when he attended graduate school and because math and science teachers were in such short supply, they could get draft deferments during the Vietnam War. "Yes, Sputnik was the best thing that happened to me," Bila said.

Charter faculty and staff members posed for an anniversary: (Rear, l-r)Ezell Agnew, Ken Barron, Gus Amaru, Ralph Bottoff, Paul Niehaus, Robert Nelson, Dean Russell, Ivan Glusac. (Front, l-r) Mary Sabada, Flavia Reps, Edith Croake, Eleanor Charlton, Phyllis Bostwick.

Wayne State University had just offered him a job in teacher education when Mehran Thomson called with an offer to teach math in 1969. WCC also offered him more freedom to write than he would have had at a four-year institution, so he became the tenth instructor in the math department. "We were all hired from high schools and we were all experienced, not only in teaching, but also in developing programs," he said. "I still think that our best instructors come with junior high and high school backgrounds."

Since 1969, Dennis Bila has written thirteen books about math, taught math education for Michigan State University in Detroit, headed the Washtenaw Community College Education Association (WCCEA), and served as the mayor of Plymouth for ten years.

Don Bylsma
Sociology

A Detroit native, Don Bylsma attended Wayne State University "by accident—really." During high school, he worked in a men's-wear store. The owner's brother was a counselor at WSU, and he encouraged Bylsma to take college entrance exams. Bylsma enrolled, dropped out, then got a job at Great Lakes Steel, where he learned that students could work the midnight shift and get paid overtime. Bylsma re-enrolled.

In 1960, he graduated with majors in science and physical education. After a stint teaching the children of Army Corps of Engineers personnel in Europe, he took a teaching job in Detroit and worked towards his master's degree in sociology at Wayne State. He had actually accepted a job at Oakland Community College when a small "Washtenaw Community College" sign on East Huron Street caught his eye. On a whim, he walked into the office and WCC hired him on the spot. Later, Bylsma was awarded a Kellogg Fellowship, which allowed him to earn his Ph.D. in higher education and sociology at the University of Michigan while teaching.

"Originally, my plan was to stay at Washtenaw for two or three years, then work my way into a college presidency, but I found that my job at WCC was a great luxury," he said. "I could focus on my teaching and still spend time with my kids as they grew up. I could jockey my schedule to fit my children's schedules. I never missed a school event that I can remember. So...I stayed."

David Byrd
Architecture

"As an individual and a professional, David Byrd left his mark on his community in many ways," Lola Jones said. "He was a fine man, dedicated to helping people better their lives."

Through the years, Byrd's endeavors and creative solutions to design problems made headlines in regional papers. He designed the furnishings for the Huron High School Career Center, which opened in 1974, and his students built the carrels for the school. He designed the ceremonial mace used in special WCC ceremonies. In April of 1975, *The Ann Arbor News* reported on an invention Byrd created with another Washtenaw Community College instructor. The headline reads "Energy Machine or Dud?" The story shows some of the tremendous scope of interests and talents the architectonics instructor brought to his classroom:

> Solar energy, fusion power, geothermal energy—forget it! Two Ann Arbor African-American men claim to have invented an energy machine which is superior to any of these potential power sources.

> David R. Byrd and Johnny Clarke, instructors at Washtenaw Community College, were scheduled to leave for Washington, D.C., this week to discuss their invention with the U.S. Energy Research and Development Administration (ERDA).

> Byrd, chairman of the Ann Arbor Human Rights Commission (HRC) and former Washtenaw County commissioner, is an instructor in architecture in the WCC Technical and Industrial Division. Clarke, a local licensed builder, is a part-time instructor in construction technology at the college.

The Instructor of Architectural Technology and former president of the Huron Valley Chapter of the Architectural Institute of America was the subject of an in-depth *Voice* profile in November 1974, which noted, "A tremendous amount of David Byrd's energy and time is spent in behalf of Ann Arbor's minority and low income citizens."

Eleanor Charlton
Secretarial Science

"I've been working at WCC since it opened its doors," Eleanor Charlton said. After earning her bachelor of science degree in social science and her master's degree in business education, she worked at Midland Senior High School, Ferris State University, and Eastern Michigan University before meeting a former EMU colleague, Art Lamminen, in the post office one day. WCC's new Director of Business invited her to come to the Community College and set up the secretarial department. She submitted her application and was hired in 1966.

Edith Croake
English

When Edith Croake joined the faculty, she interviewed with William Cherniak in his living room while his daughters played at their feet.

Edith Croake became the Community College's youngest faculty member when she was hired at the age of twenty-four in 1966—and she had absolutely no idea that she would keep the same job for four decades.

She had earned her bachelor's degree in English from the University of Michigan in 1963, at a time when there was a great demand for high school teachers. National Defense loans were available with low interest rates, so she applied to Northwestern and earned a master's degree in education and a second master's in English while teaching in a Chicago high school.

When her husband received a fellowship in Ann Arbor in 1966, the couple moved back to Michigan. Edith put a compass to a map of southeastern Michigan and drew a circle around the area within thirty miles of Ann Arbor. She applied to every high school within the circle, as well as to the new Community College. She received two job offers: teaching science, German, and English at Chelsea High School, or teaching English at WCC. She took the WCC job—"with a little trepidation"—knowing that she'd be teaching many people older than she was.

Chairman William Cherniak hired four full-time faculty: Edith Croake, William Elliot (who was finishing a Ph.D. at the University of Michigan and left after a year), Diane Peters (who was working on a doctorate at Michigan and left after two years), and Fred Wolven (advisor for the student newspaper and early creative writing publications; he stayed fifteen years). Several years later, a team of English professors from the University of Michigan came to talk about a new Doctor of Arts in English program they were preparing to launch. President Ponitz asked if members of the English Department would be interested. Croake raised her hand. While teaching, she earned her doctor of arts.

It didn't take long for Croake to become absorbed in her job at WCC. "I loved it—I still do," she said. One Friday, when she forgot to bring her paycheck home, her husband joked, "Just what I always feared: you love your work so much that you forget to get paid for it. Remember, I'm an unemployed graduate student!"

The first year, she often went home so exhausted that she could barely move. A "very traditional bride," she struggled every night to put dinner on the table, but at least one time she found herself too tired to eat. She was dealing with a new job in a new college and a wide assortment of students, some of them with special needs. "We weren't immune from the traumas of those who had participated in the war," she said.

Faculty and staff members also shared personal triumphs and tragedies. One snowy day, Vern Albright's wife dropped him off at WCC and drove away. Her car later went out of control on the "S" curve on Geddes near Prospect, and she was killed. One of Croake's students flipped his car over on Interstate 94 and was killed. She sent his papers to his parents with a note and one day they visited her, crying, to thank her. A woman from India discussed how absolutely astonished she was by the American concept of women, how it differed from her cultural traditions. ("Feminism was alive and well here in the '60s," Croake observed.) She told Croake that she would take American ideas back home with her. "I don't want to say that every moment of those early years was emotion-filled, but we were very close to everyone else," Croake said. "Their tragedies and victories became ours, too. It wasn't just the faculty who had the sense of excitement, of 'can do.' It was the students, too."

Betty Finkbeiner
Director, Dental Assistant Program

As soon as she learned that she had the WCC job, Betty Finkbeiner climbed into her car to investigate the outlying communities where her students lived, so she could understand their environment and their commute. Her first class of nine women remember convincing her to go to the Wolverine in Chelsea for one of the bar's renowned burgers, "just to get to know the area." Decades later, she was still in touch with those students.

Finkbeiner had been in practice as a dental assistant for ten years when she decided that her next career step should be teaching. She had originally interviewed for the job as head of the Dental Assistants' Program before it started, in 1967, but when she learned that the dentist she was working for had cancer, she decided not to leave. After he died, she taught at Ferris State College for a year, then learned that the WCC position was once again open. She was interviewed and hired in 1969. "The College gave me more than a terrific job," Finkbeiner said. "The College introduced me to my husband."

Finkbeiner has written a dozen textbooks for her field. "When I started teaching, there were very few materials and what was available was out-of-date," she said. "I set out to fill a vacuum."

Andrew Ford
Director, Technical & Industrial Division

On September 13, 1967, *The Voice* revealed some interesting facts about the early life of Andrew Ford, Director of WCC's Technical and Industrial Division:

School Dropout Makes Good

By Mrs. Grace F. Davis

Andy Ford came to WCC via the Detroit Public School System.

Ford, born in Detroit in 1935, started his first paying job while in elementary school. At 11 he became a hat check boy at a local dance hall, then stepped up to scraping gum off the dance floor and on to short order cook. Four of his summers were spent working in a fishery.

Ford became a drop-out at 16 because he was bored with school and joined the Marine Corps. As soon as his age was discovered he was discharged and sent home. He worked part-time for the Land and Forest Department in Ontario, Canada, felling diseased trees, and then went to Cass Technical High School, taking a Mechanical Drawing Curriculum.

The following summer he worked as a cow puncher on a ranch in Montana and lived with the Sioux Indians. He learned many of their customs and became quite an authority on their tribal dances. Later he was one of the founders of the Michigan Indian Dance Association.

While attending Wayne State University, Ford held as many as five jobs at a time, along with a normal academic load. He had his own dance band combo and a job as an audio visual repairman for the University. Summers were spent as a horseback riding counselor, as well as working for the Chrysler Corp. as a draftsman from 1953 to 1957. Ford earned his B.A. and M.A. during these busy years.

Many years after that article was written, Andy Ford continued the story, "When Paul Hunt first approached me in early 1966, I was a public school administrator and a university teacher-educator. I had taught industrial education in the Detroit public schools and at Wayne State University. At that time, I was looking at viable offers from Ohio State, Cal Tech, and Central Michigan, and I wasn't interested."

But Paul Hunt didn't give up easily. The first Dean of Occupational Education had been appointed to oversee all occupational programs, and he needed a strong and experienced Director of the Technical and Industrial Division. He kept hounding, Ford kept declining, but finally, in May 1966, he agreed to interview as a courtesy. "When I got here, though, I had a complete change of attitude," Ford said. "I found that people were serious about occupational education. I asked myself how many times I'd have the chance to help launch a new college and decided I wanted to sign on...for a few years, then I'd move on." The "few years" stretched into twenty-four years. He retired in 1990.

Pogliano called Andy Ford "the best administrator I've worked under. "You could count on him to go to bat for you," he said. "If you believed in something strongly, you'd go in, sit and argue for hours, and then he'd give you what you asked for. 'Just so you really feel strongly about it,' he'd tell me afterwards."

Don Garrett
Culinary Arts & Hospitality Management

Don Garrett's former co-workers fondly remember the stories that he would tell about his grandmother's cooking and how much he enjoyed spending time at her house. His former students remember that he never expected more from them than he did from himself. He would tell them, "You all start this course with an 'A.' What you do with it is up to you."

Garrett began his food service career in the United States Army, in between earning the Bronze Star, Army Accommodation Medal, National Defense Service Medal, and the Vietnam Combat and Service medals. After his discharge, he studied food in a more formal setting, at Washtenaw Community College. His teaching career began here in 1975, and he continued to receive accolades and awards, among them the College's Dr. Morris J. Lawrence Jr. Award.

The driving force behind the College's lengthy accreditation process with the American Culinary Federation Educational Institute, Garrett held the Ann Arbor Culinary Association's title "Chef of the Year" and served a term as governor of the Michigan District Optimist Club, whose motto is "a friend of youth."

"He was an exceptional human being and he merited every award he ever received," Trustee Richard W. Bailey said.

Don Garrett went into Culinary Arts after being inspired by his grandmother's cooking.

Dan Gray
Welding

"Welding was a good, solid program supervised by Dan Gray," Roger Bertoia said. "He was an extraordinary man. He didn't come to college teaching through the traditional route; he didn't have a bachelor's degree, but he was a terrific teacher. He opened my eyes to the fact that teaching is a gift and it's a gift that classroom training doesn't always give."

Char Hanson
Speech

Speech Instructor Char Hanson is remembered fondly by generations of students for her fun and innovative teaching methods.

Many early students mention Char Hanson's speech class as one of their highlights. She began each semester by telling her students "The Hanson Rule of Education: There's nothing to stimulate your interest in higher education like the job you would have without it." "Many of my students had been out in the real world and they realized what education could offer them," she said.

Hanson had earned a bachelor of arts degree in English from the University of Michigan and then a master's degree in speech. She was one of the teachers hired on a part-time basis after the first Registration left WCC administrators scrambling for more teachers. "I have always gotten my best jobs at the spur of the moment," she said. With a three-year-old son at home, she was happy to limit her schedule to three classes a week; a year later, however, she went full-time, but managed to schedule some evening classes so her husband could watch their son.

Mehran Thomson was among many who called Char Hanson "the social soul of the College." Hired in 1969, she retired in 1988 after two decades teaching and planning fun social activities. "There comes a time when you know that it's time to leave, but I loved my years at WCC. I continue to keep in touch with friends and go back frequently."

Judy Hicks
Library

Judy Hicks remembered her first day at her new job as though it were yesterday. Hired to help WCC's new Library Director Harold Young establish the new College's library, she got lost in Ann Arbor trying to find the 204 Huron Street office on a dreary, rainy day. When she finally managed to park, she left her lights on, and her car battery died. "I remember wondering if this was really a good thing for me to do," she said.

A 1964 high school graduate, she had worked with Harold Young in the University of Michigan-Dearborn library until Young was hired by WCC. He asked her to give the new College a try. She has been a cataloguing technician in the library ever since.

Fred Horowitz
Art

Fred Horowitz grew up in New Haven, Connecticut, graduated from Yale with two degrees (Bachelor of Arts in English and Bachelor of Fine Arts in art), then came to Ann Arbor to work on a Master of Fine Arts degree at the University of Michigan. He taught at Schoolcraft College until a WCC job opened in the summer of 1968. He was thirty years old when Bill Cherniak, head of the English Department, hired him to teach studio and design courses. "Initially, I planned to stay at WCC only a few years and then move on. However, I was divorced and had a young son and didn't want to leave the area," he said. "I was happy at WCC, particularly with the students, and more and more happy as the years went on. I felt that I was very, very lucky to be here."

A Yale graduate, Fred Horowitz came to WCC intending to stay a few years but ended up devoting four decades to the college.

Guy Hower
Counseling, Financial Aid, Student Activities

"Whether you're a staff member, administrator, or faculty member, you've got to have the right temperament to start in a school where everything is new," Guy Hower said. "In the early years, we had no rules, no policies. We winged everything."

In 1962, Hower graduated from the University of Michigan with a bachelor's degree in business. For the next three years, he taught cooperative occupational training at Rochester High School. A National Direct Student Loan allowed him to return to the university full time for a master's degree in counseling. In April 1966, he read a WCC job ad, and decided to apply. "As soon as I was hired as the first counselor, we started registering students," he said. Like many other WCC administrators, Hower changed positions several times over the years, from Counselor to Director of Counseling, Director of Athletics, Director of Student Services, and Director of Financial Aid.

"Counseling hasn't changed a lot," he observed. "We still get asked the same kinds of questions. I think that's because the students haven't changed; they still come in all ages, types, and backgrounds."

Guy Hower was WCC's first counselor and through the years he has worn many administrative hats.

Lola Jones
Counseling, Student Activities

Born in Boston, Massachusetts, to West Indian parents, Lola Jones spent her childhood in Jamaica, but returned to Massachusetts when her mother realized that the employment opportunities were better in the States.

She was the first in her family to go to college, earning her bachelor's degree in sociology from Wayne State University. In 1964, she went to work for Ann Arbor's public schools as a social worker while pursuing her master's degree in counseling at the University of Michigan. Dick Nowland encouraged her to call Dave Pollock about opportunities at the new College and she was hired in 1966, balancing her career with her home life and the care of her four children. "Although working mothers weren't that common in the 1960s, there were several women at WCC doing the same thing," she said.

She took several years off for family responsibilities, then returned to WCC, this time working in Student Services. Her office brought speakers to campus, among them Eugene McCarthy and Julian Bond. "That was an exciting job," she said. "Those speakers would talk to an auditorium full of students, faculty, and community members, then sit and answer questions in a relaxed fashion."

George Kapp
Physics

George Kapp studied physics at WCC, then worked with John McGill as a lab assistant and technician. Kapp went on to earn his degree at the University of Michigan and returned to WCC to teach physics. "He was an extremely gifted instructor," Mehran Thompson noted.

Ann Cleary Kettles
Member & Chair, Board of Trustees

Ann Cleary Kettles has always loved politics. She majored in political science at the University of Michigan, then, in the late 1960s, became involved in Ypsilanti politics. By 1972, she had decided that the Washtenaw Community College Board of Trustees should have a woman's viewpoint. "My grandfather founded Cleary University in 1883, and I had family on both sides who were teachers, so there was a name recognition for me in educational circles when I ran for the Board," she said.

Running for public office takes a lot of courage, she learned. "You really stick your neck out." During the Board election in 1972, a group of Ann Arbor citizens supported Kettles and paid for her campaign ads, which she shared with Tony Procassini. Sally Buxton was elected the same year. After its first seven years, the Board of Trustees welcomed not only one woman, but two.

"I ran for election six times, always as a non-partisan," Kettles said. "Running was fun, but also hard work. Raising the money for advertising was the hardest part of the election process for me. The first time I ran, a committee from Ann Arbor raised the money for advertising and I spent very little, just to have cards printed and mailed. The women's movement helped me during that election; I did very well. The second time I was on my own and I advertised all over the county; by that time I was invested in the Board, and I really wanted to win. I did very well in that election, too."

While working on the Board, Kettles was also juggling four children, a new marriage, and a challenging career at Eastern Michigan University. She served on the Board from 1973 until 1984, chairing the Board for two years. She stepped down when her career became more demanding, she said. "I had started as a secretary in the nursing department, then I rose through the Academic Advising Department, serving as an advisor, then coordinator, assistant director, and director." She earned her master's degree in guidance and counseling before being named interim Registrar. In time, she served as Eastern Michgan University's director for the Department of Records, Registration, and Advising.

"I have had regrets about leaving the Board, but I've stayed connected to the College," she said. She went on to serve on the boards of Washtenaw Technical Middle College and the WCC Foundation.

"I am very pleased and comfortable with what we accomplished on the Board in the early years," she said. "The people I served with on the Board have been a blessing in my life. It's a wonderful experience to be part of something as valuable to the community as WCC."

Harry Konschuh
Vice President

Born and raised in Canada, Harry Konschuh earned his undergraduate degree in math and physics from the University of Alberta, then taught in a high school until he decided to move to Lansing to work on a master's degree in math and physics at Michigan State University. He returned to Alberta and teaching until 1963, when he landed a job at Lake Michigan Community College. Konschuh quickly moved through the ranks until he was appointed Vice President of Instruction.

In 1972, WCC hired him as Dean of Employee Relations. He became the first administrator to be named Vice President, heading Human Resources and then Administration and Finance. "My job supervised faculty, facilities, information systems, security, finances, budgets, purchasing, tuition decisions—everything but instruction," he said. He arrived on campus with the reputation of having fired the entire

Harry Konschuh became the first WCC administrator to be named vice president.

faculty at Lake Michigan Community College over labor disputes, and he quickly spearheaded the administration's negotiations with faculty and staff associations.

Like many others, Harry Konschuh discovered that WCC could change personal lives just as much as professional lives; he met WCC Director of Library Services Adella Scott Blain on campus and married her some years later.

Arthur Lamminen
Divisional Director, Business & Industrial Management
The Voice published a profile of Arthur Lamminen:

Ex-Business Executive Heads B & M Division

Arthur J. Lamminen, Divisional Director of Business and Industrial Management, has had a variety of interesting experiences.

Lamminen was born in Virginia, Minnesota, and moved to Detroit shortly after. He attended the Henry Ford Technical Industrial School system where he studied industrial technology and engineering.

Lamminen worked for the Ford Motor Co. in the Research Laboratory, Dearborn. He was a pioneer in the industrial uses of the soy bean and other agricultural products of which oil paint and plastics are made....

During his rising years of success Lamminen was married in the Martha-Mary Chapel in Greenfield Village. The Lamminens were the first couple to be married in this Chapel. Henry Ford, Sr., sponsored the wedding himself as he was a personal friend....

In 1954 he went to Tri-State College in Angola, Indiana, taking 20 and 25 credit hrs. per term on a quarter basis, and received a B.A. in 1956. In 1957 he received his master's from M.S.U. He then started his Ph.D. at M.S.U. and was Administrative Assistant to the Associate Deans, and then Assistant to the Dean of the College of Business and Graduate School of Business Administration.

In 1961 Lamminen went to E.M.U. as a member of the Department of Management faculty in the College of Business, and in 1964 he was appointed Chairman of the Department of Management.

Lamminen came to WCC as B. & M. division director because the College's philosophy paralleled his personal philosophy...."We will do everything possible to help the student to help himself succeed."

A powerhouse of energy and enthusiasm, Morris Lawrence Jr. made the study and performance of music exciting and exhilarating for his students.

Dan Laursen
Geology

A science teacher who had taught at Jackson Community College, Dan Laursen was living in Denmark at the time Mehran Thomson called him about a WCC job opening. "Dave Ponitz had been complaining about us not looking far enough away for people to hire, so when a colleague found out I was interviewing Dan, he told Ponitz, 'Thom's off to Denmark.' That caught his attention!" Thomson said with a grin. "I actually phoned Denmark. Dan became leader of my science group." An outstanding teacher, Laursen was a world-renowned expert on Greenland, seashells, and stamps. His stories about being a former Resistance fighter during World War II are still told on campus.

Morris Lawrence Jr.
Music

Morris Lawrence Jr. was a giant of a man who had a passion for music and great gifts for performing, composing, and teaching music. He was an early proponent of incorporating African-American musical traditions into the College curriculum. In April 1971, Lawrence wrote in *The Voice*:

> One of the most dominant cultural characteristics of the Black people that has lasted and grown the test of time is our MUSIC. The music of the Afro-American Culture is also integrated with

many other music cultures of the world and rightly so. ETHNO-MUSICOLOGY deserves to be...within the realm of music courses...To fully understand and appreciate the music, one must know the peoples who produce that music.

Morris Lawrence produced great music. Born in 1940, in New Orleans, the birthplace of jazz, Lawrence played the clarinet in his high school band and became one of the Royal Dukes of Rhythm; he called B.B. King, Papa Salastan, and other blues and jazz stars his friends.

Lawrence graduated from Xavier University in New Orleans with a bachelor of music degree in 1961, then received the Oliver Ditson Scholarship to the University of Michigan School of Music. He played the contra-bass clarinet in the university's symphony and marching bands and earned his master's degree in 1962. His "street degree," as he loved to call it, he earned "from a lot of great and beautiful people in the music world." WCC's Director of Music played contra-bass clarinet for the Ypsilanti Greek Theater Orchestra and began composing and arranging music for a wide variety of performances. His rich baritone voice became familiar to midwestern audiences.

While working on his doctorate at Michigan, he served as Director of Music for WCC as well as Ann Arbor's St. Thomas School. Under his direction, the WCC Band would perform at the Labor Day Jazz Festival every year and at University of Michigan football games.

Lawrence's melody to "Number One" was performed on radios around the nation in the 1960s. He wrote the music for the hit tune "Hello, Strangers," which Barbara Lewis recorded, and "Groove Me," sung by King Floyd. Lawrence also wrote the textbook, *Music of Afro-American Culture.*

"Morris was a giant by several standards," Ron Zeeb said. "He stood six-foot-two-inches tall, weighed perhaps three hundred pounds, and had an enormous intelligence and gift for music. He could play the saxophone and trumpet extraordinarily well—every bit as good as Benny Goodman." One day Zeeb walked past Lawrence's music-filled classroom and heard him urge his students, "Listen to the clarinet...*feel* the clarinet...Now, listen to those drums!"

"Morris Lawrence was an outstanding member of the faculty. He came here early and he ran an excellent band," Don Bylsma said. "Morris was everywhere good music could be heard. He was exceptionally gifted. He was also a good friend. When I moved to Ann Arbor in 1970, he helped us with our move; I remember him hauling our washing machine into the house single-handedly."

In an article for *The Ann Arbor News* published on January 7, 1994, and entitled "Morris Lawrence Taught His Students More than Music," John A. Woods offered a vivid portray of Morris Lawrence's teaching style:

> In 1977, as a student in Morris Lawrence's Creative Improvisation and Songwriting class, I sat goggle-eyed as "Doc" Lawrence—all 300-plus pounds of him—shook, shimmied, and sashayed while demonstrating the New Orleans cake walk.
>
> His infectious enthusiasm would not allow him to sit still as he described how mourners in New Orleans would somberly march to the cemetery during funeral processions.
>
> With breathless energy and tumbling words, he would paint a verbal portrait of the traditional march as the mourners and musicians slowly stepped to the beat of a bass drum and muted horns playing the old hymn "Just a Closer Walk with Thee…"
>
> Ask any of the thousands of his students and they will tell you that he taught more than music. His classes offered lessons in perseverance, patience and honesty in your music and your life….

Jon Onye Lockard
Art

When Fred Horowitz was asked to teach an appreciation course on African-American art for the Black Studies Program, he interviewed African-American artists in Ann Arbor and ordered appropriate slides and books in preparation. One day he met Jon Lockard, "who was quite eloquent, very knowledgeable, and very talented," Horowitz said. "He had a lot of ideas about how the course should be taught. I thought that he would be a suitable candidate for the position and invited him to meet the Black Studies Committee." After he finished his presentation, Lockard was hired full-time, not just to teach the class, but also some studio courses.

Burton C. Lowe
Mechanical Technology

"I've taught in most of the plants in this area," Burton Lowe said, listing Ford's Rawsonville, Ypsilanti, Saline, Milan, and Brighton plants, as well as at Matco Technology and a ball-bearing plant, among others.

A Connecticut native, Burton Lowe graduated from Cass Technical High School in Detroit in 1947, and enrolled in trade school. "I had a mechanical background and I couldn't afford college," he said. In 1948, he was offered a job with Ford and stayed for two years, until the Korean War broke out and his Naval Reserves unit was called to active duty. He returned to Ford in 1953, completed his apprenticeship, and started attending Wayne State University. He was thirty-eight years old and twenty hours short of his degree when he was hired to teach industrial technology at WCC. "I never did finish my degree—I've been too busy," he said.

"Pay didn't make a difference to me when I came here," he added, explaining, "I wanted to teach. I thought I could be a bridge for people to get better jobs and work their way into a better life. I liked the fact that this new Community College wanted to bridge the gap between industry and academics, also. We all did a pretty good job of it."

John McGill
Physics

"John McGill has been very special to the history of WCC," according to Mehran Thomson. "He always kept an eye out for students and for others who needed extra consideration." Hired as a math instructor, McGill created a program for people with special needs, with activities centered around computers. The program became known as PAHISM (Project Assistance for Handicapped Students in Mathematics). "Without John, I doubt if WCC would have a handicapped program."

Bill Moy
Psychology

Bill Moy was the motivating force behind the establishment of the child care program for children of WCC students. "When you're twenty-three and twenty-four, nothing is difficult," he said. "Everything is challenging and exciting. In the early days at WCC, we made do—that was part of the challenge. In the 1960s, we were very idealistic, very socially focused. We were part of the Kennedy-Camelot dream."

After earning an undergraduate degree in psychology from Valparaiso University, Moy enrolled at the University of Michigan for graduate work and spent the summer before working at the university's Fresh Air Camp at Patterson Lake, which specializes in working with emotionally impaired children. He returned to the camp the next six summers and during the school year worked with emotionally impaired children at the Hawthorne Center in Livonia. One night, WCC Counselor Jim Jones called one of Moy's friends about a teaching job in psychology at the new College. The friend referred Moy to him.

Bill Moy taught part-time at WCC in 1967, then became full-time in 1968, while he was still working on his Ph.D. "When I came, I had no grand plans for the future," Moy said. "I was all focused on the excitement of what we were doing, what we were creating. I had already decided that this was a good place for me because I was much more committed to teaching than to research and publishing."

Mike Pogliano
Architectural Drafting

A native of the Upper Peninsula, Mike Pogliano earned his degree from the University of Michigan School of Architecture in 1964, then worked for two local architectural firms until he became a registered architect and opened his firm, Architects and City Planners.

Pogliano filled out an application for WCC as soon as he heard about the new College, and was hired part-time in 1968, full-time in 1969. Through the thirty-three years in which he taught, he continued to maintain his architectural practice.

When Pogliano arrived on campus, his department consisted of himself and David Byrd. Pogliano taught industrial drawing courses and worked with people in the architecture and construction trades. "Dave Byrd was a high-strung black man, and I was a high-strung Italian and we would argue for hours on end," he remembered. "People who didn't know us well would hide under tables, thinking they were about to see a fist fight break out, but once we were done, we'd leave the place arm-in-arm. We had great respect for each other. We both believed that if someone believed in something enough, it was worth arguing about."

Dave Pollock
Executive Assistant to the President, Dean of Students, Acting President (1975)

Born in South Bend, Indiana, Dave Pollock enrolled in the University of Michigan on the eve of World War II, then spent nearly four years in the Army. When he returned, he earned a degree in political science with a minor in history. His first job after graduation was at the university. He left to edit a small magazine, was hired by the Burroughs Corporation, and eventually returned to the university. He was working in the Community Relations Office when the community college idea began circulating and he was instrumental in its establishment. Pollock was the first person Dave Ponitz hired.

"At first, my title was Executive Assistant to the President and I had no job description. I did everything I (or anyone else) could think of," Pollock said. Later, he became Dean of Student Affairs. When the first Dean of Administration left, he moved into that job and was responsible for outside contacts, the catalogue, special events, and working on administrative issues. When Dave Ponitz left the College in 1974, Pollock became interim president. Under Gunder Myran, he worked as Executive Assistant to the President.

Robert A. Reeves
Speech

In 1959, Robert Reeves earned a degree in speech communications from Eastern Michigan University, then taught government and speech classes in Germany when he was stationed there with the Third Army. After leaving the Army in 1961, he took a teaching job in Ypsilanti offered by "Slim" Ardis. "He was a great guy, very compassionate and concerned about people," Reeves said of the future WCC Trustee.

In 1964, he went to Detroit to teach and finish a master's degree in speech pathology. In 1968, Herb Martin's wife told him about the new Community College, and Reeves filled out an application for a summer job. Bill Cherniak, chairman of the English department, offered him a full-time teaching position, however, saying, "You'll be on the ground floor of something exciting, and you'll have a chance to grow along with the College. It's a great opportunity."

"I listened to him and joined."

Reeves was active in collective bargaining—on both sides of the table, first as a faculty member and then as an administrator. He served as president of the WCCEA and ended his career at WCC as Associate Vice President for Human Resources.

Flavia Reps
History

"Out of the first fifty faculty members hired, few were women. I was one of them," Flavia Reps said. "I came with seven years of teaching experience, including four years at a college in San Diego."

A history major at St. Joseph College, she earned her master's degree from Georgetown and was working on the East Coast when she happened to read an advertisement in *The New York Times* for teaching spots at a new community college in Ann Arbor, Michigan. She applied and was hired on the spot, but wondered why she was discouraged from visiting the new campus at Willow Run—until she

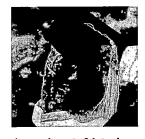

A passionate historian, Flavia Reps launched an oral history project about the College in the 1980s.

moved here, saw it, and heard about its condition during the summer of 1966.

A memorable history instructor, Reps practiced what she preached. In the 1970s, she launched an oral history project to preserve first-person memories of WCC's early days. For the nation's Bicentennial, she developed a seven-week course on the American Revolution called "Images of an Era," with groundbreaking courses on women's roles in the American Revolution, science and medical advances, music of the era, and a comparison of other nations' revolutions.

Kathleen Scott
Library

After earning her undergraduate degree in English with a teacher's certificate from the University of Iowa, Kathleen Scott went to graduate school for a master's degree in library science. She moved to Ann Arbor in June 1971.

At that time, WCC had no library director and no librarian, but the College needed a library professional for its accreditation. With the North Central Association of Colleges and Schools on its way to campus, WCC had to act soon. Scott spoke with Dean of General Studies John Wooden and learned that there might soon be a job available, if the Board of Trustees approved of the position. But, Wooden cautioned, if she were offered another job, she should take it, because

Monumental changes in the library have taken place during the four decades Kathleen Scott has reported for work.

A place for reflection, study, and learning, the library has moved several times over the years.

nothing about the WCC position was certain. Shortly afterwards, the Trustees did endorse two librarian positions, and on September 1, 1971, Kathleen Scott and Margot Orr started to work. They had full faculty status.

"Margot and I were pretty much on our own in the early years of the 1970s. In some respects, that was rather nice," she added. "The library remained rudderless for many years, neither funded nor staffed properly. When we moved to the Student Center Building, things began to change. Finally, the facility looked like a library and was staffed by professionals. In 1975 and 1976, the WCC library really started to take shape as a seriously thought-of, funded, situated library."

The many changes that have occurred in her profession and within WCC's library/media center facilities have prevented any boredom, Scott said. "I've always felt challenged."

Larry Slepsky
Physical Education

"Larry Slepsky was a physical education teacher who made a difference in students' lives," Don Bylsma said. "He built the baseball field almost single-handedly."

Jim Strayer
Biology

"Jim Strayer was one of the best teachers you could imagine," Mehran Thomson said. His field was biology. His son, Ross, followed in his footsteps; he now teaches biology at WCC.

Stuart Susnick
Government, Anthropology

Stuart Susnick's background is legendary at the College. Before coming to Ann Arbor, the Brooklyn native had been a taxi driver in New York City. He earned his bachelor's degree in political science and English in 1968, and was hired to teach at WCC "on the strength of my bachelor's degree and some limited teaching experience," he said.

"Coming to the College all happened by sheer coincidence," he explained. While visiting Ann Arbor friends, Susnick met the wife of Dr. Bob Plummer, the Director of WCC's Social Sciences Division, who told him about the new Community College. Susnick decided to apply. "I was a high-risk hire, but they took a chance on me," he said. "I started teaching in September of 1969, and I found the work congenial. I've been here ever since. I found this to be a good place to interact with students."

Mehran Thomson
Director, Exact Sciences

Son of an EMU professor of sociology, Mehran Thomson was raised in Ypsilanti. After earning his bachelor's degree in science, he taught in high school while running a television installation business. When he married, he looked for a "real job" and took aptitude tests while interviewing with a defense contractor. "I answered the questions honestly, rather than saying what I knew they wanted to hear," Thomson said. "Then I received one-million dollars' worth of free advice: 'You don't want to be an engineer.'" He was told that the only job that fit his criteria would be a professor.

So, in the late 1940s, he earned his teaching certificate at the University of Michigan and taught physics at Ypsilanti High School until the Army drafted him for the Korean War. He spent two years in White Sands, New Mexico, shooting rockets.

When he returned to Michigan, he decided that he didn't want his teaching job back. "I'd been making $2,400—the highest-paying teaching job I could find, while my wife was making more money as a secretary," he said. He took courses towards a master's degree in physics and then one day drove past a brand new high school in Redford. On an impulse, he popped in. He was hired on the spot to teach math and plan the new science labs. "The school was full of incredibly enthusiastic young teachers led by a fantastic principal. We created a remarkable high school." Thomson taught there ten years, becoming involved in educational circles. When he was hired at WCC, he was vice president of the Michigan Science Teachers Association.

Thomson walked into his interview at the College thinking it was a part-time job. He walked out as Divisional Director of Applied Sciences.

"I had great fun helping to set up a brand-new high school. At WCC, I had a comparable situation," he said. "There's nothing in the work world as much fun as starting something from scratch."

Thomson brought many fellow teachers to WCC. "Percy Mealing became my first lieutenant and bulwark," Thomson said. "He came to my attention through Andy Ford, who had come to WCC from the Detroit school system, where Percy and his brother Bob taught. I

Mehran Thomson, Director and later Dean of Exact Sciences, helped hire many faculty members during his tenure.

Lois Thomas, Manager of Manimark, the College's food vendor, was a familiar face to hungry students.

brought Percy in to teach physics, but he ended up running the math department." Thomson also hired John McGill to teach physics, Janet Hastings and Dennis Bila to teach math, and Dan Laursen to teach science, among many others. "The hiring bonanza came to a screeching halt during year three or four," Thomson recalled. "Until that time, I was free to identify my needs and go out and hire someone. Then I hired a math teacher from the University of Michigan-Dearborn and introduced him to President Ponitz at Registration. Dave shook his hand most cordially, but later told me, 'You've got to let him go.' From that point on, we had to get permission before interviewing or hiring anyone for a faculty job."

Mehran Thomson retired in 1984, at the age of sixty two. Six months after he left, Roger Bertoia entered a one-year training program and Harry Konschuh asked Thomson to fill in. "I had a ball. I knew that we had great teachers in General Studies, but suddenly I was administrating T&I and discovered just how terrific the welding, computer tech, and auto people were," he remembered. "Roger later told me it took him two years to shape his people up after I was through with them! I ended up with a great respect for Roger."

John Wooden
Director, General Studies (1966-67), Dean (1968-79)

John Wooden was also interviewed and profiled by *The Voice*:

> John P. Wooden...is a man of many experiences....He was a "roughneck" in the oilfields of Oklahoma. He has worked as a reporter for the International News Service and was one of the last correspondents to leave China before it became completely under communist rule. Wooden worked for a Japanese newspaper and for a newspaper in Minnesota. Being a radio disc jockey for stations in Minnesota and Seattle, Washington, in 1951, brought further excitement. The job he remembers most was being a paratrooper in World War II during which he spent months in a hospital after being badly riddled with bullets.

After World War II Wooden found himself going to the University of Wisconsin on the G.I. Bill to become an engineer....Two years later he decided engineering was not his field and he switched to the social sciences.

Wooden has been affiliated with several institutions of higher learning....In 1965 Wooden came to Ann Arbor and worked at the U. of M. as Assistant to the Director of the Center for Study of Higher Education while doing graduate work in higher education.

Douglas Woolley
Registrar

The success or failure of the first College Registration fell squarely in Douglas Woolley's lap. As the first Registrar, he had designed the students' one-page application form, and he processed every computer punch card completed during the three-day period. "He was trained well for the job," Mehran Thomson said.

After graduating from Michigan State University, Douglas Woolley had been responsible for setting up Central Michigan University's tabulating department (now known as the Registrar's Office). Two years later, he returned to MSU as a data processing specialist. In 1963, he was named the University of Michigan's Director of the Registrar's Office. During that time, Woolley became involved in getting out the vote that would endorse the funding necessary for the new Community College. "I was very much in favor of the idea of the Community College and its mission," he said.

Once David Ponitz was hired, Douglas Woolley asked if WCC needed a Registrar. He was hired in April 1966. "At that time, the entire College consisted of Dr. Ponitz, Dave Pollock, Don McEwen (director of counseling), Lloyd Van Buskirk (business manager), and me," he remembered.

"I joined the administration at Washtenaw Community College because I believed strongly in its philosophy of helping students—I still do."

Ron Zeeb
Business

Ron Zeeb is a fifth-generation Dexter native who has never gone far from home—except for the one year, ten months, and twenty-one days he spent in the U.S. Army. He earned a marketing degree from Eastern Michigan University in 1958, managed a sales floor for Jacobson's for seven years, then returned to EMU for his teaching degree. Shortly afterwards, he heard about the new Community

College and spoke with several new faculty members. They stressed the "fierce commitment" the College was looking for in new hires. "That approach sounded good to me," Zeeb said. Art Lamminen, "an exceptional man" who headed the business department, hired Zeeb in 1968.

"Everyone who came to WCC was looking for something different, but we were all there to help," Ron Zeeb said. "I believe that's the reason the College survived and flourished."

■ ■ ■

"It's impossible to list all the people who have made a difference at the College, as much as we'd love to do it," Edith Croake said. "Whether they stayed for decades or just a few years, each administrator, faculty, and staff member made important contributions, contributions that helped make the College successful."

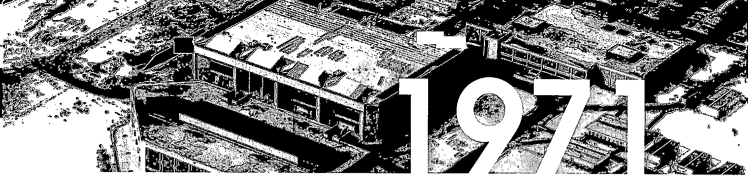

- U.S. conducts large-scale bombing raids against North Vietnam. Fighting in Indochina spreads to Laos and Cambodia.

- First installments of the "Pentagon Papers" appear in *The New York Times.* Seventy-five percent of those polled oppose the publication of the classified papers chronicling American involvement in Vietnam.

- The Supreme Court mandates busing as a means of desegregating schools.

- Returning Vietnam vets meet opposition back home. Two thousand protest the war by throwing away their medals on the steps of the Capitol.

- The 26th Amendment to the U.S. Constitution, allowing 18 year olds to vote, is ratified.

- Inflation in U.S.: 5.7+ percent. Unemployment: 5.9 percent.

- Vietnam: U.S. troop strength: 152,000; U.S. dead: 45,543.

History & Politics

- On the big screen Americans are watching *A Clockwork Orange, The French Connection, The Last Picture Show, Carnal Knowledge, The Summer of '42, Diamonds Are Forever, Klute, Shaft, Bananas, Dirty Harry.*

Movies

- Shows premiering: *All in the Family, The Sonny and Cher Comedy Hour, Columbo, Cannon, McMillan and Wife.* Television specials include *Brian's Song, The Selling of the Pentagon, The Pentagon Papers, Elizabeth R, and The Six Wives of Henry VIII.*

Television

- Hit Songs: "How Can You Mend a Broken Heart?" "Rainy Days and Mondays," "Joy to the World," "Maggie May," "Got to Be There," "Theme from Shaft," "Ain't No Sunshine."

Music

Books

- Best-Sellers: *The Exorcist* (William Peter Blatty), *The Passions of the Mind* (Irving Stone), *The Day of the Jackal* (Frederick Forsyth), *The Betsy* (Harold Robbins), *The Winds of War* (Herman Wouk), *The Drifters* (James Michener), *Rabbit Redux* (John Updike).

- Pulitzer Prize winners: *Angle of Repose* (Wallace Stegner), *Neither Black nor White: Slavery and Race Relations in Brazil and the United States* (Carl N. Degler), *Stillwell and the American Experience in China, 1911-1945* (Barbara Tuchman), *Eleanor and Franklin* (Joseph P. Lash), *Collected Poems* (James Wright).

Fashion

- "Hot pants with midis used as a cover-up, pants with suspenders and cuffs, bare midriffs with a knit, velvet, or brocade vest, tie-dyed shirts, halters, high and low boots, denim dungarees adorned with patches, butterflies, or stars, and macramé belts make the fashion scene. Women hobble on wedge and platform shoes.

- Hair is short or long, layered in the shag or gypsy cut. Teasing and spraying are out.

Fads

- Gourmet foods, jogging, tote bags, directors' chairs.

New Words

- Think tank, demo, lib, body language, gross out, hot line, hot pants, right on, sexism, up front, workaholic.

Quotes

- "I've suffered more as a woman than as a black." —Shirley Chisholm

- "Eliminating the patriarchal and racist base of the existing social system requires a revolution, not just a reform." —Premier issue of *Ms* magazine

- "Every senator in this chamber is partially responsible for sending 50,000 young Americans to an early grave." —Senator Eugene McCarthy

The Voice lists the year's highlights:

- Students demand better food on campus. Art Department Instructor Fred Horowitz advises, "If Servomation cynically continues to give you crap when your body craves food, skip the machines and bring your own stuff from home."

- Faculty offices, 25 temporary classrooms, the Learning Resource Center and its 30,000 volumes are moved to the new campus. Workers push to complete the T&I and LS&A buildings, pave roads, and install equipment.

- Occupational Studies accounts for 60 percent of the student body. Occupational Studies programs rise to 70. Sixty percent of all students are part-timers, 80 percent have a job outside school, men outnumber women 3:1, the average age of students is 24, while the age range extends from 17 to 70. Among WCC's students are 600 veterans.

WCC in
1971

Chapter 6:
Views from the Trenches

TEACHING & PREPARING STUDENTS FOR VOCATIONS

Establishing the Occupational Education Division and its programs required much more effort than hiring faculty members and providing equipment, materials, and classroom space. Dean of Occupational Studies Paul Hunt and Technical & Industrial Division Director Andy Ford had to pick their way among prejudices and traditions to get the support of industry members.

"We didn't start out to change the world. Our role, however, was to be a change agent for individual students, to offer them educational opportunities that would lead to professional careers," Andy Ford said. "We had an influence on the social dynamics of the community, but that wasn't our primary focus."

When the College opened in 1966, Ford was supervising eleven full-time faculty members and between fifteen and twenty part-timers. Classes ran six days a week, fourteen hours a day.

Every program started with an analysis of what its students would need to know when they walked out of WCC and into a new job. Then the Occupational Education administrators designed each program around those needs. "For instance," Ford explained, "everybody needs keyboarding skills. We inserted a course on keyboarding wherever it was appropriate." By creating composite classes with students coming from many different programs, the College could increase its efficiency. When changes were necessary, administrators could adapt quickly, dropping or adding individual courses rather than entire programs. This way they could respond quickly to changing vocational requirements and technology.

Because Washtenaw Community College was founded with a mission to provide trained workers for local industries and businesses, instructors and equipment had to be state-of-the-art and up-to-the-minute, which can be an expensive proposition. Roger Bertoia remembered the concern among General Studies instructors that more money went into the occupational side of the curriculum. "They were justified in believing that," he said. "It takes more money to buy the equipment and hire the faculty with industrial and teaching backgrounds."

Each occupational program was designed and supervised by an Industry Advisory Committee. One of Ford's first tasks was to introduce himself and the College to the construction unions and contractors—some of whom were markedly unfriendly to the idea of WCC offering training programs in the trades to anyone who paid tuition.

"When we opened, the one significant industry missing from WCC's programs was construction," Ford said. "At that time, the traditional labor unions here were not open to all people; often they would only accept offspring of existing members. There were also gender and racial barriers. The College opened with a "y'all come" attitude and offered instruction to anyone who wanted it, much to the distress of some old-timers in the trades. There were confrontations, arguments, and some hostilities, but we didn't back down."

When the College opened, construction programs faced racial and gender barriers.

Washtenaw Community College has always been dedicated to the educational and vocational advancement of all students.

Eventually, Ford did find people within the unions and among the contractors who had decided that change was necessary. Henry Landau, a future Trustee and father of another, was one of them. "He spearheaded the formation of a committee dedicated to affirmative action in the construction trades," Ford said. "We met several times a month with Department of Labor officials, along with union representatives, to develop the programs and break down barriers."

The plumbers and pipefitters were the first trade to embrace the College; they sent several members to a special WCC welding class. "Welding would be our pivot point," Ford said. "Little by little, the other unions followed suit in various degrees. The College, of course, was committed to admitting all interested students regardless of race or gender, which wasn't always the case in construction locals."

WCC's welding program quickly gained national renown. Most of the pipefitters who worked on the Alaskan and Canadian pipelines were trained and certified at the College. The Welding Program's

Concentrating on his work, a drafting student prepares for his future career.

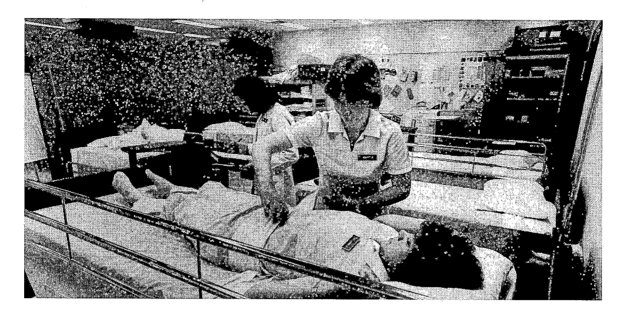

graduates receive certification to work in atomic energy, petroleum, gas, and oil lines.

David Byrd, who headed the Architectural Drafting Program, asked Ford to work with him to develop and organize a African-American contractors' association, with the College providing hands-on experi-ence and the necessary training to get a contractor's license. Ford agreed, but it wasn't a decision made lightly. "David and I had our lives threatened several times in the early days and received some nasty calls at night," he remembered. "We figured it went with the territory, but we also were careful and didn't do anything stupid. David came from Washington, D.C., and I grew up in Detroit and had taught in the inner city for ten years, so we both had had experience with rough times." Eventually, the situation improved—although to this day some unions and trades are still only marginally involved with WCC because they have problems with some of the College's admissions policies, according to Ford.

The challenges in establishing Occupational Studies didn't end there. When a program requires a license or certification, particularly in the case of medical and dental programs, either the state or the professional organization (and sometimes both) dictate the program's educational needs. "They set the criteria and we add our input after that," Ford explained. In the days when the College was new, the federal government was in the process of implementing and upgrading exacting workplace rules and regulations. The occupa-tional programs not only had to satisfy Occupational Safety and

Nursing students occasionally turned to classmates when they needed practice in basic medical techniques.

Health Administration (OSHA) standards, they also had to satisfy the State of Michigan's Public Health and Public School requirements—"which were actually more stringent," Ford said.

Inspectors routinely visited campus, particularly in the days when new buildings were rising or undergoing renovations. The automotive, auto body, and welding programs were prime targets for inspections. The College suffered through several major difficulties in meeting different requirements. For example, at one time, OSHA required fire extinguishers to be available on the floors, while the Michigan fire regulations required them on walls. In the early years, OSHA requirements for grinding and buffing couldn't be met within the College's facilities, so the program was forced to put the grinder-buffer machine into storage.

"At first, we had more flexibility to change as change was required," Ford said. "Now, bylaws, regulations, and external pressures have resulted in the loss of some flexibility in teaching and learning."

The Occupational Education faculty was relatively small and close-knit. They worked closely with the other departments to build the curriculum. English, math, and other core courses were often scheduled around the time blocks necessary for the occupational programs. "We knew we were all part of building something together that was brand new and we counted on each other's experiences in the past to help us do our best job," Bertoia said.

As the College went through its first ten years, advisory committees helped design and build each occupational program. Professionals from Ford, General Motors, Hydramatic, and local engineering and architectural firms volunteered for the committees. Bertoia remembered spending three hours or more a week meeting and talking with committee members as the College prepared for its first academic year. Once the programs were launched, meetings dropped back to once a month.

In addition to working with advisory committees, many occupational teachers spent between four and six hours each week on the road visiting shops and businesses. "We felt it was crucial that we learn the industry's expectations and what employers in each field were expecting for training and skills when they filled jobs," Bertoia said. "We built our curriculum to meet their needs."

Occasionally, industries would donate equipment to the College, but it was usually equipment they no longer used. "Our goal was to have the same equipment and standards as the leaders in the industry," Bertoia said. "In Occupational Studies, there's no choice but to keep up with—or, if we could, ahead of—industry and its new and changing standards."

The curriculum was designed to give students several classes that they might not use immediately, but would need in their profession within three to five years. "We were aiming for long-term currency, so we needed state-of-the-art equipment, software and machines to serve each of the industries we represented."

MEMORIES OF THE EARLY DAYS OF OCCUPATIONAL TEACHING

Roger Bertoia was a young instructor when he was hired by WCC and he spent long hours considering and discussing the best ways to convey the material and enable his students to reach their professional goals. "Many of these people were already working and they brought their day-to-day workplace experiences into the classroom," he said. "That made the classes extraordinary teaching and learning experiences. We all learned together and benefited from each other's experiences. The things I'd been taught in school about building curriculum and working in the real world all fell into place in my classroom."

Lester Morgan worked hard with local tradesmen to develop WCC's Welding Program into a nationally recognized and renowned program.

Welding, drafting, automotive, electricity and electronics, and the machine shop numbered among the strongest occupational programs during the College's first ten years. Some classes ran six hours long; others ran for three hours twice a week. Classes started as early as 7 a.m., and ran until 10 p.m., at least five days a week, but often on Saturdays, too. Part-time faculty members were responsible for as much as forty percent of the teaching load. WCC invited people working in industry into the classroom so they could give students up-to-the-minute workplace experiences.

Although classes kept the same names over the years, the curriculum changed almost yearly as standards and technology changed and computers were introduced to different professions. "I've hired most of the Occupational Ed faculty, including the health folks, and we all acknowledge that a patient is no different than a piece of steel on a lathe when it comes to creating a program that trains excellent professionals," Roger Bertoia said. "Our primary goal is to make sure that we offer every student a good educational experience."

Architecture

The instructor of Architectural Technology and former president of the Huron Valley Chapter of the Architectural Institute of America was the subject of an in-depth *Voice* profile in November 1974, which noted, "A tremendous amount of David Byrd's energy and time is spent in behalf of Ann Arbor's minority and low income citizens."

David Byrd initiated a course study for minority contractors who had failed in business because they didn't understand business management techniques. The four-year course taught blueprint reading, estimating, surveying, math, business administration, and remedial skills. Another program headed by Byrd trained the "hard-

"In the early days, we were all shoot-from-the-hip people," recalled Andy Ford. *"We had to be—there was so much to do and so little time."*

core unemployed" for careers in construction. To give on-the-job training, Byrd designed houses that the trainees built—literally, from the ground up under Byrd's supervision. The architect also conducted his own architectural practice, working on an eighty-unit high-rise apartment building for the elderly and a multipurpose neighborhood center in a low-income area of Ann Arbor, among many other projects.

Secretarial Science

When the College first opened in 1966, Secretarial Science boasted two faculty members and a classroom full of manual typewriters. "When I begged for electrics, we were allowed to purchase only a few,"

In 1966, Eleanor Charlton (seated) found manual typewriters in her first Secretarial Science classroom. Recruited by a former colleague, Divisional Director of Business and Industrial Services Art Lamminen, she has seen technology and curriculum change almost yearly through the decades.

Eleanor Charlton recalled. As computers became visible in the work place and business procedures changed dramatically, the department struggled to keep up with the times. "We have always required new materials and equipment almost every year so that our program and our students could stay on top of what was happening in the business world," Charlton explained.

Automotive, Welding

Bill Figg was a member of the first class of students enrolled in Washtenaw's Automotive Program. He switched to welding, left to pursue a musical career, and returned in 1973 to teach in the welding program.

"Back in 1966, we didn't have the connections with Ford Motor Company that our automotive program would later form, so there were no apprenticeships available," he pointed out. "Before that could happen, we had to teach the community and industry what this Community College was all about."

The automotive and welding programs took up residence in an old Sealtest distribution plant on Carpenter Road and remained there for nearly a decade. "Those buildings were matchboxes made of old dried-up wood. It's a miracle they didn't go up in flames," Figg remembered. For the first few semesters, teachers and students often had to improvise their lessons; equipment was sometimes hard to come by. "In fact, when the first semester started, we had no equipment at all," Figg said, adding dryly, "As a student, you quickly learn that it's hard to do welding with no equipment and no materials."

He remembered helping to unload the first machines from the trucks. "We had only oxyacetylene tanks until then," he said. The auto center had an old loading dock attached to it, and after eyeing its possibilities for weeks, the students and faculty

The inner workings of a data processing printer are studied by an attentive—and very diverse—class of students.

members decided to cut it up in order to use the materials for the metallurgy classes—"that's how desperate we were," he said. "But, despite some strong drawbacks, the students just went with the flow. In some cases, we didn't know any better. In other cases, we knew the instructors and College were doing the best they could."

In the 1970s, when he returned to WCC, he discovered that many of the students in the automotive and welding programs were adults upgrading their skills. "Often it was a family experience," Figg said. "Husbands and wives would come together to learn to ride motorcycles. We had a father and daughter come to learn how to build a boat. I myself worked nights with my father, who ran Elak-Trak Welding Company here in Ann Arbor."

The College had been offering welding for nearly ten years before the first female student enrolled in the program. "Barbara Gonigan was the first female student to take welding in order to pursue it as a career," Figg said. "That was in the mid-1970s."

Despite memories of the welding program's rough start, Figg said, "WCC was a totally positive experience for me. Looking back on it, we put up with a whole lot—working out of books because we had no tools, in particular—but somehow everyone together made it work."

Dental Assistant Program

Betty Ladley Finkbeiner and Joe Chasteen took charge of the Dental Assistant Program at the beginning of its second year on campus. They were determined to create a program so state-of-the-art that it would set the baseline for the profession within the state. "I felt we were doing something different, breaking new ground, when we established our exceptional clinical practice program," Finkbeiner said. "We wanted our students to have one hundred percent success in getting a job and in getting an appropriate salary."

In the fall of 1969, the thirty first-year students and twenty second-year students spent the first few weeks reviewing professional standards. "Dr. Chasteen and I told the students that our goal was to make every one of them immediately employable in a job where they would be happy," Finkbeiner said. "Maintaining the highest standards was the foundation of our program."

Betty Finkbeiner (second from left) has written the textbooks used in the Dental Assistant Program and the programs taught at many other schools around the country.

Respiratory Inhalation Instructor Carl Hammond (third from left)worked closely with students. WCC's Respiratory Program was active on campus until the 1980s.

Another goal was to instill a good self-image, so each student would understand his or her ("99.5 percent of our students are women") sense of self-worth. Finkbeiner openly discusses salaries and the practical aspects of the job, as well as its technical requirements. Dental assistants in Washtenaw County earn significantly more than those in other parts of the state and many professionals attribute that to WCC's program.

As soon as they arrived, Chasteen and Finkbeiner visited local dental offices to establish a clinical rotation program where students work for three weeks in a specialty office and two general practice offices. They also established a collaborative program with the University of Michigan Dental School; WCC students still work at Dental School clinics and university dental students reciprocate by working in WCC's clinic. At one time, dental assistant students treated Willow Run children in a collaborative project with the Interfaith Council of Churches. In later years, dental assistant students sponsor a Children's Dental Health Day with the campus day care center.

Many changes within the Dental Assistant Program are direct results of changes in the profession. When WCC's program began, dentists practiced "wet-finger dentistry," without using latex gloves. The Willow Run facilities were rudimentary; now the class complex is designed to look just like a professional office, and classroom walls are lined with lead. Originally, the program owned one X-ray screen, which was moved from room to room when X-rays were taken. For oral evacuation, students held a basin that they emptied with bare hands. For many years, no infection control procedures existed; gloves and masks would come later. In 1968, no videos or copy machines were available to provide educational materials. Textbooks were outdated. So were most filmstrips. By her third year at WCC, Finkbeiner began writing handouts, then texts.

The impact of OSHA, new ergonomic equipment, computerized charting and record-keeping, as well as on-line education have revolutionized the program, which has been compressed from two years to one. "The field is very, very dynamic. We can now take intraoral photos with miniature cameras and transmit them to the patient's records instantly," Betty Finkbeiner said. "We can teach students

Accounting, bookkeeping, and office procedures have been revolutionized over the years. It has become difficult to find an office or business in southeast Michigan that doesn't boast at least one WCC graduate.

three hundred miles away the same course materials we teach here in Ann Arbor."

Soon after she arrived, Betty Finkbeiner realized that she was encouraging her students to get a bachelor of science degree, so she should practice what she was preaching. Through the University of Michigan's "Two-Plus-Two" Program (which no longer exists), she enrolled in the Allied Health Program in the School of Education with her associate's degree and earned her bachelor's, then master's degrees.

Mechanical Technology

Burton C. Lowe recruited businesses and students to the field of mechanical technology and to the College. If enough students signed up for instruction, Washtenaw Community College would bring its classes to a plant. Lowe's encouragement brought many of those same students to campus over the years. "Many have thanked me. All I had to do was show them the way and they took off," he said.

Teaching mechanical technology begins with blueprint reading and an introduction to the College's Machine Shop. "Computers revolutionized our field, but people still need to know how to read blueprints," Lowe said. As students progressed into advanced courses, the technology became more complicated and challenging. "Technology has changed, but theory doesn't change and teaching methods haven't really changed, either," he said. "We do the best we can to reach each student where he stands."

Lowe said "he" because, although he has had memorable exceptions, the great majority of mechanical technology students were white men. "In my area, there are probably ten white students for

For more than thirty years, Cornelius Reeves has worked in the College's Power House, which was one of the first three buildings erected on campus.

every black student. It's still like that; for some reason, not many women or blacks go into this area," he said, estimating that the ratio of men to women was probably 50:1 in the program's early days.

"I've had more outstanding students than I can count, and I still keep in touch with many of them," he added. "I can go into almost any plant in this area and see students I once taught. The kids came with all different backgrounds and they were hungry for what we were teaching. That was the challenge and that was the fun of teaching."

Business

"My teaching was a back-to-the-basics approach," Ron Zeeb said. "I knew how to teach and I had worked in the business world."

In 1968, the Business Department consisted of six faculty members (Eleanor Charlton; Paul Kokkales; Jerry Patt; Robert Paulson; Bella Reddick, later Bella Parker, Dean of Business Education; and Evelyn Wilson), with Zeeb hired as a co-op person who would teach several classes and help place students in jobs. He visited businesses to establish a connection with the College's students. "Often, however, businesses wanted free help rather than offering entry-level opportunities that would pay students competitively," he discovered. "I remember the early years as being a struggle to form a connection between the businesses and our students."

Eventually Zeeb taught classes in marketing, salesmanship, introduction to business, and business law. "I continued to study, so I could anticipate questions and develop projects or activities that would help me bring across the points," he said.

Arthur Lamminen, Director of Business and Industrial Management, originally developed the curriculum with the help of the instructors. Remnants of the old curriculum still exist, but the field has seen great changes, thanks to technology and revolutionary changes in the business world.

Over time, the department frequently discussed the role of a core curriculum. "We all felt strongly that students, no matter what their field, should have basic courses that would help them in life," Zeeb said.

■ ■ ■

"The faculty was—and is—wonderful and the Board did everything we could to support and encourage them," said Ann Cleary Kettles. "Because the College had been founded on the need for occupational training, we were committed to strengthening and supporting the occupational focus. After all, this is the kind of education people can't get anywhere else in Washtenaw County."

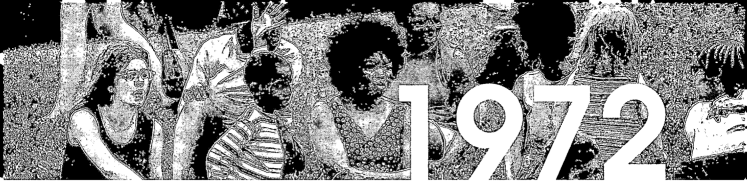

- Alabama Governor George Wallace enters Democratic primaries and wins in Michigan. He is later shot and paralyzed.

- North Vietnam launches major Easter offensive.

- U.S. bombs Haiphong for first time since 1968, mines Haiphong Harbor.

- Democrats nominate George McGovern for president and Thomas Eagleton for vice president.

- Last U.S. ground troops leave Vietnam.

- Break-in at Democratic headquarters in the Watergate building. Five are caught.

- Henry Kissinger and Le Duc Tho talk in Paris. North Vietnam accepts cease-fire, but South Vietnam's President Thieu rejects plan. U.S. resumes bombing of Hanoi and Haiphong.

- U.S. military draft is phased out; army becomes all-volunteer.

- Congress passes Title IX, which entitles women to participate equally in all areas of sports.

History & Politics

- Nielsen's Top Ten: *All In the Family, Sanford and Son, Hawaii Five-O, Maude, Bridget Loves Bernie, The NBC Sunday Mystery Movie, The Mary Tyler Moore Show, Gunsmoke, The Wonderful World of Disney, Ironside.*

Television

- Americans flock to the theaters to see *The Godfather; Cabaret; Deliverance; Sounder; Sleuth; Lady Sings The Blues; The Candidate; The Poseidon Adventure; Cries and Whispers; Play It Again, Sam; Last Tango in Paris; Deep Throat.*

Movies

- Radios endlessly play, "Let's Stay Together," "I'd Like to Teach the World to Sing," "Oh Girl," "Lean on Me," "Where Is the Love?," "Alone Again (Naturally)," "Anticipation," "Last Night I Didn't Get to Sleep at All," "I'll Take You There."

- Grammy Awards: "The First Time Ever I Saw Your Face" (Roberta Flack); *The Concert for Bangla Desh* (George Harrison et al., album).

Music

Fashion

- Influenced by President Nixon's trip to China, women wear lacquer-red colors, silk evening pajamas, lotus and patterned silk gowns. Pants are out, beltless chemises and two-piece sweater dresses are in.

- *Esquire* announces that men's "peacock revolution" is at a peak, with hip huggers or flared and cuffed bell bottoms. Suits appear in large herringbones, colorful prints, and plaids. Interesting displays of chest hair appear. Men wear British "bobby" coats in navy blue melton with silver buttons. The unisex clothing revolution begins.

Fads

- Health food, acupuncture, pinball, Jesus freaks, transcendental meditation.

Quotes

- "Everywhere new hopes are rising for a world no longer overshadowed by fear, and want and war."—Richard Nixon on the SALT signing

WCC in 1972

The highlights of the year, according to *The Voice*:

- WCC launches an educational program with Milan Federal Correctional Institution. Financed by the federal government, the program is the first of its kind.

- The College starts the year with a $500,000 deficit and then learns that the state is considering cutting its contribution to WCC by 23 percent. Governor Milliken's cutback proposal is vetoed, however.

- Twenty-one faculty and staff members are given release notices, then reinstated. Speaking for the faculty union, Marguerite Eaglin termed the rehiring delay "inhumane."

- Theft and students' failure to return books results in a 10 percent loss of the WCC library collection. The books most at risk are those dealing with religion and psychology; all the library's Bibles disappear.

- The Board approves a $5,161,088 budget, 51 percent of which is collected through the county's tax levy, 27 percent through state aid, with $200,000 from gifts and other sources.

- Fall registration hits 4,401. County students pay $310 for 31 credits; out-of-district students pay $465.

- Study shows 26 percent of College employees and 17.2 percent of students are "non-white," versus the county-wide average of 8.4 percent.

WCC in 1972

Chapter 7:
Teaching Reading, Writing, & Arithmetic

One incident from Washtenaw's first year at Willow Run speaks volumes for the kind of educational institution this new Community College aimed to become. Edith Croake's freshmen composition classes were studying a collection of essays that included an excerpt from Hitler's *Mein Kampf*. The instructor had written notes about the book on the board during class discussion and after class, a custodian walked up to her and said, "I have heard Hitler's name. I want you to help me read the rest of what's on the board here." That custodian learned to read.

"We had no reservations about sharing our knowledge with anyone who wanted to learn," Croake said. "I loved that—we were all in this new experiment together."

Unlike the Occupational Education Programs, which were constantly adding new equipment and new training techniques to each program's curriculum, General Studies Programs often required the same tools teachers had been using for generations: pens, pencils, paper, chalkboards, and an occasional overhead or movie projector. The focus was on enriching students' lives and preparing them for higher education. As in all classrooms, the instructors' personalities and dedication made classes memorable.

"My management style is to remove obstacles and let people do what they can do. Great things came from that," retired Divisional Director Mehran Thomson said.

The Community College had been founded with the commitment to offer counseling to every student. When the College first opened, Dick Nowland, Guy Hower, and Lola Jones struggled to serve 1,207 students who had largely been neglected by qualified advisors until

WCC appeared. These were students who had not been successful in high school and students trying to better their lives, either by beginning over again or by doing something no one in their families had done before. "Our job was much more than giving advice about courses," Lola Jones said. "We were here to know the students and help them in any way we could. Initially, counseling was not just a job description, it was a mission for us all. This was a new organization and we were forging new ground with a whole new population." Often, counseling relationships started by arranging for remedial courses to bring students up to the point where they could succeed in a college setting. "Our most important job was to encourage students to feel that this was something they could do. After all, it was a very big step for many students," Jones said. "They needed bolstering."

Faculty members were also part of the counseling process. Every week, small groups of students met with a faculty member or administrator to discuss common issues, problems, or the hot topics of the day. Bill Figg was in President Ponitz's first counseling group. "These were designed to help the students' awareness of who they were and what they wanted and to enhance their self-esteem," Jones said. The College targeted women as a special needs group and established the Adult Resource Center, which Lola Jones headed. The biggest challenge for most students in the early years was economic, according to Jones. Whether they came from rural farms or city neighborhoods, many students struggled to pay the nominal tuition; some also struggled with home and social issues. The College's counselors and social workers had access to community resources and often connected students to social service agencies and other people who could offer help. "We kept track of how some of our students did in later life," Lola Jones said. "We had some wonderful success stories."

Lawrence Radick was fluent in many languages.

Augustine (Gus) Amaru was hired to teach Political Science.

James Strayer taught Life Sciences.

MEMORIES OF TEACHING GENERAL STUDIES CLASSES

Spanish

In 1967, when Rosalyn Biederman was hired to teach Spanish, students used a text for oral drills, a workbook for written assignments, notes they took as the instructor wrote explanations and examples of grammar on the chalkboard, and audio tapes (now audio CDs). "Unlike occupational classes, little has changed in language instruction over the years," she said. On the other hand, much has changed in terms of the College's commitment to language instruction. In 1967, WCC offered first-year instruction in French and

Spanish. The Foreign Language Department consisted of Larry Radick, a talented linguist proficient in a half-dozen languages, and Biederman. Now the department includes three full-time, and eleven part-time instructors. When Rosalyn Biederman began teaching, foreign language courses were part of the the Communication Arts Department. Now, she chairs the Foreign Language Department. "We have come a long way!"

She takes pride in the rigor of the Foreign Language Program and the excellence of the staff. Students who complete four terms of Spanish or French at WCC are accepted at the University of Michigan as having completed their foreign language requirement. She also takes pride in her relationship with the students.

"I've always spent a lot of time with my students and enjoyed getting to know them," she said. On a regular basis, Biederman and her students go on field trips together to eat Mexican food, take in a movie in Spanish, see performances of the National Theater of the Performing Arts, celebrate holidays with in-class fiestas, and share other broadening experiences. Since 1975, she has arranged trips into the Spanish–speaking world for students to see ruins and historic locations while steeping themselves in the local cultures of Mexico City, the Yucatan, Oaxaca, Cuba, and Spain. "I've always found teaching fun—and it's always an adventure," she said.

Math

Dennis Bila believes that community college students are the easiest and most enjoyable age group to teach. He knows. He has taught a wide variety of ages. "The most difficult teaching is at an elementary school, because the students' attention span lasts no more than seven to ten minutes," he said with a smile and shake of his head. "Junior high isn't much easier because those students are so peer-oriented and they are going through so many personal changes. The high school teaching load is tremendous. Yes, community college is the easiest."

Teaching math is entirely different from most other disciplines, he pointed out. "In literature, sociology, and psychology classes, students can hold discussions and arguments with their instructors, but when I start writing on the board, people start taking notes and listening." Although the same math principles have been taught for a hundred years, technology has changed. Bila credits the calculator with revolutionizing the teaching of math.

At WCC, Bila teaches both ends of the spectrum: newly enrolled students who have weak math skills and the most advanced math students enrolled in multivariable calculus and differential equations. "When we hire for positions at WCC, we hire people capable of teaching all levels, although eighty percent of our students come to us with high school-level capabilities or below," he said. In the early days, math would have a large enrollment in the fall, but sometimes only two students in winter. It was a challenge to establish advanced classes, but faculty members remained optimistic. "That was during the Vietnam War era and there was a great need for engineering students," Bila said. "We only taught the advanced classes at night. The University of Michigan and Eastern Michigan professors didn't teach at night, so we'd get a lot of their students in our classes. We still do. It took about three years before the advanced classes were going strong."

Merrill McClatchy's speech classes showed rather than told students their strengths and weaknesses.

One of the department's greatest achievements has been the math lab, Bila believes. He authored or co-authored several of the books still used there.

Sociology

The turbulent 1960s and '70s were great times to be a sociology and psychology instructor. Don Bylsma's classes included "Marriage and the Family," "Man and Society," "Delinquency," and "Social Problems," as well as the traditional introductory classes. Later, he taught courses related to other disciplines, such as "Medical Sociology."

In the College's early days, general education classes ran either one and one-half hours twice a week or three hours once a week. All faculty members were required to teach at night, starting at 7 p.m. In the early days, instructors might teach until late at night and then return to campus for a 7 or 8 a.m. class. One of the early contracts stipulated that instructors would have twelve hours off.

"Washtenaw Community College was blessed with the right people at the right time in the right place," Bylsma said. "We stumbled, we stammered, we were clumsy, and we tripped, but we made our way, and we did very, very well."

English

"The air seemed full of intellectual energy in the early days," Edith Croake said. "To someone who had just finished an expensive M.A., it was an exciting idea to take courses for free. I improved my typing while taking a class from Bella Reddick (later Bella Parker, Dean of

Business). I took an anthropology class from Kelly Schutmatt, and a math class from Charlie Belknap, who had the office next to mine in the Quonset hut. I'd ask him for help with my homework."

In 1966, the English Department consisted of five faculty members, headed by and including William Cherniak. Originally, Croake, a twenty-four-year-old woman, taught only writing courses because the department informed her that she was "too young to teach literature." "Looking back on it, today's young woman would have said, 'Go jump in the lake!' but in those days, I accepted it," she said.

Croake has enjoyed the tremendous variety of her classes, particularly the literature classes, she said. "I also feel a strong commitment to teach composition. Everyone needs to express himself or herself well. As active citizens, we should all be able to present an argument to influence decisions and to help work out a solution to problems." Although she never intended to stay for four decades when she was hired in 1966, Edith Croake soon discovered that she fit well in the Community College setting. She appreciated the camaraderie among the faculty members and the variety of people in her classes. "I have had every category of student you can think of in terms of age, socio-economic backgrounds, and educational backgrounds. That's a wonderful challenge."

Through the years, she watched her department grow to sixteen full-time members. In 1976, the department opened the heart of English composition instruction: the Writing Center.

Speech

Most disciplines, vocational as well as general studies, required basic skills. Speech was essential, WCC administrators believed. After teaching in a variety of places, Char Hanson quickly learned that there were strong advantages to working in a community college. First, there were no disciplinary problems whatsoever. "When people are paying their own way, they're serious about what they're doing," she said. In addition, unlike four-year colleges and universities, the community college had no publish-or-perish pressure. "Faculty members are free to concentrate on teaching. I liked that."

In the early days, faculty members were pretty much on their own in designing classes and making department-wide decisions. "There was a sense of great immediacy

Char Hanson was renowned for her innovative teaching methods.

"Portrait of an Art Class." Generations of WCC art students have been admitted to leading fine arts programs around the nation.

and, sometimes, urgency, in getting things going," Hanson said. She remembered enjoying the feeling that each faculty member could walk into the classroom, close the door, and forget that the outside world existed. "I don't know if I taught with a sense of humor, but I'd like to think I did," she said. "I love teaching. I love being in front of an audience. I used to say that my chief qualification as a speech teacher was my high boredom threshold. I learned a tremendous amount from my students: everything from hitchhiking to embalming methods. I enjoyed helping my students identify what they knew that no one else knew."

Her students' first assignment required a magic trick. "That teaches them the three primary elements of effective speechmaking: the audience, the message, and you," she explained. "When they're doing magic, they concentrate on how the trick works and they can forget themselves." For their second speech, they had to lie, then be honest. "That teaches how much harder you work when you're lying," she said.

One of Hanson's favorite stories is about a young married woman who had to give a speech that would be televised. ("Television was a very handy method of showing students their strengths and weaknesses.") Before class, fellow students found the woman crying in the hall. Hanson told her that if she didn't want to give a speech, she wouldn't make her do it—"but just come in and listen." She went in, sat down, and by the end of the class, she was ready to give her speech—and she did a fine job. "I'll never forget her final speech, which began with her dressed in longjohns," Hanson said with a grin. "She demonstrated how people in the U.P. dress for winter. I consider that student a great success story!"

Art

"At the beginning, I had the feeling that our course load and approach to teaching could be fluid. Our courses were what we made of them. No one told us what to do or how to do it," Fred Horowitz said. Things began to change at the end of the first five years, he said, when the school seemed to take a collective breath and settle into a routine.

Psychology

"The early years were exciting times," Bill Moy said. "We taught on the run, quite literally out of the trunks of our cars. We brought our own books and materials to hand out, and we unloaded them from our cars every night before we taught. The facilities at Willow Run were makeshift. The best things out there were the stencil machine and, next to that, the ditto machine. That was the extent of our technology. We gave a lot of handouts. We knew that many of our students just didn't have time to visit a library or the money to buy lots of books."

Whatever the faculty did in those early years, they did with "enthusiasm, a sense of excitement, and a commitment to building something new," he said. "We had a 'let's do it!' attitude about everything."

The College's faculty members have always made it a point to listen to colleagues and develop programs to fit needs. "That was one of the beauties of this college—it still is," Moy said. He developed a psychology seminar for people in dental health, to give them models to help them deal with their patients from the perspective of applied psychology. Later, he worked with the Math Department, teaching statistical courses. "The variety and flexibility of our College offer faculty fine opportunities to expand, grow, and never become bored," he said.

INNOVATIONS IN THE ART OF TEACHING

The Math Lab

Divisional Director (later Dean) Mehran Thomson considered the Math Lab, which opened in the fall of 1966, one of the College's significant innovations. "We had gotten the germ of the idea from another community college in Southfield, but we developed it and wrote all the materials," he said. "Faculty members Don Ross, Ralph Bottorff, and Denny Bila were key players. Percy Mealing wrote many of the tests."

The lab relied on self-guided learning. WCC instructors developed units for everything from arithmetic to advanced algebra and students met in small groups to work on the units at their own pace, ask questions when they needed to, then take tests when they felt prepared. "It was a great achievement," he said.

The Testing Center

Washtenaw Community College pioneered another innovation when department heads began studying time management in classrooms and calculated how much time was taken away from instruction by test taking. Their research led to the creation of the Testing Center. Steve Vass, an economics instructor, George Griswold, a chemistry instructor, and Thomson decided to provide a place where students could take a test without consuming class time. "It's a teacher help that doesn't exist in most places," Thomson said. "The idea worked especially well after we moved to the new campus."

Outreach Centers

Over the years, Washtenaw Community College established outreach centers in Chelsea, Ypsilanti, Hartland, Ann Arbor, and Saline to bring the College's classrooms and teachers out into the outlying communities. Generally they were open at night. There was no central administration to run them; divisional directors would each adopt a site and make sure it was staffed. WCC established a policy that night students—both in outreach centers and on campus— deserved the same quality of instruction as day students received.

Putting Research to Work

"It has always been my heart-felt conviction that people lecture too much and students learn when they're involved," Thomson said. When he was in high school, he invented "the involver," a control panel for each student with red and green buttons. When a student pushed the red button, it meant he had a question on the material. Years later, he had each row of seats in one of WCC's lecture halls wired so a similar device could be installed. (It never has been.)

WCC worked with University of Michigan researchers to help improve teaching methods and interaction between teachers and students. Observers went into WCC classrooms with a check sheet to record what was happening every minute: lecture, questions, discussions, and paperwork. They gave the results to the teachers, not as an evaluation, but as a way to help them think about

Walking a mile in another's moccasins was one way to teach methods of anthropological studies. Here a class works hard to erect a teepee. The LA Building is in the background.

the use of their time and their teaching methods. "WCC had great teachers," Thomson said. "Still do."

Campus Daycare

One teaching aid that freed young parents for classes was the campus daycare center. "Washtenaw Community College worked hard to remove obstacles from students' lives so they could learn unimpeded," Dave Pollock said. One important example of this was a ground-breaking innovation: the daycare center for students' children.

In 1968, the College transformed a Quonset hut into a staffed daycare center. When the state came for an inspection, officials told WCC that the center would have to close. "We said no," Pollock remembered. The state officials said they wouldn't fund the daycare center because it wasn't the College's business. WCC told the officials that the College was in the business of providing quality education to people—"and daycare was one aspect of that business."

"I remember David Ponitz getting livid at the state officials and telling them we would pay for the daycare out of local taxes," Pollock said. "We eventually won that battle." WCC was the first and only community college to start a nursery program, according to Bill Moy. While teaching child psychology courses, he realized that his students would benefit from observing real, live children. As Moy envisioned it, the daycare program would have three benefits: providing actual hands-on experiences for students to understand theory in a prag-matic way; an opportunity for parents to attend school without worrying about childcare; and, "good, sound empirical data for our students and parents in educating them about childraising."

Moy presented the proposal to Director of Social Sciences Robert Plummer, who was enthusiastic. So was the Board of Trustees. "We started with five children, but the nursery grew tremendously fast," Moy recalled, adding that there were some challenges in establishing the nursery. WCC had to get the physical layout approved by the Health Department, which required costs relating to a physician. Once again, Moy turned to friends at the University of Michigan. The head of pediatrics, Joe Balbus, came and certified the center and he graciously served as the campus pediatrician on call for many years.

In the late 1960s, Bill Moy was coordinating the lab, teaching four courses, supervising the nursery—and "getting run down." He decided his emphasis should be on teaching; that was when one of his clinical supervisors from the University of Michigan, Shirley Bell (later she married Coordinator of Black Studies Alvin Roberts) was hired as the first day care center director. "When we moved to the new campus, we built a Family Education Building to house the nursery, and professionally I moved from a concentration on child development to mental health," Moy said.

"The daycare center was a blooming success," Dave Pollock said. "I have no idea how many women were able to receive training and education just because we had that option available for them, but I'm sure it's high. Daycare was one of WCC's real creative accomplishments, an example of meeting the needs of our students."

A Cooperative Program
with the Federal Correctional Facility

The College launched a program with the Federal Correctional Facility in Milan and the women's prison in Ypsilanti, allowing prisoners to attend classes on campus, with the agreement that they wouldn't fraternize with other students and WCC wouldn't stigmatize those students by making them give the prison as their address. In the early days, as many as twenty prisoners attended classes at a time. Eventually, WCC instructors went to Milan. Char Hanson remembered the great difficulty teachers often faced trying to enter the class building. "I remember one night when my key didn't work on the outside door," she said with a grin. "A student said that he thought a window might be open in the library and offered to get us in. I later wondered if he was serving time for breaking and entering, but I prefer to think that he was so anxious to learn that he couldn't wait for class to start!"

One report about the federal correctional facility praised WCC for offering the most advanced training available at the time. "There was an occasional down side," Pollock admitted. "Two students stole faculty cars and got as far as Pittsburgh before they were picked up."

Numerous Successes Mixed with a Few Failures

"In the early days, we were open to just about every new and innovative idea that came our way, and not every one turned out to be a good idea," Pollock admitted. "We hired our administrators and faculty members with the understanding that they would be teacher-counselors and we expected great things of them—sometimes too much. We asked everyone to hold weekly discussion groups with their students on topical issues, such as the Vietnam War. There was almost one hundred percent resistance to this idea. I remember I had one session with my students to talk about family life and one quickly pointed out, 'I'm going through a divorce. Who am I to talk about family life?' That was a real bomb. Judging it idealistically, the discussion group was a great idea, but we should have thought it through much more thoroughly. In the enthusiasm to get everything underway, we occasionally leaped too quickly."

The media classes have been popular training grounds for students who have gone on into careers in broadcast journalism and public relations.

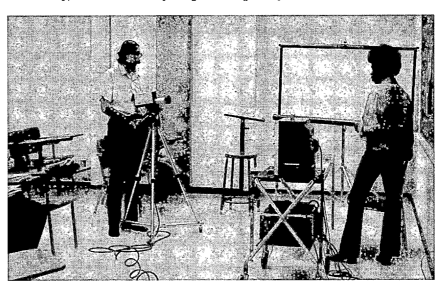

1973

■ President Nixon ends wage-price controls he imposed in 1971 except in food, health care, and building industries.

■ Watergate claims world-wide headlines. John Dean implicates the President. Spiro Agnew resigns amidst investigation of income tax evasion. Gerald Ford replaces him.

■ The U.S. and South Vietnam sign a cease-fire agreement with North Vietnam and the Vietcong. American losses, 1965-75: 45,948 in combat; 303,640 wounded; 10,298 deaths from non-combat causes. South Vietnamese losses: 184,546 dead; 495,931 wounded. Vietcong and North Vietnamese deaths: 937,562; civilians killed: 415,000. Maximum American troop level during the war (1969): 543,000.

■ Militant Native Americans seize hostages at Wounded Knee, S.D.

■ According to a Gallup poll, 25 percent of all consumers (50 million people) participate in boycotts against food inflation; groups like Operation Pocketbook set up pickets with signs reading "Nuts to Butz" and "Nix-on Beef."

■ Gross National Product: +7 percent. Inflation: +7.6 percent. Unemployment: 4.9 percent.

History & Politics

■ Pet rocks, CB radios, martial arts, backgammon.

Fads

■ Top Box-Office Stars: Clint Eastwood, Ryan O'Neal, Steve McQueen, Burt Reynolds, Robert Redford, Barbra Streisand (first woman), Paul Newman, Charles Bronson, John Wayne, Marlon Brando.

■ Opening in theaters: *The Sting* (Academy Award Best Picture), *American Graffiti, The Exorcist, Sleeper, Save The Tiger, Serpico, A Touch of Class, The Way We Were, Scenes from a Marriage.*

Movies

■ *Once Is Not Enough* (Jacqueline Susann), *The Odessa File* (Frederick Forsyth), *The Best and the Brightest* (David Halberstam), *Marilyn* (Norman Mailer), *Pentimento* (Lillian Hellman), *The Living Bible* (Kenneth Taylor), *Dr. Atkins' Diet Revolution* (Robert C. Atkins), *The Joy of Sex* (Alex Comfort).

Books

Fashion

- For men, the Mark Spitz look is in: loosely brushed black hair, dark mustache, slim figure—elegant but casual—wearing a decorative sports shirt over jeans or hiphuggers. Knit turtlenecks are worn with flared slacks. Business dress becomes more casual; sleeveless sweaters replace vests. Print shirts, patterned jackets and ties with polka dots, plaids and solid colors are in style. The "Great Gatsby" look abounds, with white hat, white shoes, open shirt, wide pants, slim jacket. The "chunky" shoe is popular.

Education

- The University of Texas, Arlington, offers a college belly dancing course.
- The University of Miami, Coral Gables, is the first to offer an athletic scholarship to women.

WCC in 1973

The Voice reveals the year's highlights:

- A controversy erupts over boxes of books. Between July 1972 and January 1973, thousands of dollars of books are received by the WCC library, but few make their way to shelves because no one was employed to process them.
- A student questionnaire reveals that students want more social sciences classes (124:50), want a more ecologically oriented plan for the campus (168:19) and a cigarette machine in the Student Union (105:91), think the Black Studies Program is comprehensive (78:37), and would like to see more night and summer classes (168:12).
- By fall, work is completed on a 19-acre athletic field and 4,401 students register for fall classes.
- The November 9 headlines reflect student concerns: "Nixon Should Resign," "The student union has poor atmosphere," "Student gov't at U of M. is hit by apathy, too," "Black Studies creates pride," "Energy crisis," "Shakespeare's works are anti-women," "We're better known than a few years ago."
- In their first game of the season, the Warriors basketball team sets a school record by scoring 146 points against Cassidy Lake Training School. Darrell Smith scores 19 points, Mike Smith and Larry Hunter rack up 20 points, Ed Byrd scores 18, and Keith Bond, 19 points.

Chapter 8:
Miracle in
the Apple Orchard

President David Ponitz had a way with words. His phrase *Fierce Commitment* succinctly described the intense effort required to get the College off the ground. He coined the phrase *The Miracle in the Apple Orchard* to describe the awe everyone felt when the College discovered its new home, an apple orchard halfway between Ann Arbor and Ypsilanti. When it was finally planted in its own ground "we all believed that the establishment of the school was a miracle," Betty Ladley Finkbeiner said.

The College began with a dream and an endorsement from the county voters. Now a campus would make it a reality, permanent and established. At its first meeting in 1965, the Board of Trustees outlined six criteria for identifying an appropriate site; natural beauty; at least 150 acres; access to transportation; proximity to the county's population center; price; and the consideration that in the future there may be two or three additional campuses. With these in mind, Board members and administrators began combing the county for possible locations.

In 1965, the Board narrowed the selection to eleven sites scattered all over the county. *The Ann Arbor News* reporter Mary Wallace faithfully recorded the rise and fall of various landowners' hopes and expectations. A farmer in Barton Hills had offered the College free land with the provision that he could develop adjacent property. "One of the first recommendations I made was *not* to build in Barton Hills because of its location," Dave Ponitz said. "No buses serviced the area. The socio-economic profile didn't fit with what we were trying to do. And we worried that students wouldn't be able to get there easily. We turned the farmer down."

A sign couldn't begin to express the joy College officials and students felt when the new campus broke ground.

On July 14, 1965, Wallace reported that first 75, then 150 acres of land bound by Maple and Stein roads had been offered to the College by Dr. E.M. Isberg and Associates. If the Board approved the gift, the landowners would then sell the rest of their property to a developer for residential subdivisions. "This gift offer could save the county several hundreds of thousands of dollars. We believe your decision will be in the best interests of the taxpaying public," Dr. Isberg told Board members.

Shortly afterwards, the Board received another offer of free land: one hundred acres in Webster Township on Webster Church Road, three miles west of Route 23.

"I found that property very tempting because it was adjacent to Route 23 North," Dave Pollock said. "However, we knew that we would be a commuter college and that was just too far out. "The Board of Trustees—wisely, I think—turned all the offers of free land down."

"This way they weren't obligated to anyone," added former Divisional Director Mehran Thomson.

The Trustees and Ann Arbor Chamber of Commerce Education Committee members devoted countless hours to the choice of sites for the new Community College. After doing the preliminary planning and site visits, they turned to the Washtenaw County Planning Department and University of Michigan planners for advice, not only about the permanent location of the College, but also about whether the College should have more than one campus. Together, gradually and logically, they began narrowing the field down. They looked at highway accessibility, availability of sewer and water services, property values, topographical characteristics, and present and proposed land uses in the area.

"Ultimately, I think that two factors—transportation and the population center—helped make the decision," former Trustee Evart Ardis recalled in 1982, during an interview conducted for Flavia Reps' oral history project. "We wanted proximity to the population center and good accessibility. We wanted it to be a beautiful place, where the students would feel they had a real honest-to-goodness college. We wanted some natural beauty so it could be an outdoor living laboratory. All those things came together at one particular site."

He remembered the Board members tramping across the land in the rain and mud, then flying over the site to see it from above, thanks to Trustee Ed Adams, who was a pilot. "He flew us around the county, back and forth over different sites," Ardis said. "We were looking to see the flow of traffic and topography from above. Then we went and walked over the land and decided which was the best site."

Technical and Industrial Instructor Roger Bertoia reviewed the new building plans, then frequently checked on the building's progress.

On December 22, 1965, the Board announced that it had selected the 235-acre Huron Valley Farms, located midway between Ann Arbor and Ypsilanti. Jarvis and Pearl Franzblau agreed to sell their orchard to the College for $3,500 an acre, $822,500 total. The College agreed to let them harvest one more crop of apples and use their cider mill one more season. In addition to three thousand apple trees, the farm had a natural hardwood forest, a pond, and a situation overlooking the Huron River.

"We took it as a good omen that at the entrance to the farm was a sign that said "Ann Arbor: 3 miles/ Ypsilanti: 3 miles," Dave Pollock said.

Mehran Thomson likes to tell an anecdote about the procurement of the land. "The old German who owned the apple orchard was discussing price with Dave Ponitz, and Dave wanted to dicker," Thomson remembered with a grin. "Dave suggested that the farmer sell it for less money and we'd name the first building after him. He told Dave, 'Pay me the money I want. You can name the building for yourself!'"

"We paid, as I remember, a little more than we wanted to, but in the light of inflation since then, we probably stole the property," Evart Ardis said. Dave Ponitz remembered loud criticisms for spending $3,500 an acre when the College could have had free land. The College President pointed out the farm's central location and how it could be reached conveniently by people coming from many different areas. He proved his point by driving to the farm from every town and city in Washtenaw County and clocking the time. He urged the Board to buy the entire parcel the campus would need right away. "We won't be able to afford to buy the land parcel by parcel in the future," he warned them. He was right. Thirty years later, the land adjacent to WCC was selling for approximately $100,000 an acre.

"Most of the Board was opposed to locating WCC on the free land, yet it was difficult to argue about why a tax-supported institution should turn down such a generous offer," Trustee Sam Harmon said many years later.

Like Ponitz, he did his own analysis—which he called "Center of Gravity." "I calculated the number of students from each part of the community who might be expected to come, then calculated three students per car, and determined transportation costs," he explained. "The apple orchard became significantly cheaper when it was approached in that light. Somebody always pays, you see. If we took the free land, the county wouldn't have to pay for land, but the students would have to pay more for transportation. At the orchard, the county would pay for the land, but after a certain number of years, the savings in transportation costs would begin to accrue. We never had another argument about the land decision again after Dave and I presented our findings."

When the site was purchased, the county population center was pinpointed at the corner of Washtenaw and Platt Road, and it appeared to be moving northeast. The intersection of U.S. 23 and I-94 freeways made the apple orchard very accessible.

While the Trustees were struggling to convince Ypsilanti Township to cooperate with the city to annex 120 acres of the newly purchased land so that the College could obtain street, police, and fire protection services, the Michigan Municipal Finance Commission set to work. In April 1966, the commission approved the sale of two million dollars in bonds to cover the land costs, architects' fees, site development plans, and some preliminary building costs. The following week, the College announced that it would begin to take enrollments for classes beginning in September at a temporary campus out in Willow Run Village.

As soon as the purchase of the apple orchard was official, the College invited everyone to bring their families for a huge, old-fash-

Faculty, administrators, and staff checked on the progress of the new campus frequently, looking forward to the move into brand-new buildings.

Raymond Steinbach

ioned picnic. "There was great excitement about the move," Ponitz said.

■ ■ ■

Long before the land was found, an architectural firm was hired to begin preliminary work on a campus design. After a seven-month search and interviews with thirty-four architectural firms, in November 1965, the Board announced the selection of Tarapata, McMahon Associates (later Tarapata, McMahon, and Paulson) of Bloomfield Hills. These architects had designed Arbor Village Apartments, Tappan Junior High School, and Newport Elementary School, so they were known in the area.

A green thumb was necessary in William Alexander's biology class. Here he works with students in the College's greenhouse.

Initially, the architects offered four plans for the Board's review. In May 1967, the Trustees selected a plan calling for a Z-shaped complex built of concrete and glass, but they objected to the number of trees that the architect had planned to demolish. They sent Tarapata, McMahon back to the drawing boards. "The final plan was much more acceptable aesthetically," Dave Pollock said. The buildings were tightly clustered around a mall, which was surrounded by apple trees. Apple trees also lined boulevards and divided parking spaces.

That summer, *The Ann Arbor News* reported, "A main aim in designing the permanent campus has been retention of as many as

The apple orchard provided students with a learning experience as well as cold drinks after making their own cider.

The "Miracle in the Apple Orchard" became a reality after President David Ponitz and many others spent countless hours studying blueprints.

possible of the fruit trees in the orchard and the larger trees which cover the site." The Du-Pine Company of Ann Arbor was awarded the contract for site clearance and road work.

Thomson was one who wanted to ensure the preservation of every possible tree. When the ground was being prepared for the first building, someone decided that the trees should all be cleared at once, to streamline future expansion, he remembered. "There were some beautiful old catalpa and oak trees standing and I dashed out when I saw guys with chain saws heading towards them. I had no authority, but I managed to stop them. I pointed out that they could cut down trees easily enough, but they couldn't replace beautiful big old oaks. Those catalpas are still standing and the oaks survived around the parking lots for many years."

The College also preserved the little lake where the farmer once pumped his apple mush. "In the early days, it was practically soup, very, very rich organically because of that mush," Thomson said. "Now we use it as a drainage basin to collect rain water. Over the years the water has gradually cleared. It's taken a long time."

A request for bids for the 118,000-square-foot Liberal Arts and Sciences Building was announced July 18, 1967. "Peter Tarapata had a wonderful master plan for the new campus," Thomson recalled. "Only the first one-third of his Z-shaped plan was built, though. Under Gunder Myran, the campus veered away from the initial concept."

The Exact Sciences Building had been designed as a three-story concrete frame structure, cast in place with brick inserts. Plans called for the ground floor to house electronic labs and business education facilities, the middle floor for the Exact Sciences (physics, chemistry, and biology), and the top floor to accommodate the Health Sciences programs (Dental Assistant, X-ray Technician, Physical and Inhalation Therapy, Nursing and Laboratory Technician programs). A greenhouse was planned for the penthouse. The building would also hold three lecture auditoriums, numerous seminar rooms, and faculty offices.

Shortly after that building was authorized, in November 1967, the State Department of Education approved a grant of $375,000 in federal vocational funds for constructing and furnishing WCC's Technical and Industrial Building, with construction expected to start early in 1968.

Painters worked around the clock in the last months of 1970 to prepare the new campus for the move from Willow Run. Breaks were a chance to catch their breath.

Bids for the Exact Sciences Building were received in March 1968. The architect had estimated a cost of $3.35 million. Low bidder J.A. Fredman of Pontiac received the construction contract for $3,777,000. In contrast, half the bids for the T&I Building came in below the architect's estimate of $2,282,000. Low bidder was the Dawley Company of Dearborn, which had proposed completing the project for $1,564,000.

The Board carefully planned the time when it would ask for bond money. "Ed Adams was a banker and very sensitive to the whole idea of timing in terms of the bond market and the construction," Procassini said. "That really served us well because we were borrowing at the best possible rate."

Groundbreaking ceremonies for these two buildings and the Power House were held in mid–October 1968. Officials actually set off dynamite at the ceremony. President Ponitz told *The Ann Arbor News* that he believed the finished campus would provide "a highly functional, well integrated facility, which will not only provide an environment conducive to learning, but will promote understanding between the liberal arts and technical disciplines through the organization of the campus and individual buildings."

Six months later, the Board approved preliminary plans for a fourth building. The Student Center was designed with the Learning Materials Center (library and audio-visual) on its third floor; administration offices, Student Activities offices, and classrooms on the second floor; and food service facilities and bookstore on the first floor. At the time the plans were approved, President Ponitz explained that the building would probably be completed in stages; not enough funds were available to complete the project all at once.

The President also announced that the Power House, Technical and Industrial Building, and Exact Sciences Building would be ready for the start of the 1969-70 school year. Throughout the summer of 1969, the College waited hopefully and expectantly for news that the last painting had been completed, the last door hung, and the classrooms readied for students. Most activities at Willow Run were put on hold. But Registration day came and went and contractors and administrators were still wrestling with last-minute details and problems on the new campus. Fall semester classes started on September 15, 1969, at Willow Run, due to electrical power difficulties on the new campus. Administrators hopefully predicted that within a month the problems would be resolved, but October 14 came and went, and still classes were meeting at the old campus.

The WCC library has undergone a series of transformations over the years, as library staff member Dorothy Hanna witnessed.

"Every available inch of space is in use and we are hanging onto buildings that we had hoped to be able to abandon," Dean of General Studies John Wooden told *The Ann Arbor News* after Registration. Enrollment that year rose by another 1,200 students, topping 3,600. Seventeen new faculty members had been hired, bringing the total to 134. Willow Run had clearly outlived its usefulness.

Gradually, at the very end of 1969, faculty and equipment started making their way over to the new Technical and Industrial Building. Occupational Education students began their new commute, although the automotive center remained on Carpenter Road for several more years, and a number of the health programs were housed in temporary trailers on the new grounds. "It seems to me that it might have taken six months for us all to move into the T&I Building completely," Andy Ford said. "During the transition, we continued to run classes at Willow Run. It was a while longer before the next building was completed and the rest of the college joined us at the Huron River campus."

One interesting detail of the new campus was a direct result of the flagpole incident on the Willow Run campus the previous year, when professors and student protesters fought for control. The Board of Trustees unanimously voted to spend considerably more money for a flagpole with its lanyard on the inside, which meant that "unauthorized persons could not pull down one flag and put up another."

"We have always been proud of the quality of instruction and the commitment to students that WCC has maintained through the years," said Trustee Jerry Jernigan.

THE TECHNICAL & INDUSTRIAL BUILDING

Although bids were first received for the Exact Sciences Building, the Technical and Industrial Building was planned to be the first building to open on the new Community College campus. According to Trustee Tony Procassini, "The Board was always trying to make sure that we had a planned growth. We didn't want anything done haphazardly. As one of the main reasons for establishing the College was its Occupational Education programs, we felt that the first building that went up should be the T&I Building. That was by design."

After studying the Occupational Education needs, the architect had designed a fifty-six thousand square-foot structure with a shop measuring seventy feet by ninety feet that would house "a full spectrum of machines for instruction in metals, precision measurements, testing, and industrial processes."

Working with Andy Ford and other faculty members, the architects carefully designed the building not only for its special vocational functions, but with an eye to the future, in the hopes of making the building accommodate new and as-yet-unseen changes in technology and trades. "Occupational buildings must be flexible in order to anticipate what they're going to become rather than focusing only on what is required at any particular time," Roger Bertoia said.

"Every area was reviewed and, as much as was practical, everyone's suggestions were taken into consideration, for better or worse," Ford said.

"Bricks and mortar change every institution—that's only natural," Bertoia observed. "Suddenly, planning becomes the focus, and with more at stake, you need more planning. Consequently, the institution becomes more conservative. Initially, when there is less at stake, you can respond to any situation more quickly. After the move, we all became a little less free to shoot from the hip, and yet we never knew until the last minute how many students we'd have in our classes. Meeting their needs and finding adequate space was always a challenge."

Despite the large new buildings on campus, T&I quickly outgrew its space. During the 1970s, Vietnam veterans were returning in large

Dale Fisher

numbers from the military, the economy was suffering, and local industries had downsized, which are all factors that traditionally cause enrollment at WCC to rise. In addition, federal programs like Community Educational Training Administration added to the enrollment, sometimes dramatically. Through the decade, the College was often and unexpectedly hit with huge waves of new students. "Those influxes really challenged us in our efforts to meet all the students' needs," Bertoia said.

Still, the programs flourished at the apple orchard, and the press and students gave the new College rave reviews.

"We had to be careful to design the T&I Building with an eye for the future and we succeeded quite well," Bertoia said. "It has served us well over the years."

"The day we moved to the new campus, we felt blessed," Ron Zeeb remembered. "By that time, Willow Run had become barely adequate. I can remember thinking that our new facilities were wonderful."

The Miracle in the Apple Orchard took place during the late 1960s, with three buildings under construction at once: the Power House, the Technical & Industrial Building, and the Liberal Arts & Sciences Building.

THE LIBERAL ARTS & SCIENCES BUILDING

Architect Peter Tarapata designed the first three College buildings, which rose in the midst of 235 acres once known as the Huron Valley Farms, owned by Jarvis and Pearl Franzblau. Director of Exact Sciences Mehran Thomson fought hard to retain as many trees as possible.

Mehran Thomson and his faculty members worked closely with Architect Peter Tarapata to plan the Exact Sciences Building. Designed as a series of concentric circles, it has a center core for supply rooms and the elevator. Surrounding that core are the laboratories. Surrounding the labs are the hall corridors. Around the perimeter are offices and classrooms. Pipes and duct work fill the spaces between floors.

Thomson visited science buildings around the country to study innovative designs and incorporated new elements into the College's Exact Sciences Building. One called for building the utilities into the tables used in the physics lab; the cabinetry was designed to be changeable, allowing it to adapt to different needs. The rotating stage in the main lecture hall is another innovation inspired by Thomson's research. Initially, the Board of Trustees questioned the expense as an unnecessary "frill," but Thomson argued that the stage would allow

Dale Fisher

the College to use the lecture hall continuously and without interruption. While one presentation was underway, preparations for the next could be completed behind the stage; as soon as the hall emptied out, the stage would revolve and the room would be ready for the next group. When the bids came in, the rotating stage made very little difference in cost, so it was approved. The auditorium has both front- and rear-projection screens.

■ ■ ■

The Liberal Arts and Sciences Building (LASB) was completed by the start of the winter term of 1970. The move for General Studies teachers was easy—"unlike what the people in the automotive program later experienced," Char Hanson said, explaining that when the Automotive Program finally moved onto campus from Carpenter Road, there were no parking lots. "People had to abandon their cars wherever they could find flat ground."

After two-and-a-half cramped years at Willow Run, the General Studies Program could finally stretch out on the new campus and enjoy the place. "It was really a beautiful site, in an apple orchard in the country. Hence, the phrase 'miracle in the apple orchard' and the College's apple tree logo," Rosalyn Biederman said. "In the first years, we actually got apples from those trees!"

Dr. Ponitz seemed to be everywhere in those days, making sure that everything was working and everyone was settled, Betty Ladley Finkbeiner observed. "I'd be lecturing in the classroom and then turn

Books, books, and more books are sold at the campus bookstore during the start of every new semester. Bookstore Manager Mary Johnson worked with students to streamline the process.

around and he'd be standing there, wanting to know what it was I was holding. He wanted to know the students and he worked hard to be in every nook and cranny, walking around to the classrooms, attending performances, greeting students on the first day of school, making all this work."

For the most part, early reviews of the new campus were ecstatic. Don Bylsma appreciated the convenience of the location. "There was a great sense of openness on the new campus. We suddenly felt official, established," he said. "There was a sense of space and freedom in the new buildings and the grounds."

"I remember those early days on the new campus with a sense of excitement," Char Hanson agreed. "We felt like pioneers."

On the other hand, the atmosphere had changed dramatically from the up-close-and-personal days at Willow Run. "After the close, crowded, rabbit-warren atmosphere at Willow Run, the new building could almost be intimidating," Lola Jones said. "It appeared to me to be a bit cold, with all its stretches of cement and glass and wide-open spaces." But she found the move to a brand-new building with clean, wide-open space exciting. So was the chance to see a college grow from the ground up—literally. "I can remember thinking that we'd never fill all that space—but we did, soon enough," Jones said.

Despite the wide open spaces, individual programs continued to feel part of the larger College community, Betty Finkbeiner said. "The Dental Assistant Program had a lot of interaction with the faculty in other departments. I team-taught a class on office procedures with Jerry Patt, who was in the business program. We even wrote a text-book together. Occasionally, I'd call someone in the biology department to share equipment. We all worked together for the common good of the school as well as our individual programs."

"The new space did change us," Edith Croake believed, "but we continued to have that feeling of interdisciplinary friendship on the new campus. It was just harder to run into people you'd gotten to know when the College was smaller." At first, the faculty offices in the new LASB were designed with dividers, not office walls. Edith Croake could hear everything going on in the nearby offices, and they could hear her. "People would mosey over and stand in our doorways and talk. They would offer suggestions for working with classes or students," she said. "That kind of physical structure encouraged an ongoing exchange of ideas."

She shared her area with Fred Horowitz (Art), Stuart Susnick (Social Science), Char Hanson (Speech), Priscilla Whiteford

(Anthropology), Bill Lewis (Math), and Sophie Crawford (Reading). "I enjoyed the mix of disciplines and appreciated the diverse perspectives," she said. Bill Moy shared a third-floor office with the head of inhalation therapy, the Dental Assistant Program, a biologist, and a chemist. Eventually, the area was divided into cubicles that could be locked for security reasons, but the "mix" was still appreciated. "That method kept us more well rounded; we learned a lot about others' concerns and fields," Moy said, conceding, "It did interfere somewhat with our departmental communication, however, and as the College continued to grow, that increasingly became an issue." As WCC built new facilities, the College gradually moved toward the specialization of departments as offices were located near faculty members' classrooms. The physical distance between occupational and General Studies faculty members grew. "I miss the earlier proximity. It was comfortable," Croake said.

Library and media services have seen many different homes on campus over the years.

The College's student body also grew, so rapidly that all too soon the College once again found itself overflowing with students and in need of additional classroom space. Ten temporaries appeared on the campus almost immediately, to house the overflow. "I remember teaching in the infamous 'temps,' which were individual trailers," Rosalyn Biederman said. "Many of the administrative functions operated out of the temps, as well."

From his office on the top floor of the LASB, Thomson could watch the construction of the new Student Center Building. "That was fun to watch," he said. "They poured concrete beams, tightened cables to put compression on them—that makes the structure very, very strong."

Trustee Richard W. Bailey, however, remembered some concern about the structural soundness of the Student Center's plans. Under Henry Landau's leadership, a consultant was hired to study the plans and construction methods. "We were worried about spilled concrete from those huge pours," he said. "Peter Tarapata told us he would engage 'fine Italian craftsmen' to patch it up."

THE LIBRARY

When the library and its thirty thousand volumes moved to the new campus, it first took up quarters in the Liberal Arts and Sciences Building, then, in 1976, moved to the Student Center Building. In the 1970s, the staff was small. "Hal Young was a gifted library director, but he didn't stay as long as we would have liked," Library Technician Judy Hicks said. In 1970, just after the library moved to the new campus, Young accepted a job out of state. For four years, his position remained vacant. For some months, the four clericals he hired ran the media center themselves.

At first, the library struggled for its share of the Trustees' budget. Some years, no money was allocated for the library—"and probably that problem was College-wide," Hicks said. "I remember days during the gas shortage when the College was shut down. Later we worked flex time, ten-hour days, four days a week."

In the fall of 1971, in order to meet accreditation standards, Kathleen Dodge Scott and Margot Orr were hired as the first two librarians on the new campus. They supervised the facility when it was scattered throughout the Liberal Arts and Sciences Building. The reference library, study tables, and librarians' offices were on the second floor of the building. The card catalogues, general collection, and checkout counter were on the first floor. Technical services and media areas were in different rooms off academic hallways. There was no interconnection between the spaces.

The difficulties extended beyond the library's physical lay-out. The staff was too small. *The Voice* published a picture of the technical services area bulging with boxes stacked on top of each other because no one was available to unpack them. "We didn't have the funding we needed from the state and there was a staff, or union, issue about who should unpack the boxes," Scott recalled. "Needless to say, the administration was not pleased when the student paper presented the situation to the public."

Despite the challenges of budget constraints and staffing issues, the librarians taught classes on bibliographic instruction, ordered books, maintained the collections, and supervised the clericals. "And yet the library system was so simple, compared to what we do now," Scott said.

Adella Scott (later Adella Blain) was hired as a part-time librarian in 1974, the year Margot Orr left. In 1975, the new library opened in the Student Center. The move brought a sense of permanency and order to the library. "The facility then looked like a library," Scott said. Leo Ho, a native of Taiwan, came as director and hired a secretary and part-time librarians. Media programs were started, librarians worked with faculty on instruction, and the order process was streamlined. Scott discovered that she loved teaching.

THE COLLEGE ENTERS A NEW ERA

The "Miracle in the Apple Orchard" had taken place before Ann Cleary Kettles was elected to the Board in 1972. She attended her first Board meetings in a special room in the Technical and Industrial Building until the Board Room was finished and furnished in the Student Center Building.

As the enrollment continued to grow and the College soon began bursting the seams of the Technical and Industrial Building and the Liberal Arts and Sciences Building, the Board supervised new building projects: the Student Center Building, Family Education Center, and the Occupational Education Building.

"We all learned a lot about building that we hadn't known previously," Kettles said. "I remember that we made one major mistake with the electrical wiring in the Student Center Building: when you turned one light on, they all went on. Instructors trying to use overhead projectors or show movies didn't find that very helpful. Then there was the thorny question of who would get what office; windows were a very popular commodity."

On the other hand, there were some commendable successes—large and small. "Someone was smart when they laid out the sidewalks," Kettles remembered. "They watched where the students were walking before anything was done, and then laid the sidewalks on the students' paths."

Kettles' particular interest focused on women's issues. The College had recognized from the start that women needed counseling and encouragement; shortly after the first women Trustees joined the Board, the Women's Center opened. "Many of our women faculty

Early faculty members and students remember David Ponitz as being "everywhere people were," talking to students over lunch, dropping in to observe classes, speaking to community organizations, and offering support at meetings. Here he shows a student the plans for the new campus.

members were very supportive of this project, among them Flavia Reps in History and Marguerite Eaglin in Counseling," Kettles said. "We all recognized that women needed—and still need—the opportunity to share their problems with each other in order to work them out. We had many working mothers and single mothers in our student body. WCC still does. They need a place to meet and find some support."

During the early 1970s, the Board also worked hard to get funding for the Daycare Program, which was broadened into a Family Education Center, offering classes on family issues as well as daycare. The voters backed the Center with a bond. Henry Landau, a local builder, put that package together with Kettles.

"Everything we did was for the students; they were our priority," she said.

■ ■ ■

When the dust finally cleared in the mid-1970s, the final campus design looked significantly different from the 1967 master plan;

besides the missing elements of Tarapata's "Z" design, the plan had called for a bridge between the Technical and Industrial Building and Student Center Building which was never built. It was judged to be too expensive, "In the end, we turned the original architectural plan around and put Technical and Industrial Building and Occupational Education Building on the two sides of the ceremonial entrance. As planned, there was no formal entrance to the campus. We built the staircase on the north side of the Student Center Building in order to fabricate a front door for the place," Trustee Richard W. Bailey said.

It quickly became apparent that the Board had been wise in choosing its location and buying the entire plot of land at once. Shortly after the College moved onto the former apple orchard, the surrounding lands doubled in value.

"In one sense, WCC became a better school when it moved to the new campus. We had the ability to function better," Fred Horowitz said. "The buildings were more attractive and more suitable to a college setting. It's a nicer place to attend, a place that offers a sense of pride. It's easier to offer good service when you have appropriate facilities and equipment."

In his 1982 interview, Evart Ardis observed, "With the construction of St. Joseph's Hospital and Concordia College, the College is situated on an educational and professional corridor...There probably isn't a seven-mile strip that has a much bigger concentration of higher education than that particular area."

The campus today never ceases to amaze Rosalyn Biederman. "It is huge and still very beautiful," she said. "I feel lucky to have worked in such a nice setting all of these years. Now, I wonder...is even one apple tree left out there?"

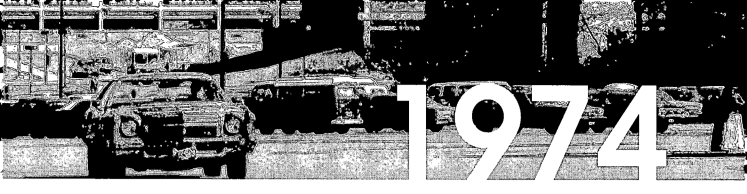

- Mao launches Cultural Revolution.

- Heiress Patty Hearst is kidnapped by Symbionese Liberation Army.

- Aleksandr Solzhenitsyn is deported from Russia.

- Grand Jury indicts President Nixon's aides Haldeman, Ehrlichman, Colson. Nixon agrees to pay $432,000 in back taxes, makes public 2,100 pages of tapes, admits "serious act of omission," resigns.

- Gerald R. Ford is sworn in as president, with Nelson Rockefeller as vice president.

- President Ford offers "earned clemency" to draft evaders and a pardon to Richard Nixon.

- The Equal Opportunity Act forbids discrimination based on sex or marital status.

- Gasoline is in short supply, car sales drop 35 percent from 1973, home construction drops 40 percent.

History & Politics

- Nielsen's Top Ten: *All in the Family, Sanford and Son, Chico and the Man, The Jeffersons, M*A*S*H, Rhoda, Good Times, The Waltons, Maude, Hawaii Five-O.*

Television

- Americans are watching *The Godfather, Part II; Alice Doesn't Live Here Any More; Chinatown; The Towering Inferno; Harry and Tonto; Murder on the Orient Express; Young Frankenstein; Blazing Saddles; Andy Warhol's Frankenstein, The Great Gatsby.*

Movies

- Hit songs: "Seasons in the Sun," "The Most Beautiful Girl," "The Streak," "The Entertainer," "Please, Mr. Postman," "Mandy," "Top of the World," "Just You and Me."

Music

- Americans are reading *Fear of Flying* (Erica Jong), *Dog Soldiers* (Robert Stone), *Sula* (Toni Morrison), *Centennial* (James Michener), *Watership Down* (Richard Adams), *Jaws* (Peter Benchley), *Zen and the Art of Motorcycle Maintenance* (Robert M. Pirsig), *All the President's Men* (Carl Bernstein, Bob Woodward), *Alistair Cooke's America* (Alistair Cooke).

Books

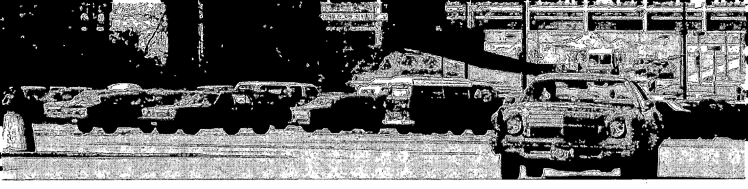

Fashion

- "Covered" and "uncovered" looks are in: string bikinis and the blanketed look with wide capes, skirts and coats that fall to mid- and low-calf, and loose blouses. Victorian camisoles are worn with skirts. Ethnic clothing is a fad. Russian-style tunics are worn with side buttons and belts; pants are tucked into boots; Chinese worker shirts, pants, and quilted vests are also popular.

Education

- Thousands bare all in the streaking fad; at the University of Georgia, 1,543 break the record for the greatest number of naked students at one time on a college campus. Hundreds at Texas Tech stay naked for hours.

New Words

- Nuke, yen, stonewalling, striking.

Quotes

- "(This nation is becoming) a nation of hamburger stands, a country stripped of industrial capacity and meaningful work,...a service economy,...a nation of citizens busily buying and selling cheeseburgers and root beer floats." —AFL-CIO

WCC in 1974

The Voice proudly carries the title "Michigan's No. 1 College Biweekly" and reveals the year's highlights:

- The baseball team finishes second in its league, with Randy Brier leading the sluggers and Vern Gowan leading the hurlers. The golf team takes third place in the Eastern Conference. The track team, only five members strong, places fourth in the conference. Tim Jennings captures the conference long-jump title with a 21-foot-10-inch jump. He is named to the Michigan Community College Athletic Association Honor Roll.

- President David Ponitz accepts a job as president of Sinclair Community College, Dayton, Ohio.

- The WCC Children's Center cares for 160 children on a part-time basis. Patricia Travis is named director.

- In November, voters approve a new funding proposal. Richard W. Bailey is elected to the Board of Trustees, while Board Chairman Anthony Procassini and William Mays Jr. are re-elected.

Chapter 9:
Let's Organize!

The College's early years were filled with excitement, professional challenges, and strong friendships, but they also contained their share of problems and disagreements. "It wasn't a time of complete harmony and bliss," Edith Croake recalled.

Many of those early problems were offshoots of the hiring extravaganza in the summer and fall of 1966, when WCC scrambled to hire enough faculty members to open the College and then again to respond to the overwhelming number of students.

"The key point about hiring in those days was that WCC didn't have a salary schedule," former Divisional Director Mehran Thomson said. "Those of us doing the hiring would find out what people were being paid and we'd offer enough to give them an incentive to move. There was no uniformity in pay—that's what led to the coming of the unions."

"This unionization might have been averted if the College had the services of a Human Resources administrator," suggested Tony Procassini, who became a Trustee in 1966. "But, then again, Michigan is a state where the unions have always been very strong."

The result? "The teachers' union came into existence because instructors felt there was no consistent salary structure," Thomson said. "They were right. In the early days, no salary plans had existed and each director made his or her own deals with the people they hired. We all got great teachers, experts in their fields, but they weren't paid in a balanced, comparable way. So, the teachers organized."

Three years before Washtenaw Community College was established, the State of Michigan authorized the formation of teachers' unions on community college campuses. In 1966, a Faculty Senate was created at WCC. The second year after the College was launched, faculty members debated about whether to join a union. After considerable discussion, they voted to organize.

"We started to unionize the first day we met as faculty members," Don Bylsma said. "Many of us here came with union backgrounds."

"In most cases, the occupational faculty led the way when it came to early union matters; they often came from backgrounds experienced in labor relations," Roger Bertoia said. "Most of us had a history with various unions and often we had to educate the General Studies people on what unions were all about. They tended to come from the ranks of antiwar and civil rights protests."

Harry Konschuh came to campus as Dean of Employee Relations. He ended his career as Vice President of Instruction and he also served as a member of the WCC Board of Trustees.

The union's arrival was difficult for some faculty members. "This was the only union I'd seen up close or been affiliated with," Mike Pogliano said. "At first, I was apprehensive, but as time and the association progressed, I could see the need for its existence."

Ron Zeeb had a similar experience. He didn't start as a union advocate, but over time he realized, "The union did more for me than I would ever have been able to do for myself in terms of working conditions, salaries, and handling grievances. My opinion about unions turned around 180 degrees, from strongly negative to strongly positive."

The faculty first met in a union hall on Packard Road. Despite some skepticism, mostly from General Studies faculty members who had had no previous history with unions, the faculty had no trouble getting the necessary signatures. The vote between the AFT (American Federation of Teachers) and the MEA (Michigan Education Association) was very close. The MEA won by one vote. ("Many people thought the AFT seemed more radical and closer to labor unions," Bylsma said.)

On January 9, 1967, the newly formed Washtenaw Community College Education Association, a union of faculty members, elected their first officers. Paul Niehaus, a biology teacher-counselor in the Exact Sciences Division, was elected president, with automotive teacher-counselor Bruce Welch as vice president, and Bella G.

Reddick (secretarial skills teacher-counselor in the Business and Management Division) as secretary. *The Voice* advisor and English teacher-counselor in the Communication/Arts Division, Fred Wolven, was elected treasurer.

In the fall of 1966, many administrative procedures were still up in the air. Although Dr. Ponitz had told faculty members they would be paid "every two weeks," they didn't know if it would be twenty-three or twenty-six payments, Bylsma recalled. He'll never forget Director of Business Lloyd Van Buskirk telling him, "It's twenty-six times a year because everyone knows teachers can't budget their money." "That's when we decided we needed a union," Bylsma said. "By that time we'd also learned that people with the same qualifications were given different salaries and that wasn't fair."

Bylsma remembered the hostility over negotiations during the early years. "It stemmed from comments and beliefs like 'teachers can't budget their money,'" he said.

There were other issues besides salaries. though. One dealt with nepotism and chauvinism. The College had allowed two brothers, both fine teachers, to work in different areas, but when a woman was denied a full-time job because she was married to a faculty member, she told Edith Croake, "Things would have been different if I'd been Merle's brother instead of his wife!"

The Association's first contract was for the 1966-67 academic year. "Lee Luchsinger, the College's business manager, gave away the farm because he had never had dealings like this before," Bylsma said. "Some of us made out well." The contract was strongly pro-teacher, but many things were not clearly defined.

At the time, Michigan's unions were the most liberal in the nation, thanks to their history with the auto industry, and many faculty and staff members—but no administrators—came with union associations. "Meanwhile, few College administrators and Board members had any experience or training with unions before meeting them across the bargaining table," Dave Ponitz said. "We were definitely at a disadvantage."

By the opening of the second school year, in 1967, Washtenaw Community College hadn't settled on a contract and negotiations started with "a very hostile fifteen-minute session," Ponitz recalled. "I remember it was a hard time for everybody," Dave Pollock added. "The union adopted the United Auto Workers' hard labor approach rather than what I'd view as a collegial approach."

Rosalyn Biederman felt the same way. "I have always felt that professional burnout here is more a result of bumping heads with administrators than wearing out in the classroom," she said, adding, "I, for one, have been a happy union supporter, however."

"During the early years, negotiations were hard-nosed and adversarial," Ponitz agreed. "It's very, very different now. By the time we reached our fifth or sixth agreement, we had finally reached a win-win situation."

■ ■ ■

A former member of the Detroit Federation of Teachers, Robert Reeves became involved in the union when he first came to campus in 1968. The day after he was hired for a teaching position in Detroit, the teachers held their first strike. "That put me in a difficult spot, but I participated," he remembered. When he joined WCC's faculty in 1968, the union was still in its formative stages—and it was very aggressive. "I was shocked at the way they almost attacked President Ponitz once," he said. "The President's office was in the old butcher shop at Willow Run and they carved their initials in his desk. They didn't back down or give quarter."

At that time, Phil Encinio was president of the faculty association and Merrill McClatchey, Don Keck, Gary Hentz, and Charlie Belknap were involved. According to Bob Reeves, Encinio later became vice chancellor at the University of California at Berkley and switched sides in negotiations. McClatchey and Keck went to New York City and rose through the union ranks. Belknap went to work for the MEA

Robert Reeves, as speech instructor, and subsequently Associate Vice President for Human Relations, served on both sides of the bargaining table.

in Michigan. Hentz was a counselor, then drafting instructor, at WCC. When Reeves showed an interest in union activities, they asked about his background and told him they needed helpers. He started immediately, working on grievances.

The second contract these association leaders signed became known in union circles as the "Green Goose." It would serve as the model for other union contracts across the state and the country. In it, salary inequities were eliminated. No one had their salaries cut, but many saw their salaries increase, and they received compensation for the past paychecks, fifty cents on the dollar.

"I studied this contract closely when I was at Lake Michigan Community College," Harry Konschuh said. "The union was very proud of its accomplishments at WCC."

The MEA had written the contract's prototype and everything about it, particularly the language, favored the union. "We studied it, we analyzed it, and we modified it," Reeves remembered. "We spent a year writing and rewriting our contract; then we started negotiating. I sat in on the negotiations. The administration had a man named Frank Dypold representing WCC; he came from industry and had no idea of what worked in an academic setting. He did an atrocious job for them."

In negotiating on management's behalf, Dypold was cautious and hesitant, while the faculty representative, Merrill McClatchey, was skilled in contract language and very adversarial. In desperation, the Board replaced Dypold with Paul Hunt, Dean of Occupational Education. "Paul had a military background and was very low-key. His job as directed by the Board was to get a contract," Reeves said. "Merrill was a skilled negotiator and Paul had no experience. There was far more compromising than management would do in later years."

That 1969-71 "Green Goose" contract was favorable to the faculty in just about every way. The counselors' quadrant payment system meant that they actually earned much more money than most of the administrators, Reeves remembered. The faculty benefited from the compensation structure. They were given more holidays and fringe benefits than any other community college faculty in Michigan. Teachers were given control of their own class schedules without input from the administration. ("Later, that authority would reside with the administration," Reeves said.) "Our success was due to circumstances, timing, and a new Board," he added.

Negotiations with union representatives on campus were "very hard," Ponitz said, because they became highly charged with emotional issues. "Initially, the union's role was to separate the president and administrators from the Board of Trustees to get what they wanted."

"In the early days, we worked very hard strategizing. We wanted to divide and conquer," Bob Reeves agreed. "Each member of the faculty bargaining team called a Board member to tell them in a very clear manner what was going on. I talked to Ed Adams and he told me, 'Reeves, we work through our bargaining team.' That was exactly what he should have said. The divide-and-conquer approach ended when Harry Konschuh came to campus."

■ ■ ■

In May 1969, *The Ann Arbor News* reporter Mary Wallace wrote about President Ponitz's censure and the "long-simmering tensions" between the leaders of the teachers' association and the administration of WCC. Although they were not engaged in contract negotiations at the time, the faculty issued a condemnation of President David Ponitz for his inability to recruit more minorities and for "aggravated problems on campus," chief among them being "the problems of our black students." The Black Student Union immediately denied the teachers' allegations and charged them with using the black students as a weapon against the administration.

Later that year, Dennis Bila was hired as a math instructor. At that time, Ed Adams was chairman of the Board and Tom Hill was the Board's negotiator. Bila immediately became involved in the Association. "Union sentiment was in my blood," he said. "My father had helped Jimmy Hoffa organize the trucking industry in Saginaw. My cousins are presidents of locals in the auto industry. In 1965, I helped organize Thurston High School."

When Bila arrived, the association's early bargaining sessions were tailored to a format familiar to former high school teachers. "Most of us in general education had a history with high school salary scales, where pay is based on degrees and advanced education credits; in high schools, faculty members are separated over five salary steps," Bila said. "The occupational faculty, which came with fewer degrees but more depth in work experience, was worried that general education would lead WCC in that direction."

They didn't, however. The College adopted a single salary schedule, taking the position that all teaching is equal, whether the instructor holds a bachelor's or a doctorate degree. "That was a defining point in the early days of the college," Bila said. "Over the years, there has been some pressure to change that position, but we never have." Just as negotiations for community colleges work differently from high school negotiations, they are also very different from negotiations in four-year institutions. "Universities make judgment calls when it comes to salaries," Bila said. "In universities, people who teach physics get paid more money than those teaching education, and men often earn more than women. WCC is different. We say—and we truly believe—that teaching calculus is not more or less important than teaching in the auto shop."

Dennis Bila became association secretary in 1970, after complaining about the new contract. "We had been given ten percent raises, which were really big, but we had given up ten percent in productivity," he said. "That amounted to having to teach an extra week a year, as I recall, because classes were stretched from fifty to fifty-five minutes. In practicality, the change meant very little, but it did represent a greater productivity, which meant that despite the raise, we were right where we had started. Most people, though, didn't see it that way."

In 1975, Bila succeeded Charlie Belknap as president and, except for three years, he served as president into the twenty-first century. Belknap often had heated and repeated run-ins with President Ponitz. Bila changed styles. "The early years were very, very difficult for both sides," he said. "Managers with a boss mentality came and went. At times, relationships would get hostile. It's very difficult for everyone involved when you bring in unions. One of our main goals was to emphasize that we're partners with the administration. We don't take orders. Here, the faculty owns the curriculum. This is not like a factory, where the president is also the CEO. Faculty and administrators share the fiduciary responsibilities. We take care of education—and we fight that battle daily."

During the Community College's first ten years, the bargaining system was based on the personality of the administrators, Bila said. "The scene was classic, just like one you'd see in the auto plants: the management was all male and came dressed in suits and ties. The union representatives were dressed in all different styles and they sat on the other side of the table with an MEA representative. Only one person from each side got to speak. It was a harsh system of negotiations, but it was the style that the MEA management trained. That's all we knew."

Ponitz remembered watching faculty members pounding the table, threatening to go on strike. "It was a different kind of logic than any I'd dealt with before. I became very frustrated in collective negotiations because they take energy away from what we needed to do with our students."

Bila remembered Shirley Roberts cautioning an early negotiating team, "We're going to walk in there now. No one smile." He hated that approach. "When you get right down to it, we're all friends," he said. "We may clash now and then, but we're still friends. During the negotiations, the people on the other side of the table might be the enemy and we'd play all kinds of games with them, but we always want any hostilities to end the minute we shake hands and walk out the door."

In 1971, the State Department of Education warned that four hundred thousand dollars might be cut from the Washtenaw Community College budget. President Ponitz issued a letter saying that because of those proposed cutbacks, the College might be forced to lay off twenty-one people. "It was a very difficult time, and it had a great impact on our collective bargaining," Reeves said. "I remember that physical education with Larry Slepsky was eliminated. We didn't like what was happening."

Ann Cleary Kettles was Board Chair at the time. Reeves and Marguerite Eaglin went to the Board and complained that they were deliberately encumbering funds and bargaining in bad faith. "Ann asked if we could work out a resolution and we eventually did," Reeves said. But not until the newspapers had a field day over the problems.

Over an eight-month period in the 1970s, sixty percent of all community college presidents in the United States were censured by their faculty. "I was one of them," David Ponitz said. "None of us had been trained in collective bargaining issues and the language was very difficult for us. I remember once the union pressed for a cost of living clause. It sounded pretty good to me, but when I talked to Bill Bott, he told me never, ever do that, that we should give a little more money instead. I hadn't had a clue."

President Ponitz was censured in 1971. He brought Harry Konschuh in to help negotiate on behalf of the Board in 1972.

"We knew that Harry was coming from an institution that had fired its entire faculty," Dennis Bila said. "He is very bright, a former math teacher, very competitive, and very, very good at bargaining and negotiations. That was a difficult period for our association."

"We knew immediately that things were about to change," Bob Reeves said. "I remember our association discussing strategies for hours on end. We even went so far as to have Harry's handwriting analyzed, to see if we could get clues about how to approach him."

■ ■ ■

Harry Konschuh arrived at Washtenaw Community College with a big reputation to maintain. The faculty knew as much about him as he knew about their "Green Goose" contract. He was notorious for having fired the entire faculty at Lake Michigan Community College during its rancorous labor disputes.

"The 1970s was a union era," Konschuh said. "WCC was having incredible labor problems. Labor relations were a mess. From the standpoint of getting salaries, benefits and union activities on track, the years 1972 to 1978 were formative years that would determine how well the Community College would be structured and functioning in the future."

At that time, WCC had four unions: faculty, custodians, administrative, and clerical.

"I came with bargaining experience from my days as a high school teacher," Konschuh said. "The Alberta Teachers Association had been organized in the 1950s, and I was on their bargaining team. I learned then that collective bargaining is a game and you've got to be able to read body language."

His first job on campus was to determine proper pay scales. "Thanks to earlier contracts, by 1972, anyone who wanted to get anything accomplished on campus had to work through union administrators," he said. WCC had hired an external negotiator named Tom Hill, who specialized in collective bargaining. His job was to help with arbitration and grievances. Konschuh worked with Hill for one contract and then took his place. "When I came, the Board—with the exception of Tony Procassini—didn't understand collective bargaining and why there was so much difficulty in creating a contract," Konschuh said. "Part of my task was to educate the Board—the faculty was way ahead of us. I spent a lot of time preparing information for them and they were very supportive."

Bob Reeves, who was the Association's chief negotiator in 1973, went into the first bargaining session with Harry Konschuh very carefully. "We'd heard that Harry was considered a night rider," Reeves said. "In fact, shortly before that day, Larry Hackney, the dean of students, went to Marguerite [Eaglin] and told her that Bob Reeves wouldn't be able to handle the new guy—'They'll rip his heart out,' he said. I was mad." When he got to the table, Reeves realized that he had never seen management prepare the way Konschuh prepared. "I knew immediately that it was a new day. Management now had someone who studied the people, the place, and the plan, and they were ruthless. It was the first time we had real bargaining." The Association soon realized that this contract would have to take Harry's language and modify it. "He only let go of his language if it was stuff that didn't count," Reeves discovered.

"So much time went into getting that awful start straightened out," Konschuh said many years later. "I can't say that the faculty wasn't serving the students; in spite of being able to do whatever they wanted, they worked hard. They were just used to a laissez-faire approach to management." Another problem area was work load for counselors. "They had the same reporting days and the same salary schedule as the faculty, with the result that you couldn't get them to work in July and August—which is when counseling is crucial for incoming students," Trustee Richard W. Bailey said. "It was years before we got the counselors on the job when we needed them." Konschuh said that the 1973 contract "actually didn't change much — but we knew that new winds were blowing," Reeves said.

From that point on, the faculty realized that the administration would be in charge. "We went to a quid pro quo basis, where if management gave something up, the faculty would have to give something in return," Konschuh said. "Basically, management got control of the language and the faculty got a little more money," Reeves added. "I remember coming out of those negotiations feeling beat-up. And I knew that going back to our members to get ratification would be tough. They were accustomed to getting their way, so we had to launch another campaign, this time with the faculty. We presented the contract in the most palatable light."

"The cardinal rule is that management could never come out publicly to say 'We won,'" Konschuh said.

In January 1975, Richard W. Bailey, a University of Michigan faculty member, took his newly elected seat on the Board of Trustees. By that time, the College administration had been so burned by association wrangles that they sat Bailey down for a talk about the history of negotiations on campus and to sound out his views.

"I think that both Dave Ponitz and Tony Procassini worried that my heart would be on the wrong side of the bargaining table because of my position at the University of Michigan," Bailey said. "I'm not sure why they worried about that, but they sat me down and talked about how I shouldn't reveal Board bargaining stands to the union. They feared I'd represent the union side. I would never have done that because I had been elected to represent the community of taxpayers. I thought it was my job to make sure our salaries allowed us to attract and retain the best people. This did not mean, to use one of Tony's favorite phrases, 'giving away the store.'"

For many years Trustee Richard W. Bailey observed the administration's slow and laborious struggle to restore management rights that had been bargained away. "When Harry Konschuh came to campus, things changed in the area of collective bargaining," Bailey said. "Hiring someone with that kind of background sends a distinct message to the faculty. Harry did a good job with labor relations here—and what faculty people initially feared never came to pass. In those early years, the faculty got (and still have) an excellent benefit package," Bailey said. Educational opportunities continue to be among the benefits offered to faculty, who have the chance to rise on the salary scale by taking additional courses. Their family members are entitled to subsidized tuition at WCC.

■ ■ ■

The union gained in benefits every year during the first decade of the College. The 1974–76 contract is actually considered the high point of the faculty's negotiations, although Bila and others could see the handwriting on the wall. "We were ahead of inflation, the salary level was good, and the benefits were good," Bila said, quickly adding, "but we were essentially just hanging on by our fingernails because the administration had brought Harry Konschuh in as negotiator.

"We learned how good Harry was in 1974," he added. "The Trustees had brought him in to get back what they felt had been given away. The faculty didn't lose anything substantive, but the administration made great gains," Bila said with a smile, admitting that he had some shouting matches with Konschuh. "We're a lot alike in our personalities. We used to run races together and we both learned that neither of us ever wants to lose," Bila said, adding, "We might have been adversaries across the table from each other, but once the negotiations ended, my wife and I would have had dinner with Harry and his wife. There are people on both sides who just don't understand that, but that's the way things should be. We're all working together for the good of the institution."

Since that 1974–76 contract, Bila said that the association has "tried to hold our own," explaining, "Some years have been harder than others. When times are difficult economically, it's hard to justify bargaining for more money, for instance. You always have to be willing to change positions; if we hadn't changed our bargaining stances, we'd be long gone today."

■ ■ ■

For the first ten years, contracts were negotiated every two years, and the battles raged over wages and benefits. During the first school year, faculty members belonged to the Faculty Senate, but that disappeared when the union arrived. Union talks cover all aspects of the faculty members' professional lives: job descriptions, working conditions, salaries, benefits, and academic issues. Eventually, WCC went to three-year contracts—"which made sense because the process is so exhausting," Bila said.

Over time, the administration added seven weeks to the faculty's base load and gave up the sixteenth hour of teaching. The school year went from two seventeen-week sessions to two fifteen-week sessions plus a seven-week summer session, making the base load thirty-seven hours. "We added more productivity and created the most productive faculty in Michigan," Konschuh said. "Then, the pendulum had to swing back. Teachers eventually were given a thirty to thirty-two-week base load and we set the number of full-time faculty members. We determined the ratio of student contact hours with part-time faculty members and said that forty percent of the classes could be taught by part-timers. My position was that we shouldn't have so many part-timers, that they should basically be a cushion between good and hard times."

■ ■ ■

The administrators' union was the second of four to come onto campus, voted into existence through the Michigan Employment Relations Commission in 1970. Douglas Woolley, the original Registrar, and Dean of Students Jim Jones convened the administrators in 1967 to discuss whether or not to organize. They called for a vote. One hundred percent were in favor—"although in later years I thought that we should have had just one no," Mehran Thomson said.

At that time, Thomson (director of math and sciences), Fred Wolven (director of liberal arts and humanities), and Al Klinehenn (the Registrar) were negotiating for the administrators. "The group subscribed to the 'golden toad theory'—they wanted to talk to the Board directly, rather than going through a golden toad that stood between us," he said. "Negotiations were a hoot. We had no power. The President hired Tom Hill as negotiator and we'd talk about God, motherhood, the flag, and working twelve months. We managed to get some pay hikes, but not much. Later, Harry Konschuh came here as business manager and he did the negotiating."

Often Thomson would switch sides of the negotiating table during the course of a week, or even a day. He would negotiate for the administrators one day and across from the teachers the next day. "One year I made it easy," he recalled with a grin. "We went into negotiations with the Board and I just said, 'Why don't we just take the same increase as last year?' Harry [Konschuh] looked at me and said, 'Done.' It was over in three minutes."

The administrators' union was bargained out of existence in the 1976. In the reorganization that followed, some administrators were moved back into the ranks of faculty, others were given administrative responsibilities with promises from the Board of Trustees to treat them fairly. Tony Procassini was Board Chair at the time. "He set the tone, insisting that the administrators would be treated every bit as fairly as if they were in the union," Konschuh said. "He kept his word." That was a turning point for WCC, he believes. "We could begin to operate and build a working institution where administrators' performance was based on management principles and not union demands."

"After the dust settled, we had no regrets," Thomson said.

■ ■ ■

The office professionals (then called clericals) were the third group on campus to organize. Judy Hicks didn't recall any battles over whether or not to go union. The clericals approached the Michigan Education Association (MEA), only to discover that they only wanted to represent faculty, so the WCC professionals went to American Federation of State, County, and Municipal Employees (AFSCME). Later, the custodial and maintenance groups joined them. (In 1993, the office professionals became members of the MEA.)

"Although there wasn't a lot of opposition to the unions among the clericals, Ann Arbor isn't a union town," Hicks said. "Most clericals, though, are from blue-collar areas where unions are important. We felt that some people were receiving preferential treatment and everyone wanted the same rights and privileges. Unions offer a means to deal with these situations. After the union came in, we saw an improvement in the way all employees were treated."

People at WCC have unique perspectives on the role of unions, views often based on more than WCC's experiences.

Burton C. Lowe, an African-American, rose through the ranks in the skilled trades at Ford in a era when those skills were most often handed from father to son and there were no African-Americans in the trades. "Blacks hadn't been given those opportunities until the union came in," he said. In the case of the Ford Motor Company, the union started in 1941.

"I was hired in 1950, and since that time I've seen a lot of major changes in policy," Lowe said. "The benefits folks in the auto industry have now are envied, yet people should look at what it took to get there. There were some hard-fought battles. I walked the picket lines many times. Any time it came to a question of economics, the union would hit Ford first, because they would buckle. Then the union would take the demands to General Motors and Chrysler."

In 1968, the people at WCC who had come from Detroit, as Lowe had, wanted the American Federation of Teachers to represent the faculty, but the academicians were more familiar with the Michigan Education Association, which believed in levying sanctions—"not using a bat to hit people over the heads during negotiations," Lowe explained. "We were outnumbered and the MEA came onto campus."

He remembers the good contracts and the bad contracts and decided long ago that the differences depended on the leaders. He often took a slightly different approach to negotiations, he said. "From my experience at the Rouge Plant, it was always my contention that we should take a strike vote at the beginning of the negotiations because that would give us leverage at the bargaining table." Throughout the association's early years, Lowe could be counted upon to get up and say, "Let's vote on a strike."

"WCC had many brilliant union leaders—in fact, I can't think of one who wasn't," Ron Zeeb said. "We were blessed with the group of officers we had."

According to Konschuh, collective bargaining brings a systematic approach to work life. "It's helpful—painful, but helpful," he said. "The Association was very important to the success of the College in its first ten years. Eventually, we got rid of the battle and settled down to work with the faculty union, which became integral to every decision and direction WCC took. I don't think that Dave Ponitz saw things that way, but the times were changing dramatically. The union really changed the educational world in the 1960s—changed it dramatically."

Eventually, the administration and the faculty reached a win-win relationship that has been maintained up until the present, Richard W. Bailey said. "Collective bargaining works extremely well now."

1975

- President Ford announces recession policy and officially ends U.S. role in Vietnam. The U.S. engages in immediate evacuation of troops, civilians, refugees. Saigon falls to North Vietnam and thousands flee by boat. The U.S. Congress approves $405 million for Vietnamese refugee aid and resettlement in U.S.

- The U.S. begins its Bicentennial celebration at Lexington and Concord, Massachusetts.

- Unemployment reaches 9.2 percent, highest since 1941.

- Cambodian Khmer Rouge evacuate people from cities, the death toll is massive.

History & Politics

- Nielsen's Top Ten TV shows: *All in the Family, Rich Man Poor Man, Laverne and Shirley, Maude, The Bionic Woman, Phyllis, Sanford and Son, Rhoda, The Six-Million-Dollar Man, ABC Monday Night Movie.*

Television

- *One Flew Over The Cuckoo's Nest* (Academy Award winner), *Barry Lyndon, Dog Day Afternoon, Jaws, Shampoo, The Man Who Would Be King, Monty Python and the Holy Grail,* and *Three Days of the Condor.*

Movies

- "Rhinestone Cowboy," "Fame," "Best of My Love," "Laughter in the Rain," "The Hustle," "Have You Ever Been Mellow?," "One of These Nights," "Jive Talkin'," "Black Water."

- Grammy Award winners: "Love Will Keep Us Together" (Captain and Tennille), "Still Crazy After All These Years" (Paul Simon), "Send in the Clowns."

Music

- *Ragtime* (E.L. Doctorow), *Curtain* (Agatha Christie), *Looking for Mister Goodbar* (Judith Rossner), *Shogun* (James Clavell), *Winning Through Intimidation* (Robert Ringer), *The Ascent of Man* (Jacob Bronowski), *Sylvia Porter's Money Book.*

Books

Sports

- Michigan falls to Oklahoma 14-6 in the Orange Bowl.

Fashion

- The Bicentennial inspires wide-shouldered pinafore dresses and other early American dress styles with high necks, fitted bodices, gathered skirts. Then there is the layered ethnic look. From Britain: Sherlock Holmes-style capes, Norfolk jackets, tartan kilts. From Russia: velvet gowns, Cossack coats, pants tucked into boots, hats with ear flaps. From France: skin-tight jeans rolled at the knee with boots. Also popular: jump suits. From China: silk, mandarin-style dresses and tunics.

- Men are wearing open shirts and leisure suits with large patch pockets. Also scarves, ascots, and string ties.

Education

- Harvard changes its 5-to-2 male-to-female admissions policy to equal admissions.

- Vandalism and violence increase in public schools. Since 1965, crimes against students have escalated 3,000 percent and against teachers, 7,000 percent.

- Governor James Rhodes and the Ohio National Guard are acquitted of all claims against them in the Kent State deaths of 1971.

- Students are dancing the hustle, bump, and robot.

Fads

- Pie throwing, dance marathons, skateboards, mood rings, Spiderman.

Quotes

- "In addition to inflation, we have stagnating productivity.People don't work the way they used to."—Arthur Burns, chairman, Federal Reserve

Some of the year's memorable moments are described in the pages of WCC's student newspaper, *The Voice*:

WCC in 1975

- In February, Dean of Administration Dave Pollock assumes the position of Interim President as David Ponitz prepares to leave for Sinclair Community College. Ponitz is presented with a red apple plaque as a remembrance of "The Miracle in the Apple Orchard," along with a worm and the inscription, "Nothing's perfect."

- WCC's Xerox representative announces that WCC's duplicating room puts out more copy than any other machine in the county: 220,000 pages per month.

- 518 students are named to the winter dean's list, 150 children are enrolled in the Children's Center.

- The Affirmative Action Committee finds that the hiring of females on campus is "the greatest shortcoming in the employment practices at WCC," but the College gets an A for hiring minority members.

- WCC is ranked second in the nation for its occupational programs.

- Gunder Myran arrives as new WCC President, 347 students leave with diplomas at the June 21 Commencement.

- The Student Center Building is completed.

Chapter 10:

Change was in the Air

The average term of a community college president is five and a half years. Dave Ponitz doesn't remember forming any plan to leave after a decade at Washtenaw Community College, but a group of business people from Dayton, Ohio, had other ideas. In 1974, they came to talk to him about their goals and hopes for Sinclair Community College in Dayton.

"Sinclair had been founded as a private YMCA college, but it had just become public when its trustees contacted me," Ponitz explained many years later. The challenge for a new president would be tremendous, he was told. Sinclair was educating twenty-three thousand students who were working for college credits and another sixty-five thousand non-credit students. Dayton was home to more scientists and engineers than any other city of its size in the country, but it was also one of the poorest cities in the country. The job of the new community college president would include helping a large population of white Appalachians, African-Americans, and Hispanics understand how education and training could make a difference in their lives.

"I had begun to realize that I couldn't stay at WCC forever. Sinclair Community College was a bigger institution than WCC, with many challenges," Ponitz said. "My goal had always been to be a big city superintendent of schools. My decision to leave was not based upon feeling unhappy or restless at WCC. It was just time to move on and Sinclair Community College offered an interesting challenge."

Dave Ponitz accepted the job in Dayton. Because another vote for a WCC levy was planned for that fall and Ponitz was in the midst of his term as chairman of Ann Arbor's United Way campaign, he asked the people in Dayton to keep the news of his career move quiet.

Inevitably, word leaked out that the new Sinclair president would come from Washtenaw Community College. "His initials are D.P.," gossip reported. People approached Dave Pollock, asking him if he had a new job, and he told them, "I've never been to Dayton in my life."

"I didn't know at the time that Dave was looking, but I sensed that he had sand in his shoes," Pollock said.

In his last interview with the student newspaper, in January 1975, President Ponitz told *The Voice* reporter, "I never believed in the cult of personality. I don't think a president makes or breaks an institution."

He went on to reminisce about his successes and failures during his ten years in office. Washtenaw's affirmative action policy, the strength of the General Studies Program, and the caring and committed faculty were all cited as successes. "In the shadow of two outstanding universities, the General Studies Program stood on its own two feet," President Ponitz said proudly, adding, "Here at Washtenaw, students are given the opportunity to succeed, not fail."

He predicted—quite accurately, as history would show—that the student population would continue to grow rapidly in job training and innovative general studies courses, that more women and retired people would be seen on campus in future years. On the other hand, in some ways, WCC was moving more slowly than he had hoped, Ponitz admitted. "I would have liked to have had the Learning Resource Center, which is being constructed now, finished five or six years ago, but problems with the master plan prevented that." He ended the interview by saying that he was glad to have been a part of the College's history. "People see the institution as a national success for what it is doing," he said.

"The story is not what I, as President, have done, but what a lot of people have done—the Board, faculty, students, and the people of Washtenaw County," Ponitz told the reporter.

Dave Ponitz left for Dayton in February of 1975. Dave Pollock, the only "founding administrator" left on campus, was named interim president of Washtenaw Community College. Lee Luchsinger, Norm Olmsted, and Lloyd Van Buskirk had all departed years before, each to become a college president or school district superintendent. Dean Paul Hunt had later followed them.

IN SEARCH OF A PRESIDENT

As soon as the President's resignation was official, Tony Procassini, Chairman of the Board of Trustees, appointed fourteen people to the College's Advisory Search Committee: Ralph Banfield, David Byrd (Technical and Industrial instructor), Frank Comstock, Albert J. Coudron, James Davenport (Exact Sciences Division instructor), WCC Counselor Marguerite Eaglin, WCC Alumnus Dewey Eubanks Sr., Helen Gooding, WCC students Lucy Gorno and Nick Watson, WCC Registrar Alton L. Kleinhenn, WCC Personnel Manager Harry J. Konschuh, Donald Parrett, and Elvira Vogel. "We tried to include students, faculty, administrators, and staff members, involved community leaders, and people knowledgeable in hiring," Procassini said. The search committee also had the help of two consultants: Joseph Consand, director of the Center for the Study of Higher Education at the University of Michigan, and Evart W. Ardis, former WCC Trustee and Director of the University of Michigan's Career Planning and Placement.

"This was, perhaps, one of the most thorough and excellent committees that I ever worked on—and I've worked on many," Elvira Vogel said in a 1982 interview for an oral history project. "This committee really represented the interests of the county." She and the other committee members realized that their job was to fill a very large set of shoes. "I think that everyone in the county felt that David Ponitz had been a great choice as a first president," Evart Ardis said in his interview for the same history project. "He had tremendous verbal skills and credibility. He met people in each of the county's communities and he made them all feel that they owned a piece of the College. He was a great outside administrator with the legislature. We couldn't have had a better person help us establish the College."

Building on what President Ponitz established, the Board decided to look—"and rightly so," Ardis added, "for someone with a different personality, because it would be hard to beat Dr. Ponitz in the areas of his great skill." They decided to focus on finding "an inside person," someone who would focus on staff development, College development, and refinement of the curriculum. "At that point, the College buildings were pretty much underway, College programs were started, and the staff had been together," Ardis said. "The Board looked for a person to help refine and develop the good start that had been made."

Procassini added, "When we were looking for a new president, we were looking for a little different skill set than Dave had. No two people are going to be alike and different people bring different job

skills, strengths, and weaknesses. We were looking for someone who could consolidate all the effort that Dave Ponitz and his crew had put together....At that time, with the College now established within our community, we felt that we needed to shift our attention from the outside to the inside." The Board also looked for someone who would commit to staying, according to Trustee Ann Cleary Kettles. "A presidential search is a tremendously long process and very time-consuming. We didn't want to go through that again any time soon."

The committee knew they had something exciting and good to offer candidates. "WCC was a very interesting place in those days," recalled Richard W. Bailey, who was sworn onto the Board of Trustees one month before Dave Ponitz left the College. "In 1975, WCC had a little more than 4,000 students and a budget of seven million dollars. There was a very strong family atmosphere here. Everyone had been hired at the same time and had shared similar experiences in getting the College off the ground. There was a sense of shared mission."

WCC has always been blessed with honorable and hard-working Trustees. Richard W. Bailey (right, front) was sworn into service on the Board one month before President David Ponitz left the College. Serving with him were (rear, l-r): Ann Cleary Kettles, Anthony J. Procassini, Sally Buxton, Phillip Wells, (front, l-r): Fulton Eaglin, and David Heebink.

While faculty and staff members speculated about what changes would come to the College with a new president, Board members set out to identify the best candidates. "We wrote ads, brochures, and pamphlets, telling people about our College and our requirements," Elvira Vogel recalled. "We also had a tremendously long list of institutions and placement services that were the recipients of our materials."

One hundred sixteen educators applied for the job. A subcommittee of the search committee reviewed every candidate's resumé closely, then reduced the number to thirty-two, who were interviewed by phone. Sixteen were interviewed in person.

Vogel remembered renting several conference rooms and conducting interviews straight through three days. "We had set up the criteria long before, and we designed a worksheet based on those criteria to help us evaluate the candidates," she said. "We had a secretarial staff available to type the person's background and previous experience so we all had that information before us when we interviewed." To their surprise—and relief—the committee members discovered that they had a firm consensus. "We were all on target," Vogel said. The committee narrowed the number of candidates to five.

Procassini and several other Board members visited the final candidates' colleges, talking to the staff, administrators, and faculty. Then the Board met and voted. "It was a unanimous decision. That's the way you want to have it," Procassini said.

Gunder Myran was asked to become the second Washtenaw Community College President.

Bailey remembered the transition as a smooth and well-run process. "It took us about a year to hire a new president and during that time Dave Pollock did a good job at holding down the fort. I don't recall any administrators leaving during that time, no turnover. Everyone was very happy with the choice of Gunder, eager to work with him, eager to see him succeed."

PRESIDENTIAL MATERIAL

"We liked Gunder Myran's ability to look ahead and plan—those were important characteristics for the College's second president and for the College's second decade," Trustee Ann Cleary Kettles said. "I became a real fan of Gunder's. He was an outstanding president. Over time, he developed the same ability Dave Ponitz had to bring people together and work with diverse groups, to establish a consensus to make things happen."

Gunder Myran was forty years old when he left his position as dean of instruction and acting president at Rockland Community College and moved into the President's office at Washtenaw Community College.

A native of Minnesota, Myran earned his bachelor of business science degree from Mankato State College in 1957, his master of arts degree in education at the University of Iowa in 1961, and his doctorate in education from Michigan State University in 1969. While at MSU, he spent four years as an associate professor in higher education, then moved on to Rockland Community College. He was offered the Washtenaw job in the summer of 1975, when his wife and three sons were vacationing at their summer home in northern Michigan. He accepted immediately and was on campus when the fall semester opened.

Gunder Myran, second Washtenaw Community College President, arrived on campus in 1975.

In September 1975, *The Voice* reported that the College's second president intended to "continue the direction of the school and its emphasis on vocational and technological programs," but also "develop approaches to keep pace with the twentieth century."

When Gunder Myran first stepped across the threshold, the College itself was stepping across the threshold of a whole new era—in more ways than one. The Vietnam War had ended and veterans were flooding classrooms, but women were coming close to equaling the number of male students at WCC. In 1966, twenty-three percent of all students had been women; in 1976, forty-six percent were women. Just as significantly, the rise in the number of women was occurring across the entire curriculum, from American studies to welding. Although the representation was smallest in the Technical and Industrial Program, women's numbers had risen from seven to twelve percent. Dean of Student Services Jim Jones credited the rise in women to the daycare center, which, in 1976, would accommodate ninety-eight children from seventy families. Another important factor, Jones said, was the women faculty members, who provided strong role models; one-quarter of WCC's faculty members were women in 1975.

"What struck me when I first saw WCC was how committed the faculty was," Myran said many years later. "They had a deep and caring concern for their students. No administration can create that level of commitment. It must come from the faculty members themselves."

During his first weeks in office, Gunder Myran discovered much to admire, but also some need for change. "Although the interim period had gone well and the College was working just fine, personnel was an issue," Richard W. Bailey said. "Years later, I learned that it's quite common on new community college campuses to get faculty members and administrators who are winners and also a fair number of duds. That's because the colleges hire so many people at once and in a hurry. WCC needed to weed out those duds. It would be up to the new president to face that issue."

Myran discovered few surprises at the College, he said later. "Dave Ponitz had been an excellent president and had done a fine job of laying the groundwork. This was not an institution in trouble. By the time I arrived, WCC was already well respected in the community, its Board and administration were providing good leadership, and the students were flourishing. The conflicts over Vietnam, students' rights, and civil rights were all in the past."

People quickly learned that the management styles of Gunder Myran and David Ponitz were very different. "Gunder's style was very much consultative. He believes that everyone wants to do a good job and that his job is to enable them to find a way to do that," Bailey observed. "People were very sorry to see Dave Ponitz go and they worried that the college would fall apart without him. But, after we gave Gunder a chance, we realized that he was a man with super vision," said Technical and Industrial Instructor Bill Figg. "We realized that Gunder would guide the College wisely."

For some, the transition between presidents was difficult. David Ponitz had hired an administrative staff full of "doers and hip-shooters," Andy Ford explained. "In the College's first couple of years, we could move overnight to respond to crises or student needs. The price you pay for this kind of situation is continuity and stability. My file cabinets in those days were never in perfect order; that's just one example of what falls by the wayside at times like those. As WCC matured, our kind of people were no longer required."

Using Evart Ardis's analogy, he pointed out, "Once the College was established, we needed store-minders and people to manage a stable, measured, solid growth of the college. That's the type of administrator that Gunder Myran was and the kind of people that he brought in. The changes were necessary, but the transition was a culture shock for those of us who had been here from the beginning."

Despite the culture shock, Ford and others at the College realized that WCC needed "a President for the next generation of growth." Over time, Gunder Myran would introduce new programs and new people, lead the way in reaching an ever more diverse group of students, excel at community relations, and help resolve union issues—"which had been at such a low point when he arrived," Bailey said.

The new President decided not to bring in a new team of administrators, but to work with the people already on campus. "I wanted the campus to maintain its comfort level, so I decided just to pick up where Dave Ponitz had left off," he said. "As situations required changes, we made them."

Washtenaw Community College has been blessed with its presidents, many faculty members and former students observed. "Our second WCC President turned out to be everything we hoped he would be," Ardis observed years earlier. "It has always offered the type of challenges that attract the best faculty and presidents," said former student and WCC lobbyist Gary Owen. "This place has high expectations and great demands—but also offers great personal rewards." Roger Bertoia added, "Dr. Ponitz laid the foundation of WCC. Dr. Myran built on it and left it in extraordinary economic health." "David Ponitz and Gunder Myran were very different, but each had his own strengths,"Ann Cleary Kettles said. "They were both good for the College at the time. Dave Ponitz was an excellent initiator. Gunder Myran turned out to be an excellent manager."

"Dr. Myran was 180 degrees different from Dr. Ponitz, but that was what the Board of Trustees had been looking for," Zeeb said. "The change in our presidents' personalities reflected the change in the College's situation and the change in the times."

By 1982, Evart Ardis had been involved in the selection of more than eighty superintendents of schools, but he told his interviewer, "I think of all the institutions that I have watched in the last fifty years, WCC was as fortunate as any in the choice of administrators. The two personalities have been, to me, most appropriate for the period in the history of the development of the College."

■ ■ ■

Three decades after his departure from Washtenaw Community College, David Ponitz pondered the question of whether he would have done anything at WCC differently.

"Lots of things," he responded. "It would have been wonderful to have started the College after having a year or two of planning, but the timing wasn't right for that. We were drawing tax dollars, and we worried that we would lose people if we didn't move quickly. Probably the biggest mistake I made was in trying to reach too far too fast. We were trying hard to fill every perceived need immediately." He also expressed regrets about the short time the administrators had to interview, hire, and introduce faculty members to the College. "We should have spent more time with the faculty," he said.

But hindsight is indeed easier than foresight. "We made some mistakes, but they were mistakes made with the best of intentions," Ponitz said. "We stressed innovation and with innovation comes risks."

FINAL THOUGHTS

Those who were present at the creation of Washtenaw Community College continue to be astounded at its success in growing from absolutely nothing. "It happened so fast," marveled Guy Hower. "When I came, there were no counselors, no school buildings, few administrators, no faculty, no catalogue. Six months later, we were serving 1,200 students."

"We stumbled, we stammered, we were clumsy, and we tripped, but we made our way and we did very, very well," Don Bylsma observed. "In 1965 and 1966, the Board of Trustees and the administration had an important choice to make: they could spend years planning and building and then open the College or they could open and then build and plan. Our experience proved that a lot of advance planning is not always the best way to accomplish something. We did a good job starting out from scratch. WCC is a marriage between the school (faculty, staff, administration, students) and the community. If we hadn't worked together as a team, we wouldn't have been so successful."

Those who came and stayed shared David Ponitz's fierce commitment to work together to make the institution succeed and to help students succeed—"and we all maintained that approach to students, to the college, and to each other through the years," Ron Zeeb said. "That's what made the college work. That attitude was so strongly established in the early years that it continues even today."

Although the "shoot-from-the-hip" early years were followed by an era of introspection, development, and refinement, Washtenaw Community College continued to maintain its ability to quickly adapt to changing times, changing needs, and changing enrollment trends. "The great thing about WCC is that every fall it changes and grows and rediscovers itself," Roger Bertoia said. Yet through it all, WCC maintains its "fierce commitment" to serve the community. "This is truly a Community College—owned, established, and supported by the community," Bill Moy said. "WCC is of the people's making and for the people's needs."

Just as the community gave its resources and efforts to start the College, the College has given back to the community, in countless ways outside the classroom. Generations of WCC musicians have performed at University of Michigan football games, community festivals, theaters, and churches. College buildings have hosted business and civic functions. The College has developed mutually beneficial relationships with thousands of area businesses, non-profit organizations, and benevolent organizations. "Sclumberger, a Belgian corporation, drew on WCC strength in computing and machining to sell products to manufacturers, and that collaborative model was followed by Eaton, General Motors, and Ford," Bailey pointed out. Many companies use WCC as a training site, sometimes drawing on WCC faculty for instructors. The United Association of Plumbers and Pipefitters has made WCC the national home for teaching the teachers who introduce new methods in the locals throughout North America. Their annual two-week on-campus experience in August brings several million dollars to the hospitality industry.

WCC now ranks as one of the state's most outstanding community colleges, according to former Vice President Harry Konschuh. "I have no question about that," he said. "There are many reasons why I say this. First of all, we have one of the best faculties in the State of Michigan. Also, our students are able to transfer easily to fine four-year universities and do well. Our graduates from the occupational programs are able to get very good jobs at good pay. Our facilities are excellent, far above other community colleges. The community support of the College is phenomenal. You can go anywhere in the state and meet expert professionals who are proud to say that they were trained at WCC."

This Community College was designed as a place where people could begin to grow and mature—and even get a second chance. Its goal was to provide people from all walks of life with the opportunity to develop and upgrade their skills in order to get good-paying jobs. "That was our mission when our doors opened and we continue to focus on that mission," Bill Moy said. "WCC has always been a great place to incubate, to develop warm, caring, meaningful relationships with faculty and staff. It's a great place to take time out to think, consider, plan, and prepare for the future."

Like many of her colleagues, Edith Croake said she has always felt fortunate to teach at WCC. "It remains one of those happy circumstances in life," she added. "I had never considered teaching in a community college, but once I was here, I knew it was the right place for me." Ron Zeeb echoed that thought, explaining, "Looking back, I would never have anticipated being in one place for so many years, but WCC became home. I couldn't have picked a better institution to work for." Guy Hower said that was because WCC has always been "stimulating, changing, and committed to doing its very best on behalf of its students."

Many former students shared Edith Croake's "happy circumstances." "I have a hard time envisioning better circumstances or situations than what happened to me at WCC—and I would say that a very high percentage of the other students during the early years would agree with me," Gary Owen said. "We were all very, very pleased with our educational opportunities. Many of Washtenaw's graduates went on to become very, very successful people."

Gary Owen was by no means the only person to begin a new life journey at WCC. Owen's journey took him from a public housing project in Alabama to the most powerful position in the Michigan legislature, as Speaker of the House. His political influence brought "Eagle Crest" to Ypsilanti and built the College of Business at Eastern Michigan University. The journeys some of his classmates chose may have been less meteoric, but equally satisfying. Bailey noted, "Dillard Roy Craiger, long-time county commissioner, obtained his GED here, certifying the talents that made him powerful in Washtenaw County. Lana Pollack was a part-time dance instructor at the College before being elected to the Ann Arbor School Board and then to the Michigan Senate. Gus Stagert, son of the University of Michigan swimming coach, was a student, then an instructor, and finally a successful entrepreneur in numerical-control machine tools." Every teacher and administrator has a list of student success stories stretching back over the years.

WCC quickly became a vehicle for upward mobility, Bailey said. "It has always been a very giving place, and everyone has worked hard to make it a place of opportunity, especially for the invisible poor." Thousands of students entered clerical jobs as confident users of word-processing and spreadsheet software, thanks to WCC instruction. Police officers and prison guards honed their skills in everything from marksmanship to crime-scene analysis at WCC. Licensed Practical Nurses gained their Registered Nurse status at the College and went on to increasingly responsible positions. Thousands of welders trained on campus used their skills to forge the Alaska pipeline. Bailey remembered a bartender at a local restaurant who studied numerical control at WCC and landed a job making $35,000— "which was more than I was being paid as an assistant professor," Bailey said. "That's what WCC is all about." A testimony to that fact is an anonymous $20,000 gift to the College from a former prison inmate/student who credits WCC with giving him a chance at a new life.

Many students already holding bachelor's—and even graduate— degrees enrolled in College classes to pursue avocations that turned into vocations. Bailey suggested that this is true particularly in the auto restoration and construction programs. One woman who came to WCC to learn how to build a dog house ended up with full-time employment in residential construction. Local photographer Lynne Pryor took a photography class for fun and turned a hobby into a highly successful business. Field biology courses have encouraged many to become active in environmental restoration. The Culinary Arts Program has prepared countless food-lovers for second careers in catering, restaurant work, or the bed-and-breakfast business. The list goes on and on.

Don Bylsma marvels at the impact the College has had on so many people's lives. He cites Gwen Arnold as one of his favorite examples. "She started as a secretary, took advantage of the free tuition at WCC, then went on to earn her advanced degree. Later, she joined the faculty here. WCC has enhanced the lives of more people than we will ever know." Rosalyn Biederman said that she found it very satisfying to realize that the College's initial devotion to the students' success "still lives in the WCC of today."

The College's counseling office did a masterful job of coordinating transfer status with Eastern Michigan University and the University of Michigan, thanks to the efforts of Ralph Banfield, former assistant in the University of Michigan President's Office. With his help, the way to higher education was paved for countless WCC students. Meanwhile, the Occupational Studies administrators and faculty closely coordinated their programs with local industries, which paved the way to careers and job upgrades for thousands of other students through the years. A significant number of WCC graduates went on to higher education and/or vocational work, then returned to teach, among them Technical and Industrial Instructor Bill Figg. "For me, WCC has been a life-changing experience," he said. "After four decades, WCC continues to building my life in positive directions. I know I'm not alone in believing that WCC changes lives."

AND THE COLLEGE MATURES...

WCC has excelled at handling situations and challenges neither foreseen nor anticipated by the first Board of Trustees, said Trustee Richard W. Bailey, who cited the Perkins Act as one example. Legislation in the 1970s provided educational opportunities for displaced homemakers (divorced or widowed women with few or no job skills outside the home), and resulted in a highly successful program at WCC. The Black Student Union and women's center are other examples of responses to changing times.

On the other hand, some challenges anticipated in 1966 never materialized. One month after WCC opened its doors on the temporary campus in Willow Run Village, an educational consulting firm told Board members that WCC should expect to handle sixteen thousand students while building a third permanent campus by 1980. Those predictions were far off the mark, but what wasn't off the mark was the College's commitment to a quality education for every student who knocked on the College doors. "I would argue that there has been great continuity over the years. The Board has always acted in unison and supported the mission of the Community College," Bailey said. For instance, WCC still offers students remedial programs, if they need them. "That emphasis was present at the start of the College and it is still there, I'm glad to say," Dennis Bila said. "We still take everyone who walks through our doors. Every once in a while there is talk of limiting who can enroll, but the Board of Trustees remains very committed to its original stand, the stand it took back in 1965. I applaud them for that."

Washtenaw's Board is extremely—and rightfully—proud of the fact that a Board member has never misused the public trust in any way. Richard W. Bailey and Ann Cleary Kettles attributed that achievement to the Board's continuity through the years and the high degree of integrity on the part of each Board member. Tony Procassini credited the first Board with establishing sound fundamental practices that served subsequent Boards well. "One of the reasons that the College has been a success and that we've gotten our millage is that the Boards have always had very, very solid people dedicated to serving the community," he said.

Traditionally, Board members have worked together amiably, with every member focusing upon a particular area of expertise. "We would defer to the people who had specific knowledge when different issues came up," Kettles said. In her era, members turned to Henry Landau for building issues, Sally Buxton and Dick Creal for educational questions, Bill Bott for community relations, and Tony Procassini for union negotiations.

Another key reason for the Board's continuing success through four decades has been its new member orientation program, Kettles said. "During the orientation, we would teach new Board members what boardship is all about. We went on retreats together to strengthen our working relationships. We quickly learned that the Board's role was not to micromanage the president, the Board has always worked through the chain of command. We believed that a Board should choose a president, back him, and help him succeed." The Board also made a policy of keeping controversy out of its meetings as much as possible. "If a Board member had an issue, we would try to resolve it at an informal breakfast meeting prior to the Board meeting. We weren't publicly confrontational," Kettles said. "We tried not to air any dirty linen in public. We wanted to present a united front to the world."

"The Trustees were very, very visible and very involved," Betty Finkbeiner said. "Ralph Wenrich was one of Occupational Education's strongest supporters. An original member of the Board of Trustees, he was integral in establishing and supporting occupational education programs. He and Trustee Ann Kettles never missed a pinning or capping ceremony."

Don Bylsma is one of many charter members of Washtenaw Community College who noted that the College was blessed with the right people at the right time in the right place. Andy Ford added, "Working all together, community members, Trustees, administrators, faculty, staff, and students built an institution that we all can be proud of, an institution that is highly respected, an institution that has filled many people's educational needs."

Board member Jerry Jernigan is a veteran of the community college system. A graduate of Mott Community College (which was called Flint College at the time), he was the first member of his family to attend college. He went on to earn his bachelor's degree from Michigan State University and a Master of Business Administration degree from Western Michigan University before becoming involved in Ann Arbor politics. He served on the City Council from the late

Trustee Jerry Jernigan is a graduate of the Community College system.

1970s until 1982, and as mayor from 1987 until 1991. After he retired, he was elected to the WCC Board of Trustees in the 2002 election, which was noteworthy for having the largest number of candidates since the first election, in 1965.

Why did he run for the Board of Trustees? "Because community colleges can make such a difference in an individual's life," he said. "It certainly did for me, just as it has for generations of kids living here in Washtenaw County." Jernigan said that he also appreciated the College's heritage established in its first ten years. "I haven't met anyone associated with WCC who isn't truly committed to the institution. WCC goes out of its way to provide everything incoming students might need: tutors, scholarships, daycare, transportation, extracurricular activities, excellent teachers," he said. "It's just a wonderful place." And it is continuing to build on the foundation laid back in its first ten years by President Ponitz and the early Boards, administrators, faculty and staff members, he added.

One of WCC's great strengths over the years has been its ability to adapt so well to change, introducing new programs, computers, the daycare center, Student Resource and Women's Center and high-tech innovations at appropriate times. "We are limited only by our own imaginations," Jernigan said. "We're fortunate enough to be sitting on the best and strongest community college tax base in Michigan. Besides the area's financial benefits, people here strongly value education. We get a lot more money from millage (which provides fifty percent of our revenue) than other community colleges in Michigan do."

Looking down the road, Jernigan predicts that WCC's Board will focus on defining the core of its existence, determining who its students are, why they're coming, and what they truly need. "We have two questions we are constantly asking," Jernigan said. "One: Are we always on the cutting edge? And, two: Where are we in terms of innovation? We want our students to leave WCC as top-flight people in whatever field they choose. We want them to have the ability to think, problem solve, and fulfill their hopes and expectations."

■ ■ ■

"I feel that community colleges are truly democracy's college," Edith Croake said. "The Founding Fathers were clear about the need to educate the populace. Every college participates in this effort, but community colleges have a special responsibility to the people who haven't had previous success academically, to those whose family members did not attend college, to those who can't afford other educational institutions, and those who are often overlooked by four-year colleges. Community colleges respond to the needs and hopes of the ordinary citizen."

Many years ago, Evart Ardis offered a benediction for the College that still rings true:

> I have a strong hope for the future. I would hope that the Community College would become even more of a community center as facilities are added, such as a little theater, auditorium, and athletic facilities. I would like to see that whenever anything significant of a county-wide nature is planned, it would likely be on the campus of Washtenaw Community College. I would hope that people throughout the county would come there often for civic, political, and social activities because I think that would make it truly a community college.... I would hope that more and more in the future, Washtenaw Community College campus would become the center of those kinds of activities.

1976

- Vietnam is reunified; Hanoi is named capital; Saigon is renamed Ho Chi Minh City.

- Democrats nominate Jimmy Carter for president; Republicans nominate Gerald Ford. Carter wins the presidency by 1.7 million votes.

- The U.S. celebrates its Bicentennial with special events around the country; more than six million people watch the Tall Ships parade up the Hudson River.

- GNP: +10 percent. Inflation: 8.7 percent. Unemployment: 8.3 percent.

History & Politics

- 31 percent of recent high school graduates enter college.

- The U.S. Air Force Academy admits 155 women; ending the all-male tradition at the U.S. military academies.

- Number of four-year colleges: 1,913

- Public—to—private school ratio of students: 7.5 to 1.

Education

- Nielsen's Top Ten television shows include *Happy Days; Laverne and Shirley; ABC Monday Night Movie; M*A*S*H; Charlie's Angels; The Big Event; The Six-Million-Dollar Man; ABC Sunday Night Movie; Baretta; One Day at a Time.*

Television

- Hit songs: "Silly Love Songs," "Don't Go Breakin' My Heart," "Play That Funky Music," "A Fifth of Beethoven," "(Shake, Shake, Shake) Shake Your Booty," "Breaking Up Is Hard to Do," "Love Is Alive," "Sara Smile," "Get Closer."

Music

- On the big screen: *Rocky, All the President's Men, Network, Taxi Driver, The Sailor Who Fell from Grace with the Sea, King Kong, A Star Is Born, The Bad News Bears.*

- Top box-office stars: Robert Redford, Jack Nicholson, Dustin Hoffman, Clint Eastwood, Mel Brooks, Burt Reynolds, Al Pacino, Tatum O'Neal, Woody Allen, Charles Bronson.

Movies

Books

- *Ordinary People* (Judith Guest), *Trinity* (Leon Uris), *1876* (Gore Vidal), *Born on the Fourth of July* (Ron Kovic), *The Final Days* (Bob Woodward, Carl Bernstein), *Roots* (Alex Haley), *Your Erroneous Zones* (Dr. Wayne Dyer), *Born Again* (Chuck Colson), *The Hite Report: A Nationwide Study of Female Sexuality* (Shere Hite).

Sports

- Pitcher Mark "The Bird" Fydrich (Detroit; American League) wins Rookie of the Year, and fans love to talk about his antics.

- Rob Lyttle of Michigan is named College All-American.

- The University of Michigan loses Rose Bowl to California, 14-6.

Quotes

- "It's the Me-Decade."—Tom Wolfe; *New York magazine*

- "This is the time of hedonism,...narcissism,...the cult of the self."—Christopher Lasch; *New York Review of Books*

- "What we've succeeded in doing in the Sixties was dealing with the constitutional issue of rights. We've won that battle....(Now) we're dealing with real equality."—James Farmer; former head; CORE

WCC in 1976

Some of the year's highlights are revealed in the pages of *The Voice*:

- 1,300 veterans enroll in the fall semester, but they face difficulties in obtaining veterans' benefits. Robert Tavernier, chairman of WCC's Committee on Veterans' Benefits, urges all students to sign a petition asking the Senate to pass Bill 969, which expands veterans' educational benefits.

- Bob Bellers, supervisor in the electrical lab, states that academics in occupational programs depends upon "a student's intellect, not their sex." Jan Werst, a student in the two-year numerical control program, notes that she has encountered some skepticism in her (all male) fellow students' attitudes, but says, "I just hope I get as good money as a man would get going into the same area."

- Twenty-six percent of WCC students are over 30 years old. There are 51 students over the age of 70.

Epilogue

What was started some forty years ago, that fierce commitment to create an egalitarian institution that would offer high-quality, low-cost education to local communities all across this country, is still the driving philosophy of community colleges today. As you have seen by reading the stories of those individuals who were there at the beginning of the community college movement, we continue to be true to our mission. It is gratifying to look back and review our path and the sources of our strength. By doing so, we are better able to understand how to proceed into the future.

Our job is not done. Every year hundreds of thousands of young people drop out of school before they earn their high school diploma; while at the same time the demand for more education in order to be economically viable continues to increase. In the past, individuals could earn a living wage by finding employment in manufacturing and other low skill jobs; now those jobs are being lost to other countries at a disturbing and alarming rate. These low-skill jobs will continue to disappear until the only option for an individual will be to become a knowledge worker.

The acquisition of knowledge and the development of up-to-date job skills are crucial for individuals and their families. They are also critical to the long-term health of our national economy. In order to maintain our strategic advantage and our societal structures, we must stop the burgeoning disillusionment of the middle class and the division of our society into haves and have-nots with an ever-growing gap between the two. This is where the community college plays a leading role. Only by building broad-based educational foundations can we hope to create and maintain a workforce that can ensure that America's standard of living will continue to grow. This will happen if community colleges continue to be empowered to offer training and retraining that provide people with job skills that enable them to adapt to a quickly changing work environment.

The challenge before us is massive. However, our forty-year history of working in this arena will enable us to succeed in helping individuals and the nation in the achievement of our economic and societal goals as long as we maintain the energy, commitment and passion for our mission.

Those Who Have Served the College...

Former Board Members

Mr. Edward Adams Jr.	January 1965–December 1972
Mr. James W. Anderson Jr.	January 1979–December 1996
Ms. Mary Claire Anhut	January 1991–December 1996
Dr. Evart W. Ardis	January 1965–December 1972
Mr. William J. Bott	January 1969–December 1972
Mr. Richard L. Boyd	January 1977–December 1982
Ms. Mary Branch	January 1999–February 2004
Mr. William M. Broucek	December 1973–December 1974
Ms. Sally Buxton	January 1973–December 1978
Mr. J. Douglas Cook	January 1967–December 1968
Mr. John W. Corey	April 1983–September 1987
Dr. Richard C. Creal	January 1965–December 1973
Mr. William J. Davis Jr.	January 1993–December 1998
Mr. Fulton B. Eaglin	January 1976–December 1976
Mr. Robert G. Forman	January 1967–December 1970
Mr. James B. Gilligan Jr.	January 1983–March 1983
Mr. Samuel T. Harmon	January 1965–December 1966
Ms. Marcia Harrison	January 1985–December 1990
Mr. Vanzetti M. Hamilton	January 1981–January 1991
Dr. David V. Heebink	January, 1971–December 1976
Mrs. Ann C. Kettles	January 1973–December 1984
Mr. Harry J. Konschuh	January 1997–December 2002
Mr. Henry S. Landau	January 1977–December 1982
Dr. Susan M. Madley	January 1983–July 1987
Ms. Nancy N. Margolis	July 1987–December 1994
Mr. William Mays Jr.	January 1975–November 1975
Mr. R. Griffith McDonald	January 1989–December 2000
Dr. Ruth H. Moorman	April 1991–December 1998
Mr. Anthony J. Procassini	November 1966–December 1992
Mr. Robert C. Ressler	August 1972–December 1974

Mrs. Judy Shelton	January 1977–December 1980
Dr. Phillip G. Wells	January 1971–December 1976
Mr. Ralph C. Wenrich	January 1965–December 1970
Mr. Kenneth Yourd	January 1965–December 1966

Current Board Members
(January 2003 through Present)

Dr. Richard W. Bailey	January 1975
Mr. Gerald D. Jernigan	January 2003
Mr. Richard J. Landau	January 2001
Mr. Roger Lane	April 2004
Ms. Diana McKnight-Morton	January 1995
Mr. David E. Rutledge	January 1997
Ms. Mary B. Schroer	January 1999

Glossary of Names

Adams Jr.	Edward	Treasurer of first Board of Trustees, 1965–1972
Agnew	Ezell	Building and Grounds staff member
Alexander	William (Bill)	Biology instructor
Allen	Jim	Student, member of the first basketball team
Allen	Wyeth	Director of the Community College Implementation Committee, civic leader
Amaru	Augustine (Gus)	Political Science instructor
Anthony	Mel	Counselor
Arcure	Catherine	Member of *Link-Up* staff
Ardis	Evart	Member of first Board of Trustees, 1965–1972; consultant for the College's first Presidential Advisory Search Committee 1975
Arnold	Gwen	Secretary; later instructor and then chair of the Business Department
Askew	Zonnie	Student, member of the first basketball team
Bailey	Richard W.	Member of the Board of Trustees since January 1975
Balbus	Joe	Head of Pediatrics at the University of Michigan Medical School, he certified the College's daycare center
Baldwin	Tom	Student, member of the 1967 bowling team; president of the Student Senate
Banfield	Ralph	Member, Advisory Search Committee seeking new President 1975
Barron	Ken	Automotive Services instructor
Belknap	Chuck	Math instructor
Belkola	Floyd	Auto Body Repair instructor
Bellers	Clifford	Physical Education, Business instructor; coached first cross country team, 1968
Berry	Rick	Student, member of the 1967 baseball team
Bertoia	Roger	Drafting instructor, later Dean of Occupational Education
Bickner	Robert	Academic counselor
Biederman	Rosalyn	Spanish instructor
Biggers	Dave	Student, member of the 1967 basketball team
Bila	Dennis	Math instructor, chair of Math Department; president of the WCCEA (Faculty Union)
Bjornstad	Mildred	Willow Run High School teacher
Boatwright	Bill	Student, member of the first basketball team
Bostwick	Phyllis	Secretary, later became the administrator in charge of Secretarial Support Services
Bott	Bill	Director of the Ann Arbor Chamber of Commerce; member of the Ann Arbor Chamber of Commerce Education Committee, member of the Board of Trustees, 1969–1972
Bottorff	Ralph	Math instructor; instrumental in establishing the College Math Lab, 1966
Bowen	Bob	Student, member of the 1967 WCC bowling team

Brakken	Bob	Student, member of the 1967 WCC bowling team
Brayton	Betty	Student, Dental Assistant Program
Brengle	Gerry	Secretary to President Ponitz, later secretary to the Board of Trustees
Bryne	Emmett	Student, member of the 1967 bowling team
Burden	Dennis	Academic counselor
Buxton	Sally	Member of the Board of Trustees, 1973–1978
Bylsma	Don	Sociology instructor, instrumental in launching WCC's Black Studies Program
Byrd	David	Architecture instructor, member of the Advisory Search Committee seeking new President 1975
Charlton	Eleanor	Secretarial Science instructor
Chasteen	Dr. Joe	Dental Assistant instructor
Cherniak	Bill	Director of the English, Speech and Language Division
Comstock	Frank	Member of the Advisory Search Committee seeking new President 1975
Comstock	Lee	Student, member of the 1967 bowling team
Cook	J. Douglas	Member, Board of Trustees, January 1967–December 1968
Coudron	Albert J.	Member of the Advisory Search Committee seeking new President 1975
Counsand	Joseph	Consultant for 1975 Presidential Search Committee; University of Michigan's Director for the Center for the Study of Higher Education
Craiger	Dillard Roy	County Commissioner who obtained his GED at WCC
Crawford	Sophie	Reading instructor
Creager	Jim	Political Science instructor
Creal	Richard	Member of the Board of Trustees, 1965–1966
Croake	Edith	English instructor
Davenport	James	Education Media Specialist, then Exact Sciences instructor; member of the Advisory Search Committee seeking new President in 1975
DeShano	Paul	Student, member of the school's first basketball team and the 1967 bowling team
DuHart	Edith	Student, member of the Jestettes
Eaglin	Fulton	Member of the Board of Trustees, January 1976–December 1976
Eaglin	Marguerite	Counselor and member of the Advisory Search Committee seeking new president 1975
Edwards	Brenda	Student, member of the Jestettes
Elchuck	Dave	Student, member of the 1967 bowling team
Eubanks	Dewey	Member, Advisory Search Committee seeking new President in 1975
Figg	Bill	Student, later became a Welding instructor
Finkbeiner	Betty	Dental Assistant instructor
Fleming	Robben	President of the University of Michigan
Fleszar	Theresa	Clerk, Registrar's Office
Ford	Andy	Director of Technical and Industrial Studies
Forman	Robert G.	Member of the Board of Trustees, 1967–1970

Franzblau	Jarvis and Pearl	Owned the apple orchard where the College located its main campus in 1966
French	Gargi	Chemistry instructor
Fulbright	Coy	WCC mailroom staff member
Garrett	Don	Culinary Arts instructor; later chair of the program
Glusac	Ivan	Economics instructor
Glushyn	Diana	Started as a staff member for *Link-Up*, eventually became Supervisor of Clerical Services
Gooding	Helen	Member of the Advisory Search Committee seeking new President in 1975
Gorno	Lucy	Student, member of the Advisory Search Committee seeking new President in 1975
Graves	Larry	Student, baseball player
Gray	Dan	Welding instructor
Griswold	George	Chemistry instructor, instrumental in establishing the College's Testing Center, later Dean of Math and Natural Sciences Division
Grzegorczyk	Phyllis	Nursing student, later became an instructor and the Dean of Health and Public Services
Hackney	Larry	Dean of Students in the 1970s
Hakeem	Ivan	Sociology instructor
Hammond	Carl	Respiratory Therapy instructor
Hanna	Dorothy	Library staff member
Hanson	Charlotte	Speech instructor
Harmon	Sam	Chair of first Board of Trustees; Board member 1965–1966
Harrington	Robert	Information coordinator for the Community College Implementation Committee
Hatcher	Harlan	President of the University of Michigan and strong supporter of the community college concept
Hawkins	Willie	Student, member of the 1967 bowling team
Haynes	Jerry	Student, member of the school's first basketball team
Heebrink	David	Member of the Board of Trustees, January 1971–December 1976
Henderson	Anna	Student, member of the Jestettes
Hicks	Judy	Library staff member
Hill	John	Student, member of the 1968 cross-country team
Hill	Tom	Hired in early 1970s to represent the College in negotiations with short-lived administrative union
Holmes	Howard	Financial supporter instrumental in funding the preliminary survey to establish community support for a new college
Horowitz	Frederick	Art instructor
Hower	Guy	College's first counselor, later Coordinator then Director of Counseling; Director, Financial Aid
Hunt	Paul	First Dean of Occupational Education
Jackson	Robert L.	Charter College employee
Jelnick	Bill	College's Business Manager; later Dean of Business Operations
Jernigan	Jerry	Member of the Board of Trustees, 2002 to present

Johnson	Mary	Manager, WCC bookstore
Johnson	Walt	Student, member of the school's first basketball team
Jones	Jim	Black Student Union representative in 1969, later a Psychology instructor, and then Dean of Students
Jones	Lola	Academic counselor, Student Activities Office staff member
Kapp	George	Student, later became a Physics instructor
Keresteszi	Mike	Library Director during the 1960s
Kettles	Ann Cleary	Member of the Board of Trustees 1973–1984; Chair, 1981–1984
Kleinhenn	Alton	College Registrar and member of the Advisory Search Committee seeking new President 1975
Kokkales	Paul	Business instructor
Konschuh	Harry	Dean of Employee Relations, subsequently named Vice President for Administration and Finance, member of Advisory Search Committee seeking new President 1975. Member of the Board of Trustees, 1997–2002
Lamminen	Arthur	Director of Business and Industrial Management Division
Landau	Henry	Member of the Board of Trustees, 1977–1982
Laursen	Dan	Geology instructor
Lawrence Jr.	Morris	Music instructor
Leonard	Sylvester	Member, Community College Implementation Committee; Washtenaw County Treasurer
Lewis	Bill	Math instructor
Lockard	Jon Onye	Art instructor
Lowe	Burton	Industrial Technology instructor
Luchsinger	Lee	Executive Assistant to the Board of Trustees
Mallory	Richard	First Purchasing Director
Mann	John	Student, later instructor in the Automotive Program
Martin	Gayle	Student, later a Dance instructor
Martin	Herb	Psychology instructor
Mayhew	Mike	Student, member of the first basketball team
McClatchey	Merrill	Speech and Film instructor, influential in faculty union
McClellan	Elwood ("Woody")	English instructor during the late 1960s
McDonald	Jim	Chair, Ann Arbor Chamber of Commerce Education Committee in late 1950s
McGill	John	Math instructor, created a computer lab for special needs students
McKevitt	John	Member, Community College Implementation Committee
Mealing	Percy	Math instructor; instrumental in establishing the College's Math Lab, fall 1966
Miller	Sue	Member of the *Link-Up* staff
Morgan	Jerry	Student, 1967, president of the Student Senate that choose the College colors of green and white
Morgan	Lester	Welding instructor
Mortensen	Gary	Student, member of the 1967 bowling team

Moy	Bill	Psychology instructor; instrumental in establishing the College daycare center
Myran	Gunder	President, 1975–1998
Nelson	Robert	Radiography instructor
Niehaus	Paul	Instructor, Exact Sciences Division; counselor; first president of WCCEA, 1967
Olmsted	Norm	First Dean of General Studies
Orr	Margot	Librarian hired in 1971
Owen	Gary	Student; later Speaker of the House, State of Michigan
Parrett	Donald	Member of the Advisory Search Committee seeking new President 1975
Patt	Jerry	Business instructor
Patton	Gerry	Dental Assistant instructor
Paulson	Robert	Agri-business instructor
Perigo	Bill	College basketball coach
Phibbs	John	Student, currently Manager of Archives and Records Management
Pittman	Bill	Head of the Buildings and Grounds Department
Plummer	Robert	Director of Social Sciences; instrumental in establishing the campus daycare center, later called the Family Education Program
Pogliano	Michael	Architectural Drafting instructor
Pollack	Lana	Dance instructor, later elected to the Ann Arbor School Board and to the Michigan Senate
Pollock	David	First Executive Assistant to the President, subsequently Dean of Students, interim President in 1975
Ponitz	David	President 1967–1975
Poole	Milton	Chemistry instructor
Procassini	Tony	Member of the first Board of Trustees, 1966–1992; Chair 1973–1981
Pryor	Lynne	Student, later a successful local photographer
Radick	Lawrence	Foreign Language instructor
Real	Mike	Student, member of the 1967 bowling team
Reddick Parker	Bella	Instructor, counselor, Secretarial Skills Department, first Secretary of the CCEA, in 1967; Dean of Business 1989–2000
Rees	Gerald	Physics instructor
Reeves	Cornelius	Power House staff member
Reeves	Robert	Speech instructor, president of the WCCEA, subsequently Associate Vice President for Human Relations
Reps	Flavia	History instructor
Ressler	Robert	Member of the Board of Trustees, 1972–1974
Roberts	Alvin	Psychology instructor, first Director for Black Studies Program, resident of the Student–Faculty Assembly
Roberts	Dianna Hale	Student, Dental Assistant Program
Roberts	Shirley	College's clinical psychologist, then Director of the first Family Education Program and later Dean of Enrollment and Student Services

Ross	Donald	Math instructor, instrumental in establishing the College Math Lab, fall 1966
Rowland	Vivian	Member of the *Link-Up* staff
Russeau	Art	Student, member of the 1967 baseball team
Russell	Donna	Member of the *Link-Up* staff
Russell	Dean	Electronics instructor
Sabada	Mary	Secretary, later became head of Personnel
Sanderson	Larry	Student, member of the 1967 bowling team
Schmunk	Charles	Student, member of the school's first basketball team
Schreiber	Nicholas	Chair of the Chamber's Citizen's Steering Committee founded by the Ann Arbor Chamber of Commerce's Education Committee
Schutmatt	Kelly	Anthropology instructor
Scott	Kathleen	Librarian beginning in 1971
Scott - Blain	Adella	Librarian, currently Dean, Learning Resources
Slepsky	Larry	Athletic Director and coach
Smith	Jackie	Student, member of the Jestettes
Smith	Roy	State Representative from Ypsilanti instrumental in identifying Willow Run as a potential site for the new College
Smith	Sherman	Student in the Automotive Program, 1969
Shure	Fred	Student, member of the school's first basketball team
Spelman	Frances	Student, 1967
Stabler	Neil	Member of the 1967 Search Committee for first President
Stager	Gus	Coach
Stein	John	Student in the Automotive Program, 1969
Strayer	Jim	Biology instructor
Susnick	Stuart	Social Sciences instructor
Tarapata	Peter	Architect representing Tarapata-McMahon Associates, developed first master plan for the College
Thomas	Lois	Manager of Manimark Food Service
Thomson	Mehran	First Director of Exact Sciences, later became Dean of Exact Sciences
Tigner	John	President, Black Student Union; Assistant Coordinator, Black Studies Program and later an instructor in Black Studies
Toggerson	Pete	Student who, together with Gerald Ulmer, suggested the name for the student newspaper, *The Voice*
Tomas	Ana	Student, 1967
Ulmer	Gerald	Student, member of the school's first basketball team; along with fellow student Pete Toggerson, suggested the name of the student newspaper, *The Voice*
VanBuskirk	Lloyd	First business manager
Vass	Steven	Economics instructor, instrumental in establishing the College Testing Center
Vogel	Elvira	Member of the Advisory Search Committee seeking new President in 1975
Watson	Nick	Student and member of Advisory Search Committee seeking new President in 1975

Welch	Bruce	Instructor, Automotive Department, first vice president of the WCCEA, 1967
Wells	Phillip G.	Member of Board of Trustees, 1971–1976
Wenrich	Ralph	Member of Board of Trustees 1965–1970
Wheeler	Kenneth	Electricity/Electronics instructor
Whitford	Priscilla	Anthropology instructor
Wilder	Oklin	Student, member of 1967 bowling team
Wiley	Joyce	Clerk, Registrar's Office
Williams	Calvin	Counselor, Director of Counseling, Dean of Student Services; current Associate Vice President of Student Services
Wilson	Evelyn	Business instructor
Wilson	Steve	Student, member of 1967 bowling team
Wolven	Frederick	English instructor; first WCCEA treasurer; advisor to the student newspaper, *The Voice*
Wooden	John	First Division Director of General Studies; later Director, Social Science Division and Dean of General Studies
Woolley	Dr. Carl	Dental Assistant instructor
Woolley	Douglas	First Registrar
Young	Harold	First Library Director
Young	Raymond	University of Michigan professor who conducted the community survey regarding support for a local community college in 1962
Yourd	Kenneth	Member of Board of Trustees, 1965–1966
Zaremba	Ernie	Psychology instructor
Zeeb	Ronald	Business instructor